electrical • plumbing • detailed instructions

—TEN POUND BOOKS—

HOME WIRING & PLUMBING

Over **600** Photos • **50** Step-by-Step Projects

CONTENTS

Copyright © 2008
Creative Publishing international, Inc.
400 First Avenue North, Suite 300
Minneapolis, MN 55401
1-800-328-3895
www.creativepub.com
All rights reserved.

President/CEO: Ken Fund
Publisher: Bryan Trandem

Printed in Singapore
10 9 8 7 6 5 4 3 2

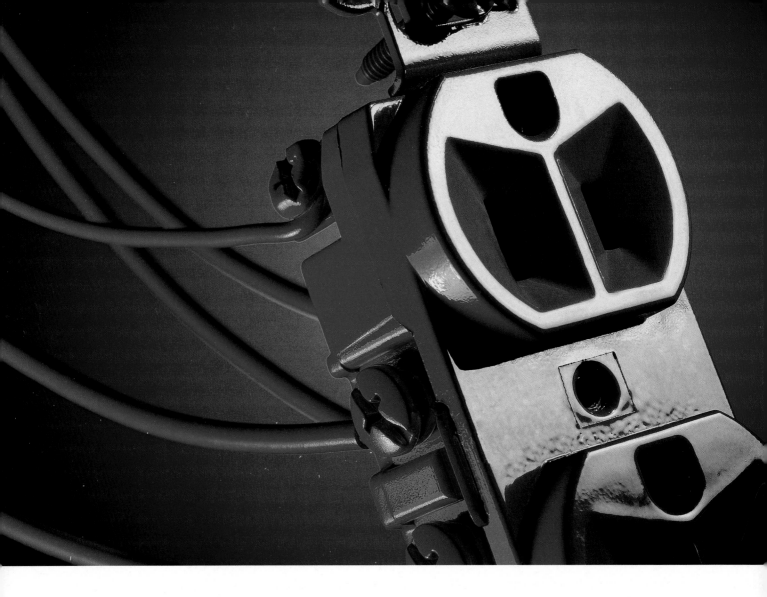

INTRODUCTION

Before you pick up the phone to call for help with your next plumbing or electrical question, pick up *Home Wiring & Plumbing* because, really, you can do it. Despite what you may think, or fear, plumbing and wiring are home improvement topics in which everyone can succeed. Even if you are a beginner with no previous plumbing or wiring familiarity you can successfully approach home wiring and plumbing repairs and installations with the help of this easy-to-use book.

Detailed directions and professional tips and secrets are presented in everyday language. Technical terms are clearly defined, parts are illustrated, and all steps are photographed so that you not only have complete text directions but you have visual guides as well. And the projects we help you with are the most common repairs and installations homeowners confront.

In the wiring section of the book, you'll learn how to put together a wiring tool kit, turn off the

power, test for current, and make wire connections, as well as gain an understanding of electrical circuits. You'll then find everything needed for that specific project, including the tools and materials required (listed and photographed), the amount of time to devote to the project, and the step-by-step instructions to get the job done.

Similarly, for plumbing repairs you'll learn about plumbing systems, as well as how to put together a tool kit and how to evaluate the plumbing in your home. The most common repair and installation projects are then explained in detail with step-by-step instructions and photos.

With this book you'll walk into the home improvement store with confidence. *Home Wiring & Plumbing* is here to help you succeed in your household plumbing and electrical repairs and installations, and save you hundreds, if not thousands, of dollars.

Welcome to Wiring 101

WIRING 101 REPRESENTS A DIFFERENT TYPE OF HOME REPAIR BOOK: YOU DON'T NEED TO HAVE ANY PRIOR KNOWLEDGE TO BE SUCCESSFUL. ALMOST EVERY HOME REPAIR BOOK DEPENDS ON YOU HAVING SOME FAMILIARITY WITH THE SUBJECT MATTER BEFORE YOU BEGIN. IF YOU HAPPEN TO BE A TRUE BEGINNER, YOU'RE ALREADY AT A DISADVANTAGE.

What do you do, then, if you have no idea exactly what an electrical circuit is, if you don't really know the difference between wire strippers and needlenose pliers? What if you don't know that the thing you've always called an "outlet" is really a receptacle, and if you have no idea of the difference between a circuit breaker and a fuse?

You reach for Wiring 101. This is the one book on electrical wiring that doesn't assume you already know a lot about the subject. But it's also a book that won't insult your intelligence and talk down to you.

Professional electricians tell us that 95 percent of all service calls involve just a few basic repairs, so chances are you really don't need a book that teaches you how to rewire your entire house. What you do need is a book that shows you the 25 most common projects you're likely to face, a book that describes the projects in careful, no-step-left-out detail, so you can get the job done with no problem.

On the following pages, that is exactly what you'll find: directions for solving the 25 universal wiring problems and projects in your home. No knowledge is assumed, and no question is left unanswered.

Despite what you might think, or what you might fear, you really don't need a lot of technical understanding to have success at most wiring projects. Of course, it's great if you understand things like the "polarity of alternating current," or the difference between a short circuit and a ground fault, but the fact is that you don't need to know these things to replace a wall switch that buzzes, or to replace an ordinary outdoor floodlight with one that senses motion and turns on automatically to make the shadows safer when you're coming home late at night.

Wiring is a whole lot easier than most people think, because when it gets right down to it, electricity behaves in very logical, predictable ways. If you make repairs in a systematic way that carefully follows the proper steps, wiring is simpler than most plumbing or carpentry projects.

With that in mind, many of the projects in this book are extremely basic. There are just a few pages devoted to learning how to make wire connections, or how a circuit works. The rest is all practical step-by-step information, beginning with the most basic of projects. (Yes, we actually do show you how to remove a broken lightbulb.) And we'll show you how to put a new plug on the end of your toaster or lamp cord. And how to replace a lamp cord that has worn through. Surprisingly, these routine problems are ignored in many wiring books. There are also more substantial projects here, such as replacing wall switches and receptacle outlets. And at the end of the book, you'll find a couple of "extra credit" projects—how to install track lighting in replacement of an ordinary ceiling-mounted light fixture, and how to add new electrical outlets with surface-mounted raceways. Although these projects are a bit more advanced, you'll be happy to find that they're easier than you imagined. From the skills you learn with these 25 projects, you'll develop the confidence you need to do almost any wiring project that comes along.

HERE'S HOW TO USE THIS BOOK:

The first two pages of each project give you the background information and any technical understanding that will be helpful to understanding what you're about to do. You'll learn about the skills required, get an idea of how long the project might take, and see all the tools and materials you'll need to gather to do a project.

Then, turn the page and begin. Virtually every step is photographed so you'll see exactly how to do the work, and along the way you'll find helpful sidebars that show you what to do if something unexpected happens, tips for using tools correctly, safety recommendations, and more. Before you know it, you'll notch up another home repair success.

It's that easy. Really.

Before You Begin:
Putting Together a Wiring Kit

Electrical tape

Toolbox

viper ROUTER BITS

Wire connectors

Lamp sockets

Lamp cord

Westinghouse
8' LAMP CORD SET

70101   SPT-1 Wire

Switches & receptacles

WIRE STRIPPER A.W.G.

Screwdrivers   Current sensor   Needlenose pliers   Combination tool

Here's pretty much all you'll need to complete most of the repairs and projects in this book. They are available at any home improvement center or hardware store.

UNLIKE SOME OTHER TYPES OF HOME IMPROVEMENT SKILLS, MAKING BASIC wiring repairs doesn't require very much at all in the way of tools and materials. Investing $30 to $40 puts you in a position to save hundreds of dollars on routine wiring repairs. We recommend that you keep a small toolbox with items dedicated to your wiring tools. That way, you can bring your kit to your work site, and will have the screwdrivers, pliers, and other things you need handy, and won't have to hunt for a screwdriver at the most inconvenient time. Here are the things we recommend for your wiring tool kit:

• **Electrical tape.** These days, tape isn't used to make wire connections, but to help label wires temporarily as you replace fixtures. Some electricians, though, do wrap a loop of electrical tape around plastic wire connectors to reinforce the connections.

• **Toolbox.** A small plastic toolbox is just fine; one with a divided tray for holding wire connectors, screws and other small items is a good choice.

• **Wire connectors.** Sometimes known as "wire nuts," after one manufacturer's product. They're used to join wires together, and you'll be using them a lot. They're color coded for convenience. Green connectors are used for bare copper grounding wires. With most manufacturers, orange connectors are used for two small wires, yellow for two or three wires, red for three or more wires. But you should follow the recommendations on the box, in case you buy a different brand.

• **Lamp sockets.** Repairs to lamps and light fixtures are very common, so you can save yourself time by having a few of these on hand. Besides, they're very inexpensive.

• **Switches & receptacles.** Because these are so frequently needed, and so inexpensive, keep a few on hand. Sooner or later, you'll need them.

• **Cord kit.** Another inexpensive item that's good to have on hand. Lamp cord kits have preattached plugs, to make rewiring a lamp very easy.

• **Screwdrivers.** Have at least two screwdrivers; one with a slot-shaped tip, the other with an X-shaped Phillips tip. It's even better to have several sizes of each type.

• **Needlenose pliers.** This tool is used for almost every wiring project, and is used mostly for bending and connecting wires.

• **Current sensor.** This clever tool tells you if the wires you want to work on are carrying electricity or not. Best of all, this new-style tool doesn't require that you touch any wires.

• **Combination tool.** This workhorse does it all: cuts cables, identifies wire sizes, strips wires. It is the single most important wiring tool you can have.

There are handful of other workshop tools you may use in your wiring projects. They include: a portable drill, a hammer, a level, a utility knife, a tape measure, and a stud finder. If you don't already own them, you may need to buy or borrow them when you get to projects that require them.

Before You Begin:
Understanding an Electrical Circuit

NO QUESTION ABOUT IT: WIRING AND ELECTRICITY MAKE MOST PEOPLE JUST A LITTLE NERVOUS. Understanding a bit about how electricity behaves in the wires that run through your house will help take away a bit of the scary mystery, and will also give you some confidence to make these repairs. So let's take a short tour of your electrical system. You might even carry the book along with as you walk through your home looking for the things we describe.

Electricity is really nothing more than a form of magnetism running through wires. Electrical energy is obviously invisible, but it's useful to think of it in much the same way as you'd think about water flowing through plumbing pipes. Like water, the electricity is present but not really moving until you "open the faucet" by turning on a light switch, or turning on the motor for an appliance.

Problems occur when the wires (the "pipes") carrying current become broken or blocked, or if they "leak" electricity outside the system. If you're ever been shocked, you know one result of electricity leaking outside its wires. Because flowing electricity generates heat, leaking electricity can also cause fires. These are the reasons electricity makes people a little nervous: it's an invisible energy, it can cause shocks, and it can cause fires.

Fortunately, the system has lots of safety features built in to prevent these problems. And to stay perfectly safe while making repairs to the system, all that's necessary is for you to shut off the flow of electricity in the wires you want a work on. This is very, very easy to do, as you'll soon see. Let's start the tour:

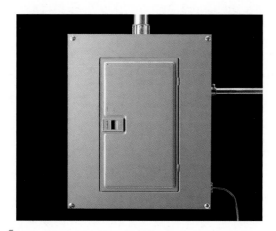

1 For all intents and purposes, your electrical system begins for you with the **main service panel.** Usually this is a gray metal box located in a utility area of your home—the basement, the garage, or a utility room. Sometimes, though, it might be located inside a wooden wall cabinet in a finished basement room.

2 Inside the service panel are rows of toggle switches. These are **circuit breakers**. They serve two functions. First, they protect wires from having too much current flowing through them. If you've ever had a circuit breaker trip and lights go out suddenly, you've experienced this safety feature. Secondly, the circuit breakers let you shut off the power to wires when you want to work on them.

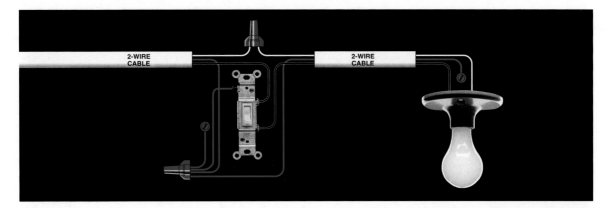

3 Each of the circuit breakers in the service panel sends and controls electricity through a **circuit**—a continuous loop of wire that runs from the service panel, out to one or more receptacles, appliances, or light fixtures, and back again. This diagram shows a simplified circuit. Even the most complicated circuits are just variations of this basic idea. Electricity changes its nature as it flows through the circuit wires. It begins as **"hot" current**.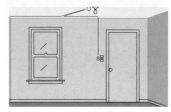
This current is under **"pressure,"** which means that it carries voltage. After the electricity does its work, by creating light or heat or moving mechnical parts in an appliance, it loses its pressure, or charge, and becomes **"neutral"** as it flows back to the service panel. The wires carrying hot current are normally black or red, while neutral wires are usually white. In addition to the hot and neutral wires, a circuit has a loop of bare copper wire (or sometimes an insulated green wire). This **grounding wire** is a safety feature that carries stray electricity back to the service panel if the other wires "leak" their electricity.

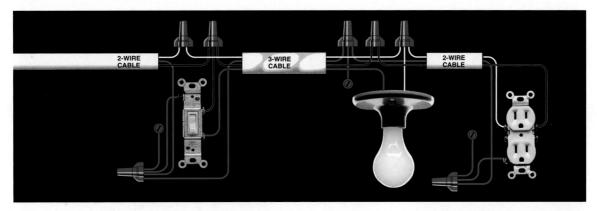

4 Here's another circuit map that shows how a more complicated circuit works. This circuit sends electricity to both a switch/light combination, and a receptacle outlet. If you follow the path of the black wire, you'll see how it works. As the black wire carrying hot current reaches the switch location, it branches, sending one black wire that passes all the way through the light fixture and goes to the receptacle. This allows the receptacle to operate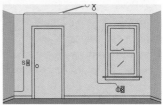
independently from the switch and light. Back at the switch, you'll see that another black wire leads to the switch. The hot current passes through the switch, then is carried to the light fixture through a red wire, which is part of a cable containing three insulated wires. From both the light fixture and the receptacle, white wires carry "depressurized" neutral current back to the service panel.

Before You Begin:
Turning Off the Power

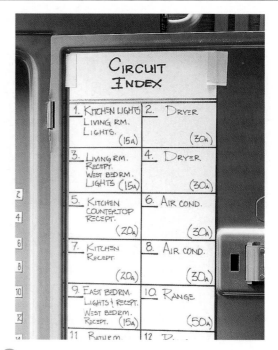

1 Find your main service panel (see page 8). Make sure there is no moisture on the floor below the panel. In very rare instances, people have been shocked when they touch a service panel while standing in water. Open the door of the panel, and look for the index on the inside face of the door. If your electrical service has been properly mapped, the index will tell you exactly which circuit breaker controls the circuit wires you want to work on. This isn't always the case, though. Sometimes you'll need to switch them off one at a time, identifying the correct breaker through trial and error.

2 With your finger, snap the lever on the circuit breaker to the OFF position. You will hear an audible click, and on some breakers a red window will appear on the face of the breaker. Now, close the panel door, and make very sure that everyone in the house knows you'll be working on wires, and that they shouldn't touch the service panel. **DO NOT** actually work on wires until you've tested for current (next page).

WHAT IF...?

If you have an older home with an electrical panel that contains fuses rather than circuit breakers, you will shut off power to the circuits by removing the fuses.

1 Locate the fuse that controls the circuit wires you plan to work on. Like a circuit breaker panel, fuse panels usually have an index that labels the circuits. The circuits that control ordinary wall outlets and light fixtures are usually screw-in fuses. The fuses for large appliances are usually cartridge fuses that fit into a fuse block you pull out of the panel.

2 Unscrew the fuse, being careful to touch only the insulated rim of the fuse.

Before You Begin:
Testing for Current

TOOL TIP

No-touch current testers are very easy to use, but they are accurate only if they are working properly. Before trusting it to test wires to make sure they are safe to work on, test the tool on a fixture that is carrying live current—the power cord on a lamp that is turned on, for example. Turn the tester to ON, then move the probe around the lamp wires until the tester glows or sounds its audible alarm. Now you know the tool works correctly, and can trust it to accurately test wires for live current.

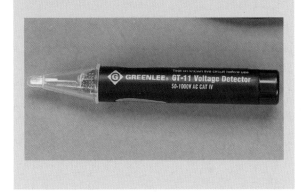

Receptacles: Remove the coverplate on the receptacle. Turn the tester on, and verify it works by testing it on wires you know to be live. Now insert the probe tip on the receptacle into the electrical box on each side of the receptacle. If the tester does not indicate current, you know the wires are now safe to work on.

Light fixtures: Loosen mounting screws and carefully lower the light fixture away from the ceiling box. With the wall switch in the ON position, pass the tip of the current tester within ½" of each wire.

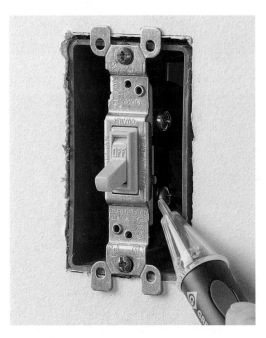

Wall switches: Remove the coverplate on the switch, and insert the tip of the current tester into the box, passing it within ½" of each of the screw terminals on the side of the switch. If the tester does not light up or beep, the wires are safe to work on.

Before You Begin: Making Wire Connections

ONE OF THE FEW SKILLS THAT IS UNIVERSAL TO MOST WIRING PROJECTS IS STRIPPING WIRES OF THEIR OUTER PLASTIC JACKETS, exposing the bare wires, and then connecting those wires to each other or to wire leads or screw connectors on switches, outlet receptacles, light fixtures, or other devices. So before moving on to any actual repairs in this book, practice the following skills:

- Stripping cables and wires
- Connecting wires
- Making screw terminal connections

- Making push-in connections
- Making set-screw connections

HOW TO STRIP WIRES

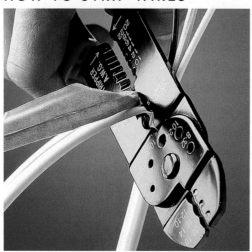

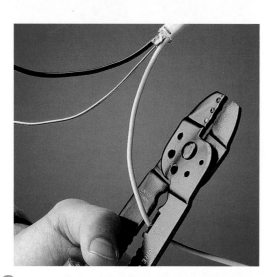

1 If you need to, cut away any plastic sheathing on the cable containing the wires, using the cutting jaws of a combination tool, or a utility knife. (If you use a utility knife, make sure not to nick the plastic jacket on the individual wires. If necessary, you can trim the wires down to size, using the cutting jaws on the combination tool.

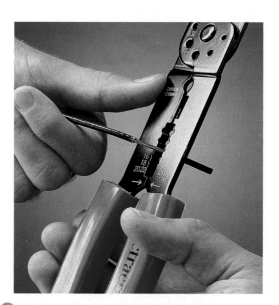

3 To strip insulation from the individual wire, select the opening on the combination tool that matches the size of the wires. In most instances, you'll be using the 12-gauge or 14-gauge openings on the tool. Open the jaws and place the wire in the correct slot, then close the jaws of the tool around it. Tug on the wire until it comes free from the insulation.

2 Determine how much wire to strip. Many receptacles and other devices come with a gauge that tells you how much wire to strip. Usually, it's about ¾".

HOW TO CONNECT WIRES WITH SCREW CONNECTORS

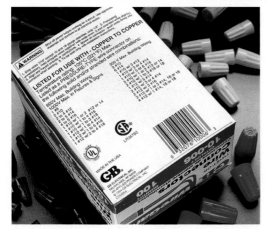

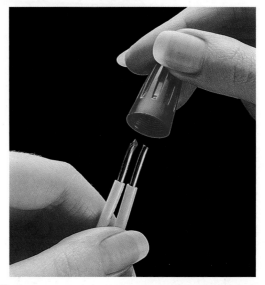

1 Screw connectors are used to join circuit wires together, or to join circuit wires to the wire leads on a light fixture, dimmer switch or other device. Choose a wire connector appropriate for the number of wires you're connecting, and for their size. Wire connector packages come with recommendations for usage. Green wire connectors are reserved for grounding wires.

2 Hold the wires together and slide a wire connector onto them. Twist clockwise until the wires are snug. You shouldn't be able to see any bare wire exposed. Tug on the wires gently to make sure they're firmly attached.

HOW TO MAKE SCREW TERMINAL CONNECTIONS

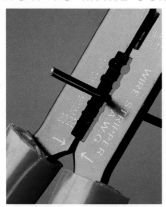

1 Strip about ¾" of insulation from each wire, using your combination tool. Choose the slot in the tool that corresponds to the wire size—this will almost always be 14-gauge or 12-gauge wire for the type of wiring you're doing.

2 Form a C-shaped loop in the end of the wire, using a needlenose pliers. Make sure the wire has no nicks or deep scratches. If it does, clip it off and restrip the ends of the wire.

3 Hook each wire around the appropriate screw terminal on the device, so it forms a clockwise loop. Attach only one wire under each screw terminal. Tighten the screw securely. The plastic insulation on the wire should just touch the screw, and the end of the wire should be under the screw, not extending beyond it.

HOW TO MAKE PUSH-IN CONNECTIONS

1 Although they are not as secure as screw connections, you can also use push-in connections on some switches. Some devices also have push-in connections. To make this connection, use the strip gauge on the back of the device to mark the wire for stripping. Use a combination tool to strip the wire.

2 Insert the bare copper wires firmly into the push-in fittings on the back of the switch or receptacle. There shouldn't be any bare wire exposed. Tug gently to make sure the wire is firmly gripped. If not, remove the wire and reinsert. If the device won't grip the wire tightly, connect the wire using the screw terminals instead.

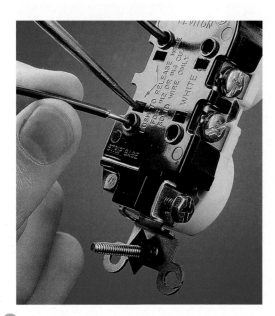

3 If you need to remove a wire from a push-in fitting, insert a small nail or screwdriver into the release opening next to the wire. The wire should pull out easily.

WHAT IF...?

A new type of wire connector looks like a twist connector, but instead uses a simple push-in action. Strip the wires to the length indicated, then simply slide the bare wires into the holes on the connector.

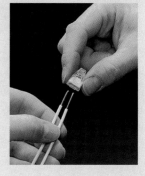

A continuity tester is a specialty tool that can be used to test lamp cords, switches, sockets, switches, and other devices to see if they are working correctly. The continuity tester is a battery-operated tool that sends a very faint electrical current through the metal components on a device, and senses whether or not there is a continuous pathway for household current to follow. If you have doubts about the condition of a device, the continuity tester offers a quick way to tell if the device is faulty or not.

Although there's only one project in this book that calls for a continuity tester, it's useful tool you might want to add to your wiring tool kit.

On lamp cords, use the continuity tester to check the pathway from the prongs on the plug to the ends of the cords.

On pull-chain switches, attach the clip of the tester to one of the switch leads, and hold the tester to the other lead. Pull the chain. If the switch is good, the tester will glow when the switch is in one position, but not in the other.

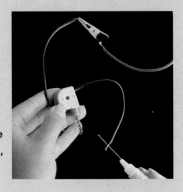

On wall switches, attach the clip of the tester to one of the screw terminals and touch the probe to the other screw. Flip the switch lever from ON to OFF. If the switch is good, the tester will glow when the switch is ON, but not when OFF.

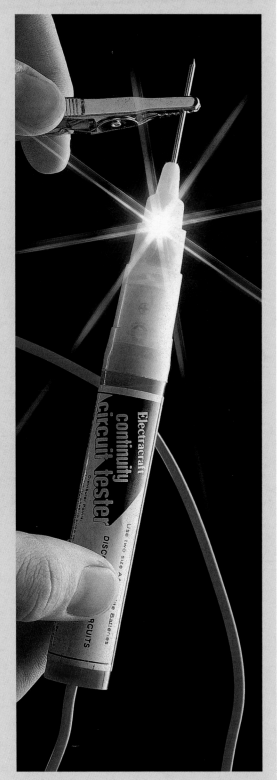

Adding a Wireless Phone Jack

1

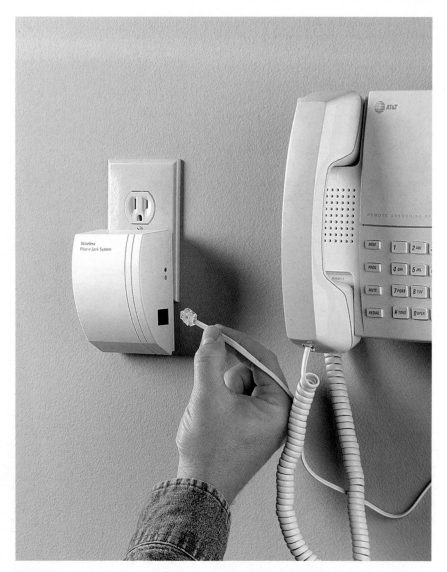

Wireless phone jack systems make it posssible to add telephone jacks without running new phone cable through walls. In a matter of moments, you can add a phone jack wherever you have an electrical outlet.

HOME CENTERS AND ELECTRONICS STORES SELL "WIRELESS" PHONE JACK KITS that use your household electrical wiring to transmit phone signals. The kits include two pieces. One is a base unit you plug in to a standard electrical receptacle and then connect to a standard phone jack. This provides a bridge between the phone wires and the electrical system. The second piece is the wireless jack, which you can plug in to any electrical receptacle in the house. To create additional phone jacks, just buy more wire jack units from the same manufacturer. Kits are sold for around $50, with extra jacks costing $20 to $30.

HOW TO ADD A WIRELESS PHONE JACK

1 Purchase a wireless phone jack kit. Most come with one base unit (A) and one wireless jack (B), which will allow you to add a phone jack anywhere you have an electrical receptacle.

Use the included length of phone wire (C) to connect the base unit to an existing phone jack near an electrical receptacle. You can plug the cord into either of the two jacks on the transceiver. The other jack lets you plug in a phone.

2 Plug the wireless jack in any electrical receptacle in the house or garage, provided it is part of the same electrical system. Plug your phone into the jack on the side of the unit.

TOOLS & SUPPLIES YOU'LL NEED

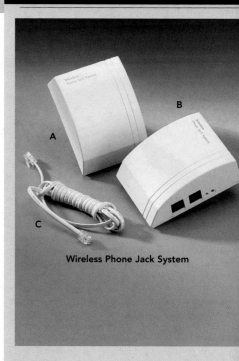

Wireless Phone Jack System

SKILLS YOU'LL NEED

• Reading package instructions

DIFFICULTY LEVEL

SKILLS LEVEL

EASY   MODERATE

Incredibly easy; you'll finish this in just seconds.

WHAT IF...?

If you want to use a computer modem with a wireless jack, consider buying a wireless model designed for high-speed modem connections. Although all wireless units can be used with computer modems, they transmit at a rate of 14.4K or so. Wireless jacks designed for computer modems, on the other hand, transmit at 56K.

Repairing Phone Jacks

2

Phone jacks are easily damaged. Whether they get smashed by an errant chair leg or their wires get rattled loose, a faulty jack can degrade the quality of the sound on your phone—or disconnect you altogether. The good news is that working on phone wiring is easy and very safe.

REPAIRING OR REPLACING A BROKEN PHONE JACK is a project that offers a lot of bang for the buck. If a phone jack somewhere in your house has stopped working or has very poor sound quality, you can probably fix it by investing $5 and less than an hour of your time.

The phone system is separate from the household wiring, and runs on a very mild current, which means you don't have to worry about shock. You don't have to turn anything off to replace a phone jack.

PHONE JACKS 101

Red
Black
Green
Yellow

Phone jacks generally have four thin colored wires in them. The wires are connected to screw terminals or to slotted brackets. The four wires are usually colored red, yellow, green and black. Connect the individual system wires to the screw or bracket connected to the matching color leads leading to the modular plug.

CHEAT SHEET

If your wires don't match the color scheme shown here, don't worry. Use this chart as a reference for connecting wires to the screw terminals:

The red terminal will accept:
- a red wire
- a blue wire (or blue with white stripe)

The green terminal will accept:
- a green wire
- a white wire with blue stripe

The yellow terminal will accept:
- a yellow wire
- an orange wire (or orange with white stripe)

The black terminal will accept:
- a black wire
- a white wire with orange stripe

TOOLS & SUPPLIES YOU'LL NEED

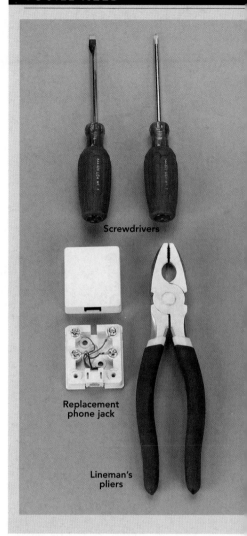

Screwdrivers

Replacement phone jack

Lineman's pliers

SKILLS YOU'LL NEED

- Making wire connections (pages 14-16)

DIFFICULTY LEVEL

SKILLS LEVEL

EASY   MODERATE

You'll likely finish this in 30 minutes or less.

HOW TO REPAIR A PHONE JACK

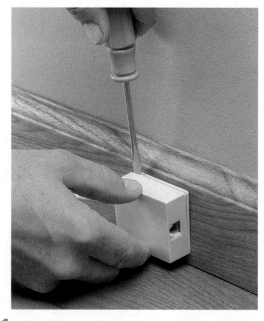

1 If the jack has no visible damage, you may be able to get it working again by reconnecting loose wires inside. Pry the cover off the jack with a small screwdriver.

2 Under the cover, you'll see six or eight wires in four colors. Each of the wires should be firmly seated under a screw terminal or in a forked metal tab. If one of the wires is loose, reattach it to the terminal of matching color. Plug in the phone to test it. If it still doesn't work, continue with replacing the jack

3 To remove the jack, first disconnect all the wires from their screw terminals or forked tabs. Then, unscrew the screws (there may be one or two) holding the jack to the wall. Tape the phone wires to the wall so they don't get knocked into the wall cavity.

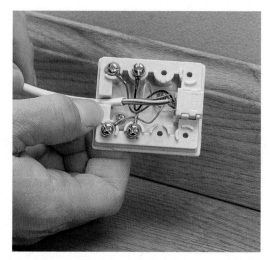

4 Take the old jack to a hardware store or home center and try to find a similar replacement jack so you can use the same mounting holes. Remove the cover from the new jack. Carefully thread the phone wire through the back of the new jack, and connect the wires to the screw terminals of matching color. Attach the jack to the wall, replace the cover, and test the phone

What if I have a *really* old jack? Older style phones used a four-pin system rather than modular plugs. New phones won't work with these jacks, so you'll need to replace them with new modular jacks.

1 Unscrew the old jack from the wall, and carefully pull it away from the wall.

2 On the back of the old jack, you'll find two or four colored wires connected to screws. Unscrew the screws to free the wires and then clip away the stripped portion of the wires. Buy a new modular phone jack.

3 If your new jack uses forked tab connectors, thread the phone cable through the opening in the back of the jack, then press each of the four wires into a forked tab that already contains a wire of the same color running to the plug-in opening. If your new jack uses screw terminals, follow the instructions on the opposite page. After all the wires are connected, plug in a phone. You should have a clear dial tone.

4 Set the jack over the old mounting holes and make sure the wire isn't being pinched against the wall. Drive the mounting screws back into the holes. Snap the cover back onto the jack and plug in your phone.

Removing a Broken Lightbulb

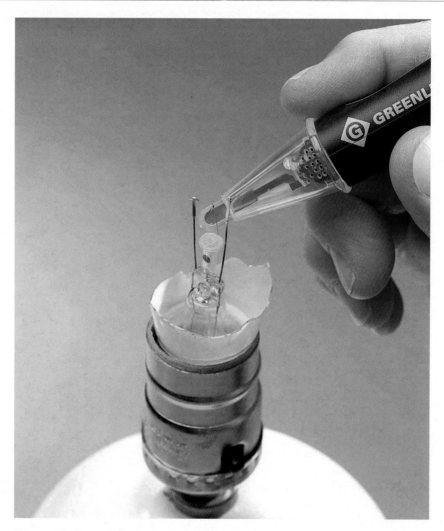

3

Even with the simplest wiring repairs, using a voltage sensor to check for power is a good idea. We'll then show you how the pros handle this job—using a needlenose pliers to remove the broken lightbulb. This technique works on even the most corroded and rusted light fixture sockets.

IF YOU'VE EVER TRIED TO REMOVE A LIGHTBULB THAT'S CORRODED AND STUCK in a fixture socket, you know that the lightbulb can easily break, leaving the bulb's aluminum base stuck in the fixture. There are several solutions to this common problem; some work better than others. For example, you may have heard of the old potato trick that suggests you push a raw potato into the broken socket and turn. But this introduces moisture and other debris into the fixture, and it doesn't work that well, especially if your broken bulb is really stuck. The bar of soap technique isn't much better. Effective methods include using a pair of needlenose pliers or a bulb extractor device, which can be found at most hardware or home improvement stores.

LIGHT SOCKETS 101

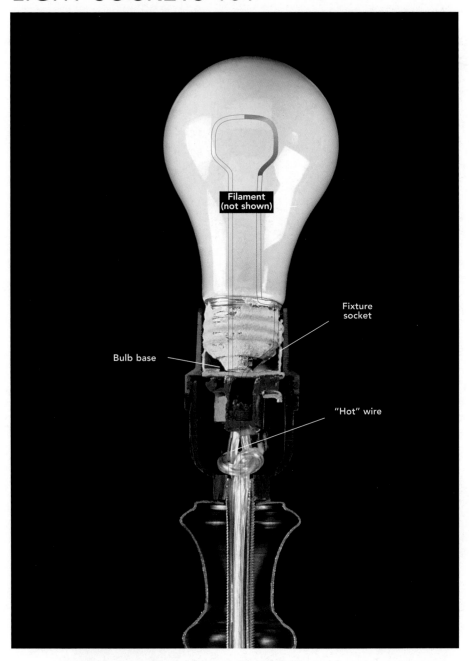

Filament
(not shown)

Bulb base

Fixture
socket

"Hot" wire

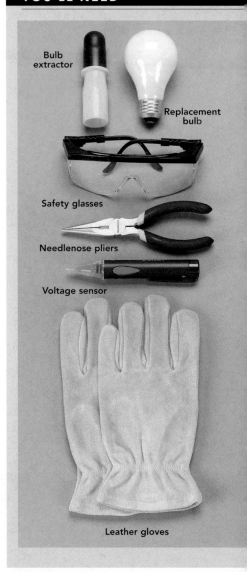

TOOLS & SUPPLIES YOU'LL NEED

Bulb
extractor

Replacement
bulb

Safety glasses

Needlenose pliers

Voltage sensor

Leather gloves

SKILLS YOU'LL NEED

• Turning off the power (page 12)
• Testing for current (page 13)

DIFFICULTY LEVEL

SKILLS LEVEL

EASY   MODERATE

You'll finish this job in just a few minutes.

Over time, the aluminum base of a lightbulb may become corroded and difficult to remove from its socket. You can almost always remove the bulb without damaging the socket. In this cutaway lamp, you can see exactly how a light fixture socket works. Current flows up into the lightbulb through the "hot" wire and through the central contact in the base of the bulb. The current flows through the filament inside the light bulb, loses its charge by producing light, then the neutral current flows back to the neutral wire through the threaded metal portion of the bulb and socket.

HOW TO REMOVE A BROKEN LIGHTBULB

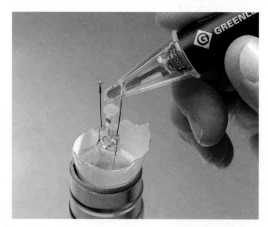

1 Before you start to remove the broken bulb, turn off the power to the light (or unplug the lamp, if that's what you're working on). Then, with the light switch in the ON position, place the tip of your voltage sensor in the broken bulb base. If the sensor beeps or lights up, then the wires are still live and are not safe to work. Check the main circuit panel again and trip the correct breaker to disconnect power to the light. If the sensor does not beep or light up, the circuit is dead and safe to work on.

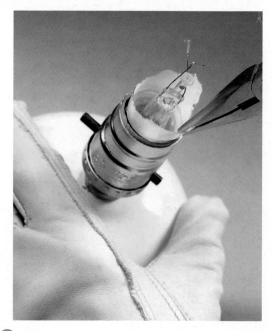

2 Put on safety glasses and a pair of heavy leather work gloves. Use your needlenose pliers to remove any broken shards of glass still attached to the lightbulb base. If you're working on a ladder, have a helper hold the base of the ladder.

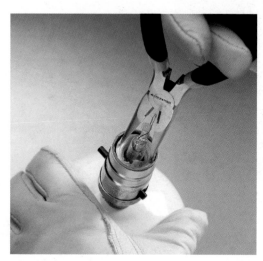

3 Insert the needlenose pliers into the broken bulb base as far as they will go. Spread the handles of the pliers firmly apart (this will cause the jaws to press against the inside of the socket), and turn the pliers slowly counterclockwise, unscrewing the bulb base. If the bulb won't budge, try wrapping the jaws of the pliers in duct tape for extra grip.

TOOL TIP

Needlenose pliers are handy for all sorts of household repairs, not just wiring. They come in all sorts of sizes. A good basic pair should have jaws around 3" long and comfortable handles.

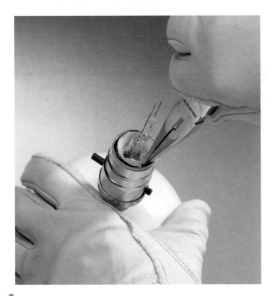

4 If the lamp is still stuck, use the tip of needle-nose pliers to grab the lip of the bulb base and bend it in slightly on one side. Grip the bent portion firmly with the pliers, and pull the base counter clockwise to unscrew the bulb.

5 If the broken bulb is in a hard-to-reach location or if you're not comfortable working on top of a ladder, you can buy a broken bulb extractor (available at hardware stores for less than $10) and screw it on to the end of a broom handle or extension pole. Simply insert the extractor into the socket. Its rubber sides grip the edge of the bulb base and give enough grip to allow you to turn the base out of the socket.

WHAT IF...?

What if the bulb still won't turn?

The base of the bulb is soft aluminum, and, if you pull hard enough, it will begin to tear much like a pop can. If you can't twist the bulb out, you may be able to create a little tear in the edge of the base. Try to fold the tear back. You'll probably rip a piece of the bulb off. Eventually, you'll have the whole socket out.

6 Once the bulb is out, wipe away any corrosion in the socket with a rag. If bulbs often get stuck in a particular fixture, use a bulb socket lubricant (available at hardware stores) to lubricate the lightbulb base and prevent corrosion. And remember, there's no need to twist hard when installing a bulb.

Controlling Lights
From a Keychain Remote

Remote kits include a plug-in receiver unit (left) and a keychain remote (right). Some models include multiple transceivers that let you connect several lamps or other plug-in appliances.

A KEYCHAIN REMOTE IS A VERY EASY WAY TO IMPROVE YOUR PERSONAL SAFETY FOR AN INVESTMENT OF ABOUT $20. It lets you turn on a lamp before you enter a dark home, or to leave it on until you're safely in your car. The receiver module plugs into any household outlet. Plug a lamp into the bottom of the receiver, and you can control the light with the keychain remote.

HOW TO SET UP A KEYCHAIN REMOTE

1 Plug the receiver into the receptacle where you usually plug in the lamp you want to control. Open the cover panel on the unit. There will be two dials, one with a "unit code" (typically a number) and another with a "house code" (typically a letter). If you're only planning on controlling one device, any code will do.

3 Plug the lamp into the unit and switch the lamp on. Test the remote by turning the lamp on and off.

2 Set the small switch below the dials to "learn." Hold one of the "on" buttons on the keychain down until the light on the unit flashes. The keychain is now programmed for this unit.

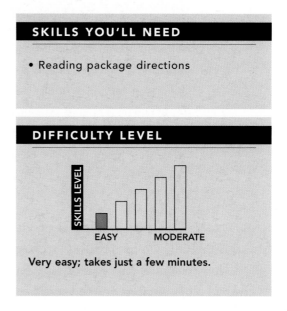

SKILLS YOU'LL NEED

• Reading package directions

DIFFICULTY LEVEL

EASY   MODERATE

Very easy; takes just a few minutes.

Replacing a Broken Plug

Different appliances and lamps have different kinds of plugs. In all cases, replacing a damaged plug is an easy task, once you identify which replacement plug you need. Appliances and tools often have thick, round cords (A, B) and heavy plugs, sometimes with three-prong plugs. Small appliances and lamps often use small plastic plugs (C, D). Some devices use "polarized" plugs (E) which have one wide prong and one narrow prong. Polarized plugs can only be plugged into a receptacle only one way.

ELECTRICAL PLUGS ARE SIMPLE DEVICES THAT TAKE A LOT OF ABUSE, and, not surprisingly, they often break at inconvenient times. You can almost always replace the plug for a tiny fraction of the cost of replacing the appliance or device. Replacing a badly bent or crushed plug can prevent a bad shock or even a fire.

PLUGS 101

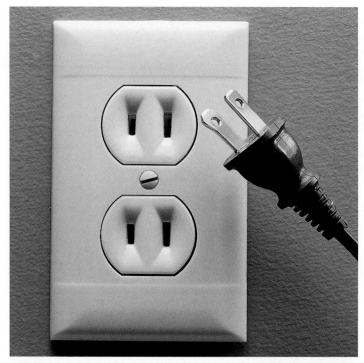

Appliances, lamps, and other electrical devices generally have plugs with either two or three prongs. The round third prong on a three-prong plug provides a path into the grounding system in your home. Receptacles in older homes might not be designed for three-prong plugs, requiring you to use an adapter (see page 33). When replacing a plug, always choose one that resembles the original.

(see page 33)

TOOLS & SUPPLIES YOU'LL NEED

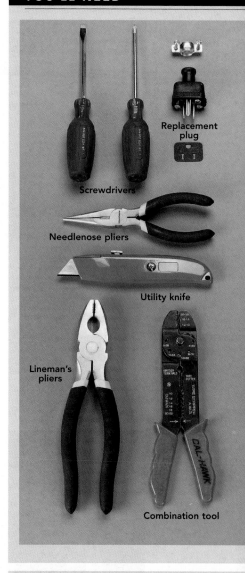

Screwdrivers

Replacement plug

Needlenose pliers

Utility knife

Lineman's pliers

Combination tool

SKILLS YOU'LL NEED

- Making wire connections (pages 14-16)

(pages 14-16)

DIFFICULTY LEVEL

SKILLS LEVEL

EASY   MODERATE

You'll need 15 to 20 minutes for this.

HOW TO REPLACE A THREE-PRONG PLUG

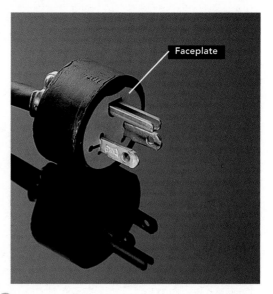

1 Use lineman's pliers to cut off the old plug. Cut as close to the base of the plug as possible. Take the old plug with you to a hardware store or home center and purchase an identical replacement plug.

2 Pry the plastic faceplate off the front of the replacement plug with a small screwdriver.

Faceplate

3 Feed the cut end of the cord through the rear of the plug so that you have about three inches of the cord coming through the front of the plug. Use a sharp knife to carefully cut the plastic insulation off the cord. Then, use your combination tool to strip about ¾" of insulation from the ends of each of the three insulated wires inside the cord.

4 Next, you'll need to tie an underwriter's knot with the black and white wires where they emerge from the plug. (See the opposite page.) This knot prevents the wires from coming loose inside the plug.

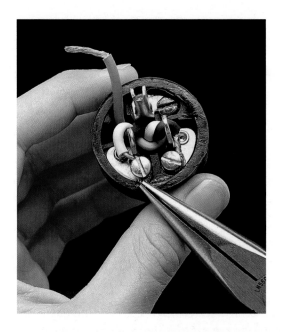

5 Now you'll need to connect the wires to the plug. On the face of the plug, you'll see three screws, one silver, one copper-colored, and a third green. Loosen the silver screw a few turns and wrap the end of the white wire clockwise around the screw. Needlenose pliers can make this easier. Tighten the screw, making sure the bare wire doesn't touch either of the other screws. Then, connect the black wire to the copper screw in the same way. Finally, connect the green wire to the green screw. When all the wires are secure, snap the faceplate into place and test the cord.

HERE'S HOW

To keep wires secure in the plug, tie a special knot in the white and black wires, called an underwriter's knot.

Create loops in each wire outwards from the cord, then feed the end of each wire through the opposite wire's loop—white through the black loop, black through the white.

Now pull the wires tightly, closing the loops and completing the underwriter's knot.

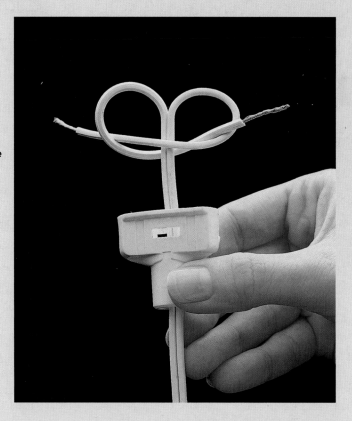

HOW TO REPLACE A TWO-PRONG PLUG

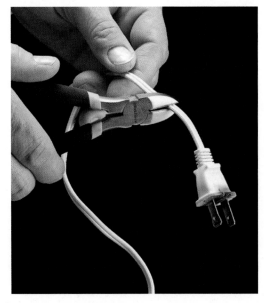

1 Use lineman's pliers to cut off the old plug. Cut as close to the base of the plug as possible and make your cut perpendicular to the cord.

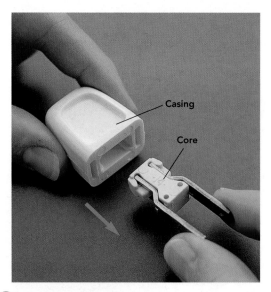

2 The quick-connect replacement plug has two parts, an outer casing and a core. Squeeze the prongs of the plug together and pull the core out of the casing.

3 Feed the cut end of the cord through the quick-connect plug's casing. Spread the prongs on the core and then push the end of the cord into the back of the core. Firmly squeeze the prongs together. You should feel two small spikes on the insides of the prongs pierce the cord's insulation. Slide the core back into the casing. The casing will hold the prongs in place. Now you can test the plug.

WHAT IF...?

What if your appliance has a polarized plug?

If the plug you're replacing had a wide prong and a narrow prong, you'll need to purchase a similar quick-connect replacement plug. When you assemble the plug, make sure the wide prong of the plug lines up with the ribbed half of the cord. The wide prong is the neutral, and will only fit into the neutral slot on a wall receptacle.

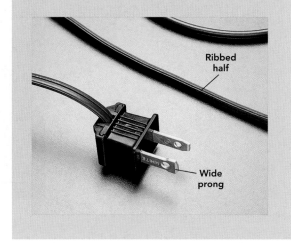

HOW TO REPLACE A FLAT-CORD PLUG

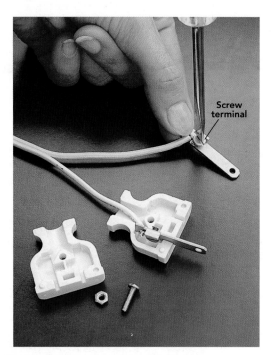

1 Cut the old plug from the cord, using a combination tool. Pull apart the two halves of the cord so that about 2" of wire is separated. Strip ¾" of insulation from each half. Remove the casing cover on the new plug.

2 Hook the ends of the wires clockwise around the screw terminals, and tighten the screw terminals securely. Reassemble the plug casing. Install the insulating faceplate, if the plug has one.

SAFETY TIP

What if your home has only two-slot receptacles and you need to use an appliance with a three-prong plug?

NEVER break off the third prong. Instead, use a grounding adapter. Make sure to attach the metal loop on the adapter to the coverplate screw on the receptacle.

A better long-term solution will be to replace this receptacle with a three-slot receptacle that is properly grounded. Turn to project 12 on page 64 if you'd like to try this.

Fixing a Doorbell

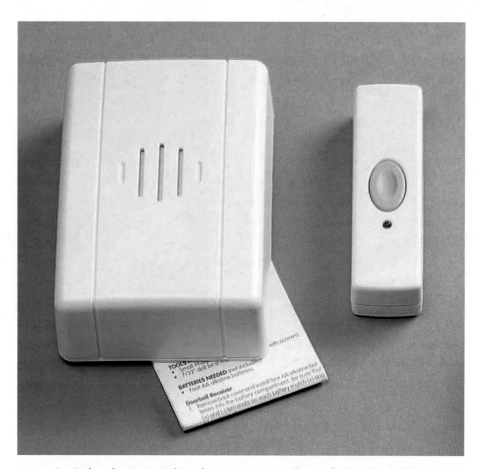

6

A wireless kit is a quick and easy way to replace a failed doorbell system. The kit consists of a battery-powered doorbell button that sends a wireless signal to a plug-in chime unit somewhere in the house. Some models come with two button units, one for the front door and one for the back.

WHAT DO YOU DO IF YOUR DOORBELL DOESN'T CHIME? The repair may be as simple as repairing loose wires or replacing a $2 button. The most common causes of doorball malfunction—loose wiring and worn-out buttons—are the easiest to fix, requiring only a screwdriver.

If the problem is with the wiring itself or the chime unit, it's generally simpler and cheaper to replace the system with a wireless doorbell kit, which take only minutes to install and cost very little.

DOORBELLS 101

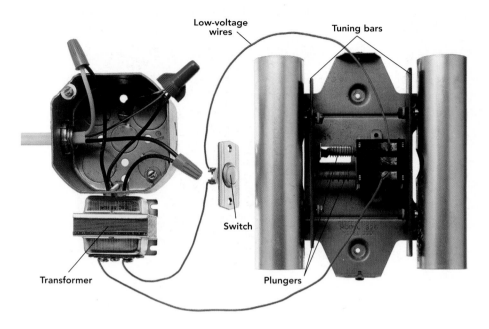

Low-voltage wires

Tuning bars

Transformer

Switch

Plungers

Repairing or replacing a doorbell is a simple project that often doesn't even require you to shut off the power. Doorbells are powered by a transformer that reduces household current to 24 volts or less. This low-voltage current goes from the transformer to the switch by the door and on to a chime unit. When you press the doorbell button, it completes a low-voltage pathway and causes the plunger to strike a musical tuning bar. To distinguish between the front and back door signals, one of the doorbell switch-and-plunger pairs strikes two tuning bars in succession, creating the characteristic "ding-dong" sound. The other switch and plunger strikes only one tuning bar.

HERE'S HOW

Rarely, it may be a loose wire connection on the doorbell chime unit that causes the problem. Remove the cover on the chime unit, look for loose wires, and tighten them with a screwdriver. More often, though, the problem will be with the push-button switch, or with a chime unit that has simply reached the end of its life.

TOOLS & SUPPLIES YOU'LL NEED

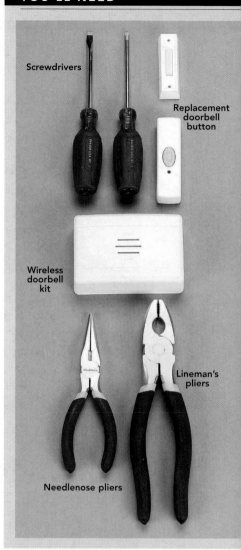

Screwdrivers

Replacement doorbell button

Wireless doorbell kit

Lineman's pliers

Needlenose pliers

SKILLS YOU'LL NEED

- Turning off the power (page 12)
- Testing for current (page 13)
- Making wire connections (pages 14-16)

DIFFICULTY LEVEL

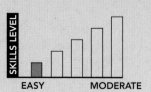

SKILLS LEVEL

EASY   MODERATE

Takes about 1 hour or less.

HOW TO FIX A DOORBELL

1 Begin by testing the button to make sure it works. Doorbell buttons are commonly the culprit. Use a screwdriver to remove the two screws that secure the doorbell cover to the house.

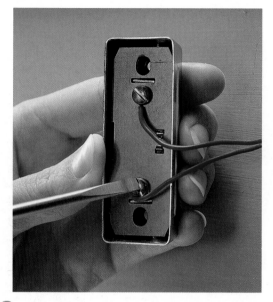

2 Carefully pull the switch away from the wall. Check the two wire connections on the back of the switch. If the wires are loose, reconnect them to the screws on the back of the button. Test the doorbell by pressing the button. Check the two wire connections on the back of the switch. If the wires are loose, reconnect them to the screws on the back of the button. Test the doorbell by pressing the button.

3 If the doorbell still doesn't work, loosen the screws on the back of the doorbell, remove the wires, and touch their bare copper ends together. If the bell sounds, the problem is a faulty button you'll need to replace (go to step 4). If the bell doesn't sound, the problem is elsewhere in the system (go to step 5). If you're replacing the switch, disconnect the wires and tape them to the wall to keep them from falling inside and getting lost.

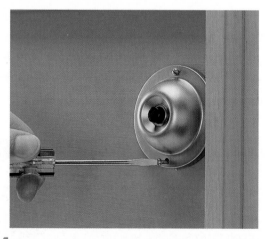

4 To replace the switch, simply buy a replacement that has the mounting holes in the same location as the old one. Wrap each of the wires around one of the screws on the back of the switch and tighten the screws. Position the button over the mounting holes and attach the new button to the wall with a screwdriver.

5 If the bell didn't ring, check the transformer, which is probably located in the basement or utility room near your main service panel. Check the two wires connected to the surface of the transformer, and reconnect them if they're loose. Test the doorbell by pressing the button. If the doorbell still doesn't sound, go to step 6.

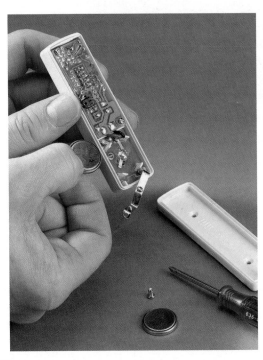

7 Install the battery into the battery compartment of the doorbell button. Go outside your front door and press the button to make sure the chime rings. If not, you may need to move the indoor receiver to a receptacle closer to the door.

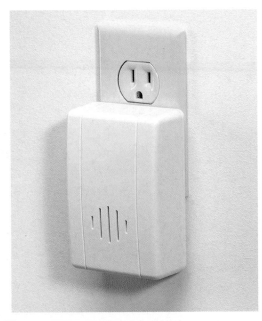

6 If nothing else has worked, now it's time to install a new wireless doorbell kit. First, plug in the chime unit to a centrally located receptacle in your house. Disconnect the doorbell switch by your door, and clip off the wires as close to the wall as possible, using lineman's pliers.

8 Mount the button to the door frame where you removed the old doorbell. You may have to drill two new holes before securing the new button to the wall with screws. Some doorbells come with double-sided tape that can be used to secure the button to the wall or to door molding. Push the doorbell button to make sure it works.

7

Fixing a Lamp Socket

Fixing an old lamp is a satisfying and surprisingly simple process. No matter what a lamp looks like on the outside, they almost always have the same electrical components.

WHEN A LAMP STOPS WORKING, IT'S OFTEN CAUSED BY A BAD LIGHTBULB SOCKET UNIT—that's the piece containing the switch or pull chain that holds the lightbulb. No need to throw the lamp away: for a few dollars, you can replace the socket and restore the lamp to like new. Replacing a socket is easy, and most hardware stores and home centers sell a variety of replacement sockets.

LAMP SOCKETS 101

Lamp sockets and switches are usually interchangeable—choose whatever type you want. Included here from top left: twist knob, remote switch, pull chain, push lever.

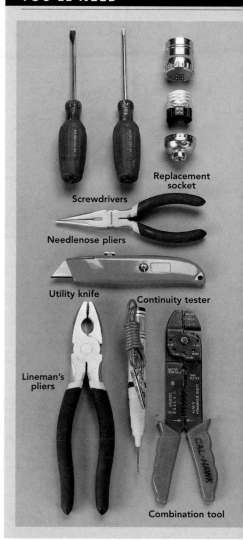

Screwdrivers

Replacement socket

Needlenose pliers

Utility knife

Continuity tester

Lineman's pliers

Combination tool

QUICK FIX

Sometimes, you'll get lucky and you can fix the faulty socket very easily. With the lamp unplugged and its bulb and shade removed, use a small flat screwdriver to pry up the small metal tab on the base of the socket. The tab should be angled slightly upward, not pressed flat in the socket. If the tab doesn't touch the base of the bulb, electricity will not flow though the bulb. Prying it up may restore the current flow. Replace the bulb and test the lamp.

Contact tab

SKILLS YOU'LL NEED

- Making wire connections (pages 14-16)
- Testing for continuity (page 17)

DIFFICULTY LEVEL

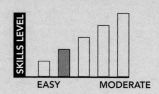

SKILLS LEVEL

EASY   MODERATE

This job takes 30 to 60 minutes.

HOW TO FIX A LAMP SOCKET

Outer shell

Insulated
sleeve

1 With the lamp unplugged, the shade off, and the bulb out, you can remove the socket. Squeeze the outer shell of the socket just above the base and pull the shell out of the base (the shell is often marked "Press" at some point along its perimeter. Press there and then pull).

3 With the shell and insulation set aside, pull the socket away from the lamp (it will still be connected to the cord). Look at the two screws on the sides of the socket. One half of the cord should be connected securely to each. If the screws are loose or if either of the wires is unattached, you've found the problem. Reconnect the ends of the cord and tighten the screws. But if the connections seem sound, then you'll need to continue by unscrewing the two screws to disconnect the socket.

2 Under the outer shell, you'll find a cardboard insulating sleeve. Pull this off and you'll reveal the socket attached to the end of the cord.

WHAT IF...?

What if my lamp is old and the shell is held in place by screws?

Some older lamps may have an outer shell held together with small screws. Simply undo the screws, remove the outer shell, and proceed as described here.

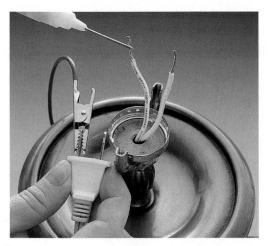

4 To rule out a bad cord as the cause of the problem, attach the clip of your continuity tester to one prong of the lamp's plug; then touch the probe first to one of the bare wires and then to the other. Do the same test for the other prong. The tester should light up once for each prong. If the tester never lights or lights on both wires for the same prong, you'll need to replace the cord. If it lights up once for each prong, the socket is the problem.

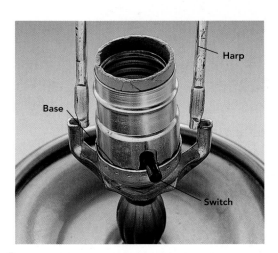

Harp

Base

Switch

6 Set the socket on the base of the lamp. Make sure the switch isn't blocked by the "harp"— the part that holds the shade on some lamps. Slide the cardboard insulating sleeve over the socket, so the sleeve's notch aligns with the switch. Now slide the outer sleeve over the socket, aligning the notch with the switch. It should snap into the base securely. Screw in a lightbulb, plug the lamp in, and test it.

5 Attach the ribbed half of the wire to the silver screw terminal on the new socket. Attach the other wire to the brass-colored screw terminal. If the stripped ends of the cord are frayed or blackened, cut them off with your combination tool and strip away ¾" of insulation to reveal clean wire.

HERE'S HOW

Here's how to buy a replacement socket. First, make sure it accepts the same size bulb (you'll be able to see this by looking). Next, if your old socket has a twist-, push-, or pull-chain-style switch, find a replacement that has the same style. (If the socket doesn't have a switch, you'll need to find a socket without one.) Finally, make sure it has the same watt rating as the old socket. Somewhere on the inside or outside of the socket, you'll find a number (between 20 and 120) followed by a *W*. This is the watt rating.

Replacing a Lamp Cord

8

Lamp cords get lots of abuse, so it's not uncommon for them to wear out. A damaged cord is a major fire and shock hazard and just wrapping it with electrical tape is not a safe repair technique. Fortunately, replacing a cord is fairly simple and much cheaper than replacing the lamp.

LAMP CORDS ARE BASICALLY ALL ALIKE, no matter what the lamp looks like. They disappear into the base of the lamp, snake through the lamp, and end at the socket where the bulb screws in, simple as that. Replacing one requires only disconnecting the damaged cord from the socket and then snaking the new cord back through the lamp to the socket.

LAMP CORDS 101

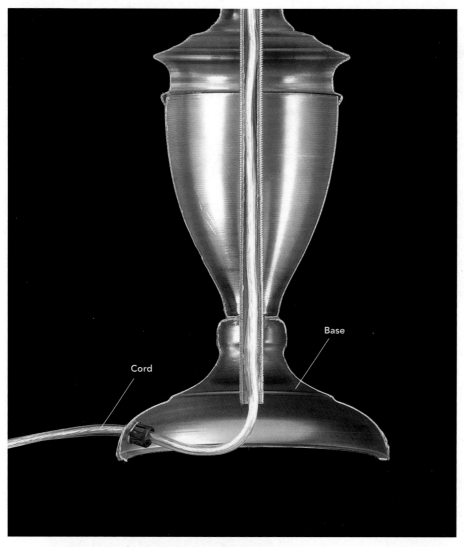

Cord

Base

Table and floor lamps are actually pretty simple. The cord runs from the base of the lamp up to the socket (which often houses the switch). If there's a problem with a lamp, it's likely either with the cord or the socket (project #7).

WHAT IF...?

What if you have a big floor lamp? It will be easier to snake the new cord into the lamp with a little help from the old one. A couple inches from the base of the lamp, cut the old cord. Tape the bare end of the new cord to the end of the old cord. Now, you pull the new cord into the lamp by pulling out the old cord through the top.

TOOLS & SUPPLIES YOU'LL NEED

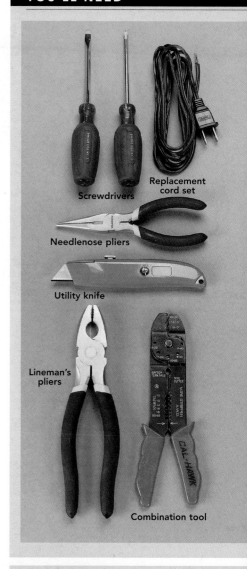

Screwdrivers

Replacement cord set

Needlenose pliers

Utility knife

Lineman's pliers

Combination tool

SKILLS YOU'LL NEED

• Making wire connections (page 12)

DIFFICULTY LEVEL

SKILLS LEVEL

EASY   MODERATE

This repair takes about 1 hour.

HOW TO REPLACE A LAMP CORD

1 With the lamp unplugged, the shade off, and the bulb out, you can remove the socket. Squeeze the outer shell of the socket just above the base and pull the shell out of the base (the shell is often marked "Press" at some point along its perimeter. Press there and then pull).

2 Under the outer shell, you'll find a cardboard insulating sleeve. Pull this off and you'll reveal the socket attached to the end of the cord.

3 With the shell and insulation set aside, pull the socket away from the lamp (it will still be connected to the cord). Unscrew the two screws to completely disconnect the socket from the cord. Set the socket aside with its shell (you'll need them to reassemble the lamp)

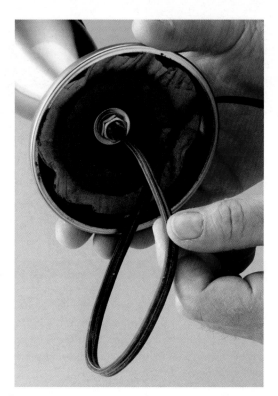

4 Remove the old cord from the lamp by grasping the cord near the base and pulling the cord though the lamp.

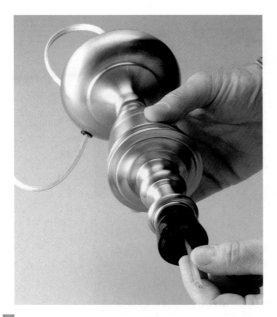

5 Take your damaged cord to a hardware store or home center and purchase a similar "cord set." (A cord set is simply a replacement cord with a plug already attached.) Snake the end of the cord up from the base of the lamp through the top so that about 3" of cord is visible above the top.

6 Carefully separate the two halves of the cord. If the halves won't pull apart, you can carefully make a cut in the middle with a knife. Strip away about ¾" of insulation from the end of each half.

7 Connect the ends of the new cord to the two screws on the side of the socket (one of which will be silver in color, the other brass-colored). One half of the cord will have ribbing along its length; wrap that wire clockwise around the silver screw and tighten the screw. The other half of the cord will be smooth; wrap it around the copper screw and tighten the screw.

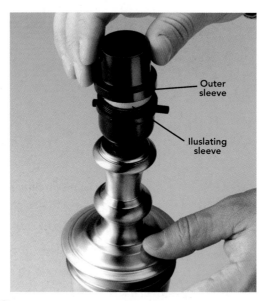

Outer sleeve

Iluslating sleeve

8 Set the socket on the base. Make sure the switch isn't blocked by the "harp"—the part that holds the shade on some lamps. Slide the card-board insulating sleeve over the socket, so the sleeve's notch aligns with the switch. Now slide the outer sleeve over the socket, aligning the notch with the switch. It should snap into the base securely. Screw in a lightbulb, plug the lamp in, and test it.

Fixing a Pull-chain Switch

9

The pull-chain switch is actually a separate piece of the fixture. It's held in place with a retaining nut and connected to circuit wires with two wire leads.

CHANCES ARE YOU'VE GOT A LIGHT FIXTURE WITH A PULL-CHAIN somewhere in your house—in a closet, attic crawl space, or maybe even your bathrom vanity. And, chances are, if you use it enough, you will eventually pull a little too hard and the switch will fail. Fortunately, you can easily replace a pull-chain switch, generally for only a dollar or two.

This is the first project where you actually touch circuit wires, so make sure you read the information on shutting off power and testing for current, found at the beginning of this book.

PULL CHAINS 101

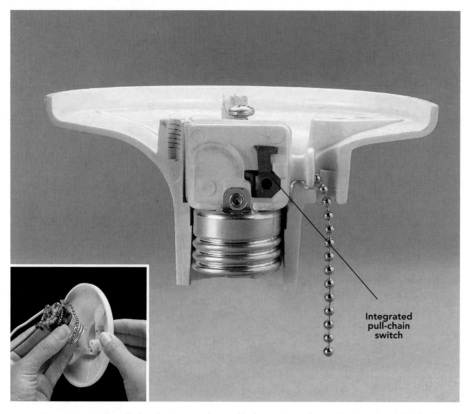

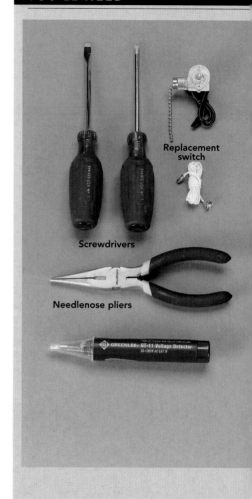

TOOLS & SUPPLIES YOU'LL NEED

Replacement switch

Screwdrivers

Needlenose pliers

Integrated pull-chain switch

On some utility light fixtures, the pull-chain switch is part of the lightbulb socket. On these fixtures, you'll need to replace the entire socket/switch unit (inset).

WHAT IF...?

If you have a light fixture or lamp with a push-button switch, replacing the switch is exactly the same as for a pull-chain switch.

Just buy a replacement switch that matches the old switch, and replace it using the same technique described on the following pages.

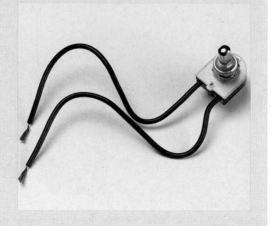

SKILLS YOU'LL NEED

- Turning off the power (page 12)
- Testing for power (page 13)
- Making wire connections (pages 14–16)

DIFFICULTY LEVEL

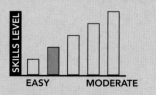

EASY   MODERATE

This project takes less than 1 hour.

1 First, make sure that switch is broken, not just the chain. If you find a short bit of chain sticking out of the fixture, pull on it to see if the light turns on and off. If so, you can buy and attach a new length of pull chain. If there's no chain left or if the switch doesn't work when you pull the remaining chain, go ahead and replace the switch.

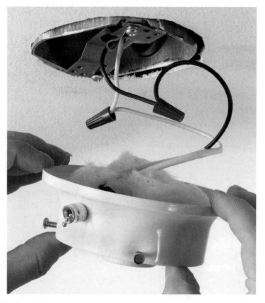

2 First, turn off the power to the fixture. Now, remove the globe and lightbulb, and loosen the mounting screws that hold the fixture to the electrical box. Lower the fixture away from the ceiling.

3 Test for current by holding your voltage sensor within ½" of the circuit wires. The black wires should cause the sensor to beep if power is present. Check all the wires for power in case the light was wired improperly. If the sensor beeps or lights up, then the circuit is still live and is not safe to work. Check the main circuit panel again and trip the correct breaker to disconnect power to the fixture. If the sensor does not beep or light up, the wires are dead and safe to work on.

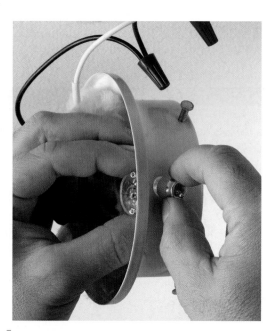

4 Hold the fixture steady with one hand and turn the knurled retaining nut at the base of the pull chain. You should be able to turn it with your fingers. If it sticks, use needlenose pliers to turn it. Once the retaining nut is off, pull the switch out of the fixture.

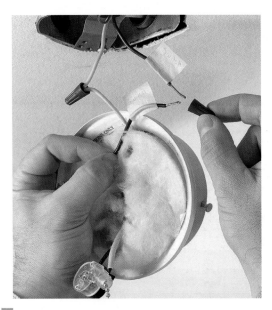

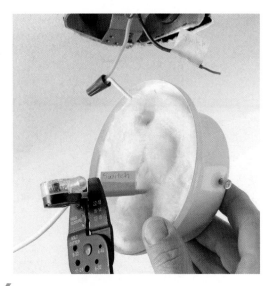

5 Remove the two wire leads coming from the switch from the wires they are attached to by unscrewing the wire connectors. On most fixtures, one of the switch's leads will be connected to a circuit wire, the other lead to the light fixture itself.

6 If the switch is part of the fixture itself, snip off its connection, using a combination tool. You'll connect the new switch to the wire you've just snipped, so strip about ¾" of insulation off that wire.

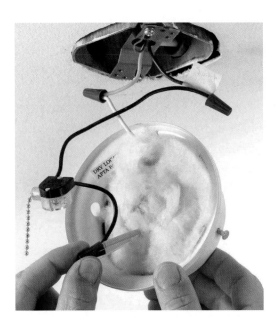

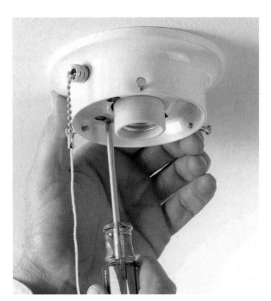

7 Attach the wire leads on the new switch to the disconnected wires, using wire connectors. Then, insert the threaded portion of the switch through the hole. Slip the retaining nut over the pull chain and thread it on to the switch until it is snug.

8 Reattach the fixture to the ceiling by holding it over the electrical box in the ceiling so that the mounting holes in the fixture line up with the screw holes in the box. Make sure all the wires are in the box and not pinched between the ceiling and the fixture. Insert the mounting screws and tighten them down with a screwdriver. Now you can replace the bulbs, restore the power, and test the fixture.

Installing a Programmable Thermostat

10

Programmable thermostats come in many varieties, but all of them will help save on energy costs. Most models have instructions for programming printed on the access plate.

IF YOUR HOME'S TEMPERATURE IS CONTROLLED BY AN OLD DIAL-TYPE THERMOSTAT, you may want to replace it with a modern programmable thermostat, which can save you up to one-third on your heating and cooling costs. Programmable thermostats allow you to set temperature levels for different times of the day according to the schedules of those living in the house. For instance, in the winter, you can program the thermostat to turn the heat up to 73 degrees in the morning when you are waking up, automatically lower the temperature to 69 degrees during the day while you are gone, then raise the temperature back up to 73 degrees just before you arrive home in the evening, then lower back down to 69 degrees again while you are sleeping.

Prices range between $19 and $120 depending on the unit's features. Some thermostats offer different programming schedules, including a five-to-seven-day schedule. When shopping, keep in mind that you might want to program a slightly different schedule for every day of the week. In that case, make sure you purchase a seven-day programmable thermostat. Also, keep in mind that some of the lower-priced models may result in temperature variations of up to nine degrees. If in doubt, get help from a salesperson at a local hardware or home improvement store to find the one that is right for your home.

THERMOSTATS 101

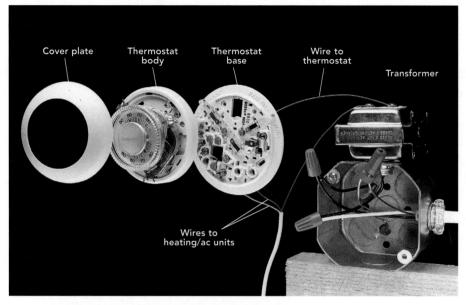

Cover plate | Thermostat body | Thermostat base | Wire to thermostat | Transformer

Wires to heating/ac units

All thermostats operate on low-voltage wires powered by a transformer, usually found attached to an electrical box near your furnace. The number of wires attached to the thermostat can vary from four to ten, depending on the complexity of your heating and air conditioning system. If you label the wires to identify the terminals they're attached to, installing the new thermostat will be a snap. There is very little danger of shock, because the wires you'll be touching are low-voltage.

CHEAT SHEET

Here's the common function of the screw connections you'll find in the standard thermostat controlling a forced-air furnace and central air conditioner.

- R = hot wire from transformer. Some thermostats have Rh and Rc connections if there are separate transformers for the heating and cooling units. Often, the Rh and Rc connections are joined together in the thermostat.
- C = common wire from transformer. Some thermostats don't use this connection.
- G = control for blower fan
- W = heating element
- Y = air conditioner compressor

SAFETY TIP

If your old thermostat has a vial of mercury in it, make sure to contact your local hazardous waste authorities to learn how to dispose of it safely. Mercury was used in thermostats from the 1950s to the 1970s.

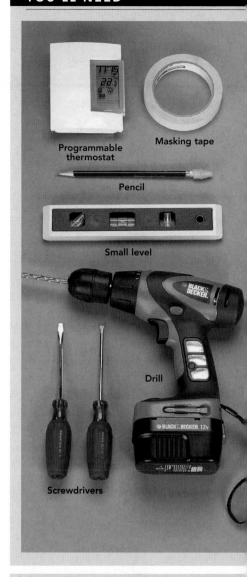
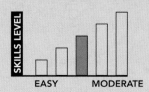

1 To remove the old thermostat, first switch off the power to the heating and cooling system at the main panel. Remove the cover from the old thermostat. In most cases, the cover will snap off when pulled firmly from the bottom. If it does not pull off, look for any small securing screws, and unscrew them to release the cover.

2 Next, remove the dial itself, which is held in place by a couple of small screws. You should be able to pull the dial off and expose the mounting plate beneath.

3 The mounting plate has several screws connected to wires (between three and eight wires, generally). There will also be two or three screws that hold the plate to the wall. Begin removing the plate by unscrewing these screws completely.

4 You can now pull the mounting plate away from the wall. Before you disconnect the wires, though, take a moment to label them according to the screws they're attached to on the mounting plate.

If you have a box-shaped thermostat rather than a dial-shaped one, replacing it isn't much different. You will remove the cover (A), disconnect the thermostat body (B), label and disconnect the wires (C), and remove the mounting plate from the wall (D). Then follow the directions on the following page, starting with step 6.

5 When all the wires are labeled, remove the plate completely by unscrewing all the screws that hold the wires. Take care not to let the wires fall into the wall cavity. Inspect the ends of the wires. They should be clean and free of scorching or dirt. If they aren't clean, clip off the stripped portion and then strip away ½" of insulation to expose fresh wire. Bend the stripped portion into a clockwise hook with needlenose pliers.

6 Now you are ready to install the new thermostat. First you'll need hang the new mounting plate. Position the plate on the wall and make certain it is level. Use a pencil to mark the new mounting holes on the wall once the plate is level.

7 Set the mounting plate aside. Using a drill, drill out the holes for the wall anchors (typically wall anchors are included with a new thermostat; use the drill bit size recommended in the instructions).

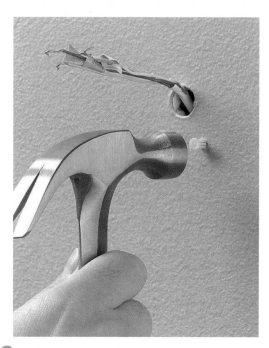

8 Press the wall anchors in the holes and push them with your fingers or gently tap them with a hammer until they are flush with the wall.

9 Reposition the wall plate over the hole, making sure that the anchors line up with the holes in the plate. Pull all of the wires through the plate. Using the screws provided with the anchors, attach the wall plate to the wall.

10 Match the labels on the wires to the corresponding screws on the new mounting plate. Connect the wires to the screw terminals on the thermostat. If the coding is different, check the instructions that came with the new thermostat to determine the wire connections for the new thermostat. There will be a table showing all the possible combinations. It's possible that one or more wires will not be used on the new thermostat. If so, tape the ends off and let them remain loose in the box.

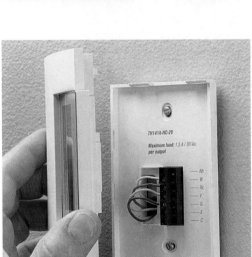

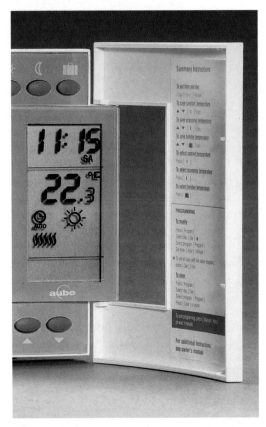

11 Install the backup batteries into the thermostat control unit, then snap the unit onto its mounting plate. Restore the power to the heating and cooling system, and test the new thermostat by turning the fan to auto and setting the temperature higher than the room temperature. The furnace fan should kick on and warm air should start to flow from the vents. If you have a cooling system, set the temperature lower than the room temperature. The air conditioner should come on and cold air should flow.

12 When you are certain that the new thermostat is working properly, follow the instructions that came with the new thermostat to program the unit to your individual needs.

11 Adding a Wireless Light Switch

Wireless switch kits are a simple and inexpensive way to add a second switch to an existing fixture.

SOMETIMES A LIGHT SWITCH IS JUST IN THE WRONG PLACE, or it would be more convenient to have two switches controlling a single fixture. Adding a second switch the conventional way generally requires hours of work and big holes in walls. (Electricians call this a "three-way" switch installation.) Fortunately, wireless switch kits are available to perform basically the same function for a fraction of the cost and effort. There is a bit of real wiring involved here, but it's not nearly as complicated as the traditional method of adding a three-way switch installation.

The kits work by replacing a conventional switch with a unit that has a built-in radio-frequency receiver that will "read" a remote device mounted within a 50 ft. radius. The kits come with a remote, battery-powered switch (it looks like a standard light switch) that you can attach to a wall with double-sided tape.

Two other similar types of wireless switch kits are also available. One allows you to control a plugged-in lamp or appliance with a remote light switch. The second type allows you to control a conventional light fixture remotely, but instead of replacing the switch, the receiver screws in below the lightbulb. This is particularly useful if you want to control a pull-chain light from a wall switch.

WIRELESS SWITCHES 101

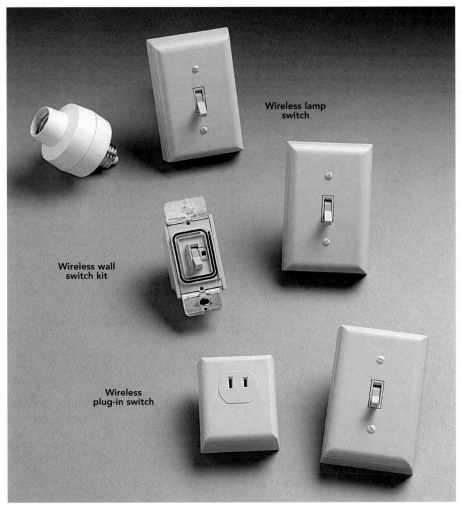

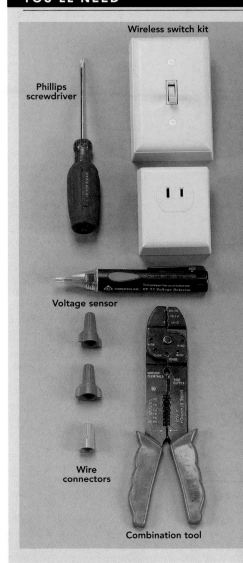

Wireless switch kit

Phillips screwdriver

Voltage sensor

Wire connectors

Combination tool

Wireless lamp switch

Wireless wall switch kit

Wireless plug-in switch

Wireless kits are available to let you switch lights on and off remotely in a variety of ways, at the switch, at the plug, or at the bulb socket.

The remote switch is a wireless transmitter that requires a battery. The transmitter switch attaches to the wall with adhesive tape or velcro strips.

SKILLS YOU'LL NEED

- Turning off the power (page 12)
- Testing for current (page 13)
- Making wire connections (pages 14-16)

DIFFICULTY LEVEL

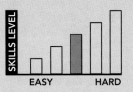

SKILLS LEVEL

EASY   HARD

This is real wiring, but you should be able to finish in about 1 hour.

HOW TO REMOVE A WALL SWITCH

1 To remove the old switch, first shut off the power to the switch. Remove the decorative cover-plate from the switch by unscrewing the two screws that hold the plate to the switch box. Set the screws and the plate aside. With the cover-plate off, you will be able to see the switch and the electrical box it is attached to.

2 Use a voltage sensor to make sure the wires are dead. Hold your voltage sensor's probe within ½" of the wires on either side of the switch. If the sensor beeps or lights up, then the switch is still live, and you'll need to trip the correct break-er to disconnect power to the switch. If the sensor does not beep or light up, the circuit is dead and you're safe to continue.

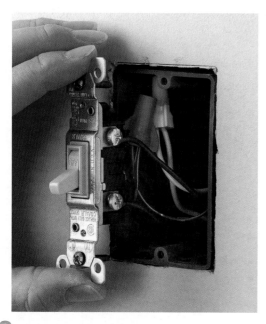

3 Remove the switch from the box by unscrew-ing the two long screws that hold the switch to the box at the top and the bottom. Once the screws are out, hold the top and bottom of the switch, and carefully pull the switch away from the box.

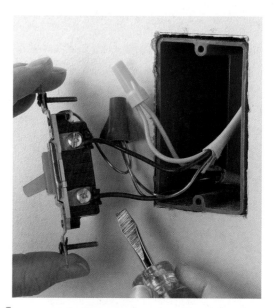

4 Remove the switch completely by disconnect-ing the wires. In many cases, there will also be two white wires connected with a wire connector in the box. You won't have to deal with these in your installation.

HOW TO INSTALL A WIRELESS WALL SWITCH

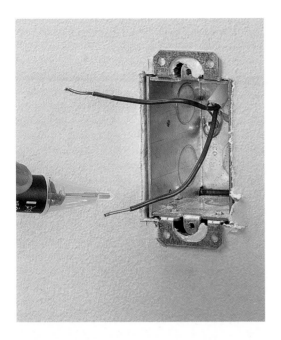

1 To install the receiver switch, you'll need to determine which wire carries current from the service panel. Bend both the wires so they are as far apart as possible. Turn the power back on temporarily. Without touching either wire, pass your voltage sensor over both. One should make your sensor beep and light up and the other won't. The one that trips your sensor carries current. Turn off the power and label that wire with a piece of tape.

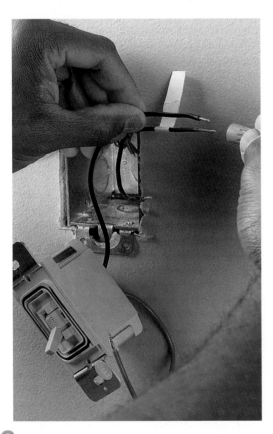

3 Once the wires are firmly connected, you can attach the switch to the box. Tuck the new switch and wires neatly back into the box. Then drive the two long screws that are attached to the new switch into the two holes in the electrical box.

2 Identify the wire lead on the receiver switch marked "line" and attach it to the circuit wire you marked with tape, using a wire connector. Connect the other wire lead on the switch to the remaining circuit wire in the same way.

4 Reattach the coverplate. Then, turn the power back on at the main panel and test the switch for operation. You should be able to turn the light on and off as normal.

5 Now you can install the transmitter switch. Install the 9-volt battery in the transmitter switch. Remove the backing from the double-sided tape on the back of the switch and place the switch on a wall within 50 ft. of the receiver switch.

6 Test the operation of both switches. Each switch should successfully turn the light fixture on and off. You've just successfully created a three-way switch installation, without running any new wires.

1 You can also purchase wireless switch kits that control plug-in fixtures. Plug the receiver unit into any receptacle.

2 The unit has a receptacle on its face. Plug a lamp or any other plug-in device into the unit (this is an especially handy way to control Christmas lights).

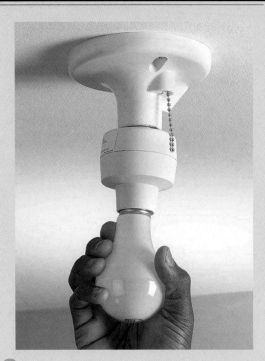

1 A third type of wireless switch uses a transmitter that screws into the bulb socket of the light fixture. If you need to control a light with a pull-chain switch or if you don't want to replace a wall switch as shown above, this is the best choice. Remove the lightbulb and thread the receiver into the bulb socket.

2 Screw the lightbulb into the receiver socket.

Fixing a Bad Receptacle

12

Since receptacles don't have moving parts, they don't wear out quickly, but they don't last forever. If a receptacle won't hold a plug or if it's hot to the touch or sparks when you pull a plug, it needs some attention and possibly replacement. If you have a GFCI receptacle (inset) see page 76 to 79 to replace it.

THE THING YOU'VE PROBABLY CALLED AN "OUTLET" IS MORE PROPERLY KNOWN AS AN ELECTICAL "RECEPTACLE." A receptacle that gets a lot of use will eventually wear out—you'll know this has happened if appliance plugs feel loose in the receptacle, or if a lamp flickers when the plug is jiggled. Another common problem is wires that work loose, causing the receptacle to stop working. This project will show you how to check the wire connections, then replace the receptacle if it's bad.

RECEPTACLES 101

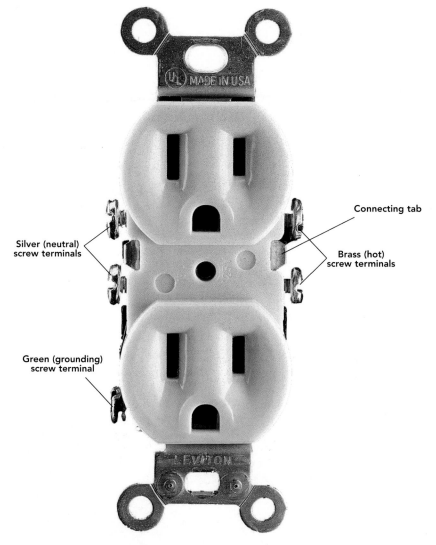

Silver (neutral) screw terminals

Brass (hot) screw terminals

Connecting tab

Green (grounding) screw terminal

Receptacles have five screws for connecting wires: two silver, two brass colored, and one green. Some installations don't use all of these screws. Disconnecting and connecting a switch is only a matter of connecting the right wires to the right screws.

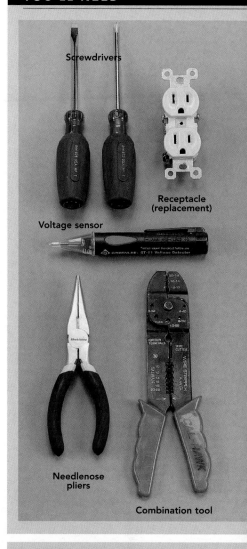

HOW TO FIX A BAD RECEPTACLE

1 Shut off the power to the switch at the main service panel. Remove the decorative coverplate from the receptacle. Set the screw and the plate aside. With the coverplate off, you will be able to see the receptacle and the electrical box it is attached to.

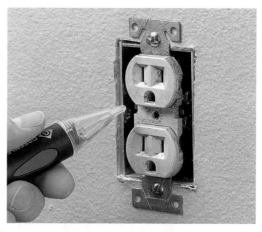

2 Use a voltage sensor to make sure that the circuit is dead. Hold your voltage sensor's probe within ½" of the wires on either side of the receptacle. If the sensor beeps or lights up, then the receptacle is still live, and you'll need to trip the correct breaker to disconnect power to the receptacle. If the sensor does not beep or light up, the receptacle is dead and you're safe to continue.

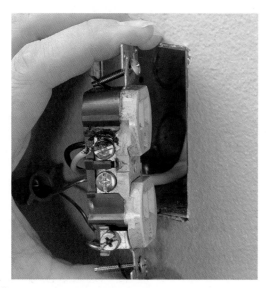

3 Remove the receptacle from the box by unscrewing the two long screws that hold the switch to the box at the top and the bottom. Once the screws are out, carefully pull the receptacle away from the box. Depending on how your receptacle has been wired, it may be connected to two colored wires and a bare grounding wire, or four colored wires and a bare wire.

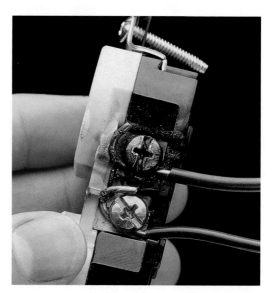

4 Inspect the screws where the wires connect to the switch. They should be tight and the connections should be clean and free of any scorch marks. If the connections were good, the problem is likely with the receptacle itself. If one of the wires is loose or if the connections are scorched, the problem is probably a loose screw causing a short circuit. You can follow the directions below to reattach the old switch or you can install a new one to be on the safe side.

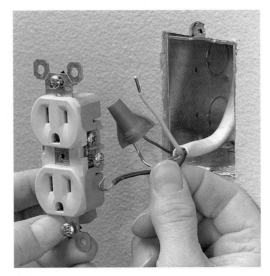

5 Loosen the screw terminals and remove the circuit wires. Inspect the wires, and if they're damaged, clip them off and strip about ¾" of bare wire, using a combination tool. Check the connecting tabs on the sides of the receptacle. If they have been snapped off, you'll need to also do this on the new receptacle, using needlenose pliers

6 Use needlenose pliers to bend the stripped portions in small, clockwise hooks. Now you can connect the wires to the receptacle. Take one of the black wires and wrap the end of the wire around one of the two brass-colored screws on the side of the switch. Tighten the screw so it's snug. If there is a second black wire, wrap it around the other brass-colored screw in the same way.

7 Now take one of the white wires and wrap the end of the wire around one of the silver screws. Tighten the screw so it's snug. Do the same for the second white wire if there is one. Connect the copper wire to the green-colored screw on the bottom of the receptacle.

8 Once the connections are made, gently tuck the wires and the receptacle in to the box so the holes at top and bottom of the receptacle align with the holes in the box. Use a screwdriver to drive the two long mounting screws that hold the receptacle to the box. Replace the cover plate. Restore the power and test your receptacle.

Childproofing Receptacles

Standard receptacles present a real shock hazard to small children. Fortunately, there are many ways you can make receptacles safer without making them less convenient.

THOUSANDS OF CHILDREN ARE SHOCKED EVERY YEAR when they insert foreign objects in receptacles. Plug-in safety caps are an effective solution, but they make receptacles less convenient. Installing a tamper-resistant receptacle is an easy variation of replacing a bad receptacle (pages 64 to 65). And there are some other simple solutions that will allow you to childproof receptacles in just a few minutes.

CHILDPROOFING 101

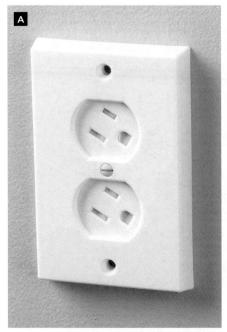

A

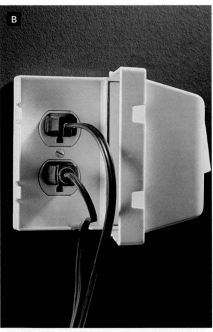

B

C

D

Safety coverplates (A) are designed so plugs need to be twisted before they can be fully inserted. Plug covers (B) replace standard coverplates and allow you to plug in lamps or other devices and then cover the plugs, preventing curious fingers from removing the plugs. Tamper-resistant receptacles (C) feature spring-loaded shutters that remain closed unless the two prongs of a plug enter the slots simultaneously; they won't open for a single pointed object, like a screwdriver or key. A very easy solution is plug-in inserts, which effectively block the receptacle slots completely.

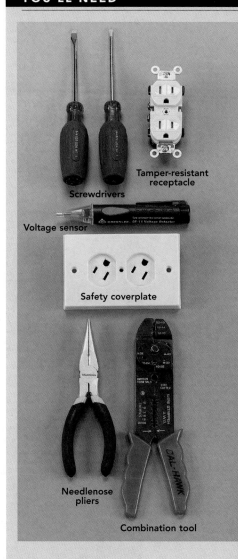
SKILLS YOU'LL NEED

- Turning off the power (page 12)
- Testing for current (page 13)
- Making wire connections (pages 14-16)

DIFFICULTY LEVEL

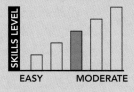

SKILLS LEVEL

EASY   MODERATE

This project will take about 1 hour.

INSTALLING A TAMPER-RESISTANT RECEPTACLE

1 Shut the power to the switch off. Remove the decorative coverplate from the receptacle by unscrewing the screw that holds the plate to the electrical box. Set the screw and the plate aside.

2 Use a voltage sensor to double-check that the circuit is dead. Hold your voltage sensor's probe within ½" of the wires on either side of the receptacle. If the sensor beeps or lights up, then the receptacle is still live, and you'll need to trip the correct breaker to disconnect power to the receptacle. If the sensor does not beep or light up, the receptacle is dead and you can proceed safely.

3 Remove the receptacle from the box by unscrewing the two long screws that hold the switch to the box, one at the top and another at the bottom. Once the screws are out, gently pull the receptacle away from the box. Depending on how your receptacle has been wired, there may be two colored wires and a bare wire or four colored wires and a bare wire.

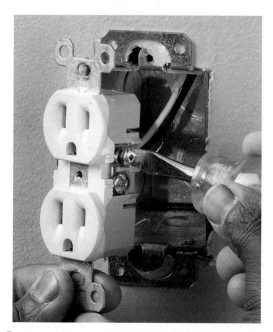

4 Remove the receptacle completely by unscrewing the screws that hold the wires. Disconnect each wire by turning the screws on the sides of the receptacle just enough to free the wires.

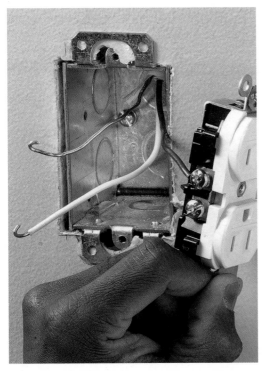

5 Clip off the stripped ends of the wires and use your combination tool to strip away about ¾" of insulation. Then use your needlenose pliers to bend the stripped portions in small, clockwise hooks. Take one of the black wires and wrap the end of the wire around one of the two brass-colored screws on the side of the switch. Tighten the screw so it's snug. If there is a second black wire, wrap it around the other brass screw in the same way.

WHAT IF...?

What if I want a tamper-resistant GFCI receptacle?

No problem. GFCIs are available with the same shutter mechanism. Follow project #14 on page 74 to install one.

6 Now take one of the white wires and wrap the end of the wire around one of the silver screws. Tighten the screw so it's snug. Do the same for the second white wire, if there is one. Connect the copper wire to the green-colored screw on the receptacle.

7 Once the connections are made, gently tuck the wires and the receptacle in to the box so the holes at top and bottom of the receptacle align with the holes in the box. Use a screwdriver to drive the two long mounting screws that hold the receptacle to the box. Replace the coverplate. Restore the power and test your receptacle.

INSTALLING SAFETY COVERPLATES

1 You can get much of the protection of a tamperproof outlet with a safety coverplate. Adding one takes only minutes and requires no contact with wiring. Remove the old coverplate from the receptacle by unscrewing the screw that holds the plate to the electrical box.

2 Hold the safety coverplate over the receptacle. Use a small screwdriver to tighten the screws.

SAFETY TIP

Push-in slot covers cost just pennies, and can be very effective at keeping kids from poking objects into electrical receptacles. Buy several packages, and use them to plug any receptacle that your child might be tempted to play with.

3 To plug a device in, push the slider aside and insert the plug. The shutters automatically snap over the slots when nothing is plugged in.

INSTALLING A PLUG COVER

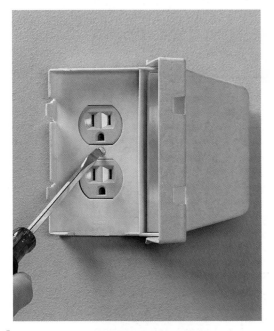

1 Plug covers are designed to replace coverplates on receptacles where devices are plugged in more or less permanently to prevent children from unplugging them. After removing the old coverplate, hold the plug cover's base plate over the receptacle and screw it in with a small screwdriver.

2 Plug in your lamp or other device and snap the plug cover into the new base plate. Cords should fit through the slots in the plug cover.

SAFETY TIP

Any receptacle is made safer by installing it "upside down" with the rounded grounding slot at the top. Three-prong receptacles are almost always installed with the round third prong facing down, but some experts recommend wiring receptacles with the third prong on top. This is because the third prong is the grounding prong and doesn't carry any current under normal operation. In theory, if something were to fall on a partially inserted plug, it would hit the harmless grounding prong and not the current-carrying slot prongs. Either way, you're wiring it right, but upside down may be slightly safer.

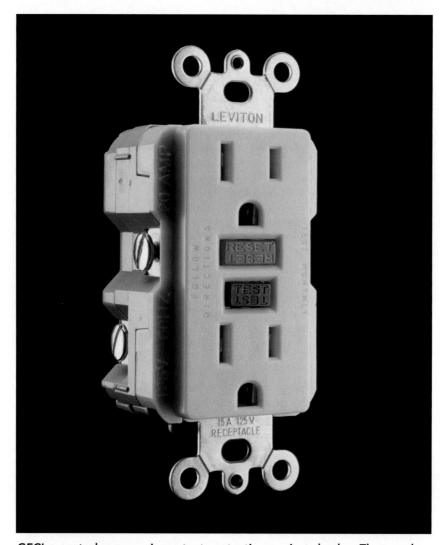

GFCI receptacles are an important protection against shocks. They work just like a normal receptacle, but they have special circuitry that helps prevent shocks. They're required by building code in all wet locations but can help improve safety anywhere.

A GROUND-FAULT CIRCUIT-INTERRUPTER RECEPTACLE (called a GFCI by pros) works just like a standard receptacle with an added feature. In the event of a short, the receptacle shuts off—"trips"—in a tiny fraction of a second. This will protect you from a dangerous shock, and this is why building codes require GFCIs in wet locations like bathrooms, kitchens, and garages.

If you need to replace a faulty receptacle in a kitchen, bathroom, or garage, replace it with a GFCI. Even if your existing receptacles work fine, you can add a measure of safety (and practice your wiring skills) by installing GFCIs. In a child's bedroom, for example, it's a good idea to install a GFCI.

GFCI 101

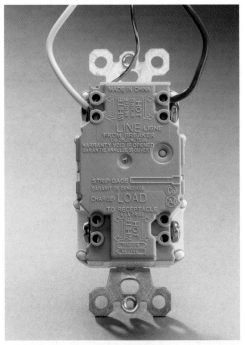

Wiring a GFCI isn't much different from wiring a standard receptacle. The main difference is that, in this installation, you'll only use one pair of the four screws, the ones labeled "line." If there were only two colored wires attached to the old receptacle, the new GFCI is attached in the same way (top photo). But If you have more than one of each color of wire connected to the old receptacle, you'll need to use a technique called pigtailing to connect the GFCI (shown in the image at left). Don't worry; it's easy and you'll see how on the next page.

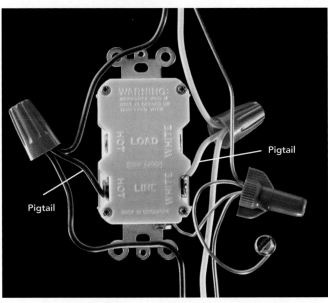

Pigtail

Pigtail

TOOLS & SUPPLIES YOU'LL NEED

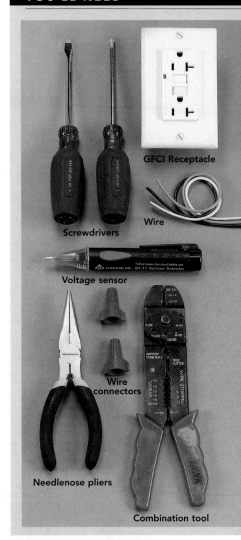

GFCI Receptacle

Wire

Screwdrivers

Voltage sensor

Wire connectors

Needlenose pliers

Combination tool

SKILLS YOU'LL NEED

- Turning off the power (page 12)
- Testing for current (page 13)
- Making wire connections (pages 14-16)

DIFFICULTY LEVEL

SKILLS LEVEL

EASY HARD

This project usually takes about 1 hour.

TERMS YOU NEED TO KNOW

LOAD—In this installation, you're ignoring the screws labeled "load" and using only the ones labeled "line." The load screws literally put a load on the GFCI circuitry of the receptacle by making the GFCI protect other devices on the same circuit (so, other receptacles on the same household circuit could also trip the GFCI in the event of a short). This sounds like a good thing and it is in certain situation. But for your purposes, it will cause a lot of "nuisance" trips, where the GFCI will shut down for no apparent reason. This is why you should use the line screws only.

HOW TO REPLACE A GFCI RECEPTACLE

1 Remove the decorative coverplate from the receptacle. With the coverplate off, you will be able to see the receptacle and the electrical box it is attached to.

3 Remove the receptacle from the box by unscrewing the long screws at the top and the bottom. Once the screws are out, gently pull the receptacle away from the box. It won't pull away easily, since the wires are still attached, so pull firmly. Depending on how your receptacle has been wired, there may be two colored wires and a bare wire or four colored wires and a bare wire.

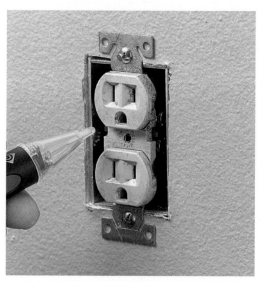

2 Before you remove the old receptacle, use a voltage sensor to make sure the circuit is dead. Hold your voltage sensor's probe within 1/2" of the wires on either side of the receptacle. If the sensor beeps or lights up, then the receptacle is still live, and you'll need to trip the correct breaker to disconnect power to the receptacle. If the sensor does not beep or light up, the receptacle is dead and you can proceed safely.

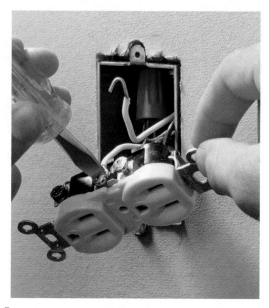

4 Remove the receptacle completely by unscrewing the screws that hold the wires. Disconnect each wire by turning the screws on the sides of the receptacle just enough to free the wires.

5 Now you can start to connect the GFCI. To begin, count the number of wires you just disconnected from the old receptacle. You'll either have three wires—one each of white, black, and bare wires—or you'll have five—a pair of white and black wires and a single bare wire. If you've got five wires, skip to steps 6A and B. If you've got three wires, clip off the stripped ends of the wires and use your combination tool to strip away about ¾" of insulation. Then use your needlenose pliers to bend the stripped portions in small, clockwise hooks and go to step 7.

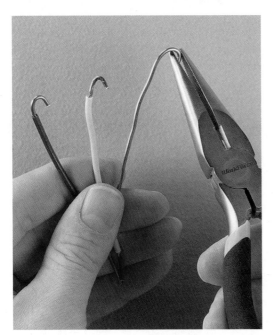

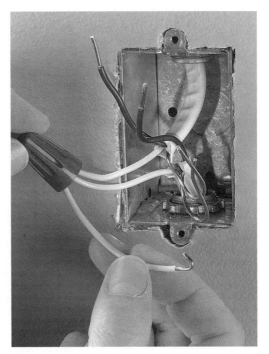

6A If you've got five wires, clip off the stripped ends of the wires and use your combination tool to strip away about ¾" of insulation. Now cut three 3" pieces of 14-gauge wire—one bare, one white, and one black. Strip about ¾" of wire from both ends and then use your needlenose pliers to make a clockwise hook at one end of each. These are your pigtails.

6B Hold the straight end of the white pigtail next to the ends of the two white wires coming from the electrical box. Slide a wire connector over the ends and twist it clockwise until the connector is snug. No bare wire should be visible. Repeat this procedure for the black wires and black pigtail, and then for the two bare wires and the bare pigtail.

HOW TO REPLACE A GFCI RECEPTACLE (CONTINUED)

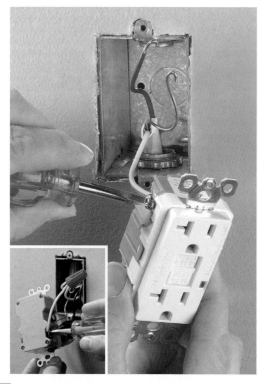

7 Connect the white wire (or the white pigtail; see inset photo) to the silver-colored screw labeled "line."

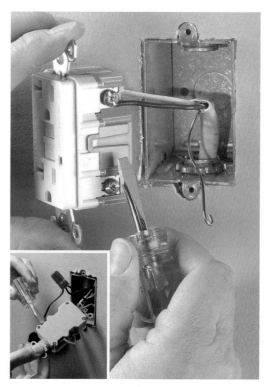

8 Connect the black wire (or the black pigtail; see inset photo) to the copper-colored screw labeled "line."

BUYING TIP

Not all GFCI receptacles are created alike. Make sure you buy one that's rated the same as the receptacle you're replacing. Many household circuits carry 15 amps of power. Receptacles for 15-amp circuits look like the one on the left. But a 20-amp circuit should have receptacles rated for 20 amps, like the one shown on the right. 20-amp receptacles have one T-shaped slot that accepts special T-shaped plugs on appliances with heavy power loads, such as window air conditioners or hot tubs.

15-amp GFCI   20-amp GFCI

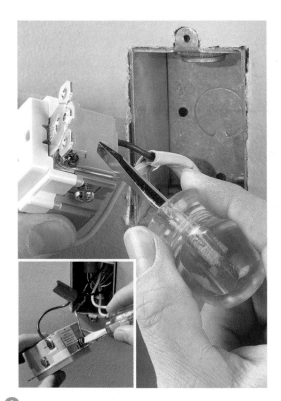

9 Connect the bare wire (or the bare pigtail; see inset photo) to the green grounding screw on the bottom of the receptacle.

10 Once the connections are made, gently tuck the wires and the receptacle into the box so the holes in the top and bottom of the receptacle align with the holes in the box. Use a screwdriver to drive the two long mounting screws that hold the receptacle to the box. Replace the coverplate. If your GFCI didn't come with its own coverplate, you'll need to buy one with a square cutout to fit the GFCI.

11 Restore the power and test your receptacle. In addition to plugging something in to the receptacle, you need to test the two buttons on the face of the receptacle. Press the TEST button. The receptacle should make a clicking noise, the RESET button should pop out, and whatever you've plugged in should stop working. If this happens, the GFCI is wired correctly and working. Push RESET and the receptacle will work again.

15 Replacing a Bad Light Switch

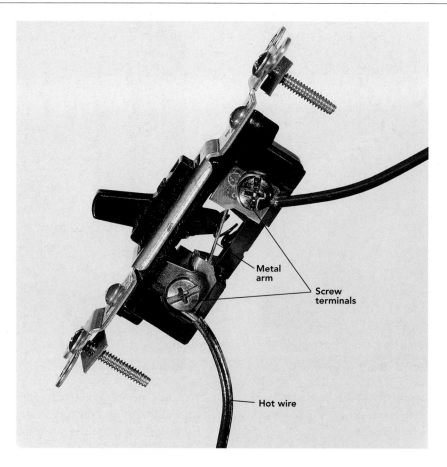

Light switches have moving parts, so they do eventually wear out or stop working reliably. As shown in this cutaway, most switches have a movable metal arm that opens and closes the electrical circuit, and eventually the metal arm loses its resilience, or snaps off. You might also want to replace a switch just because you want a new look, or to install a dimmer (see page 84 to see how).

THERE ARE SEVERAL REASONS WHY YOU MIGHT NEED TO REPLACE A LIGHT SWITCH. If the switch won't stay in position (won't stay on), if it buzzes, if it gets hot, or if a breaker trips when you flip the switch, it might be time to replace the switch. And, of course, you might want to replace the switch for aesthetic reasons or to gain the added functionality of a dimmer. Dimmers not only provide greater control, but they save energy and make light-bulbs last much longer than they would at full power.

Fortunately, swapping an old switch for a new one is a very simple project. You can easily replace the standard light switch with another standard light switch using basic hand tools.

LIGHT SWITCHES 101

TERMS YOU NEED TO KNOW

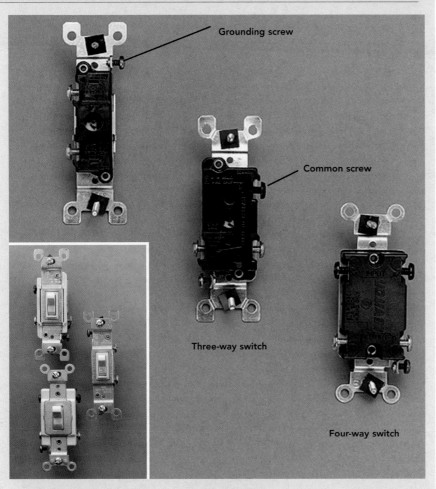

Grounding screw

Common screw

Three-way switch

Four-way switch

Single-pole switch

Wall switches come in three types, and it's crucial you buy the right replacement. Single-pole switches (left) are used when a light fixture is controlled from one switch location only. Notice that it has two screw terminals on the side of the switch (the screw on the metal strap used to connect the grounding wire isn't counted when you talk about circuit wires). A three-way switch (center) is used when a light fixture is controlled from two different wall locations. It has three screws on the body of the switch. One screw is known as the common terminal, the others are called travelers. A four-way switch (right) is used when a light fixture is controlled from three or more different wall locations. It has four screws on the body of the switch. Four-way switches are a little rare; you may not have any of them in your house.

When replacing a switch, remember to buy a replacement that matches the old switch, and connect the wires in the same way they were connected to the old switch.

YOU'LL NEED

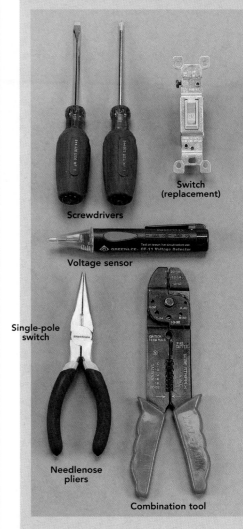

Screwdrivers

Switch (replacement)

Voltage sensor

Needlenose pliers

Combination tool

SKILLS YOU'LL NEED

• Turning off the power (page 12)

• Testing for power (page 13)

• Making wire connections (pages 14-16)

DIFFICULTY LEVEL

SKILLS LEVEL

EASY   MODERATE

Allow about 1 hour for this project.

HOW TO FIX A BAD WALL SWITCH

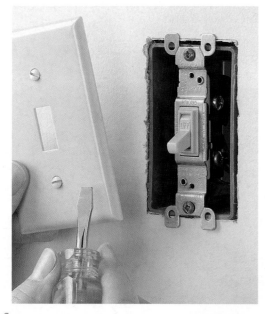

1 First shut off the power to the switch. Remove the decorative coverplate from the switch by unscrewing the two screws that hold the plate to the switch box. Set the screws and the plate aside. With the coverplate off, you will be able to see the switch and the electrical box it is attached to.

2 Use a voltage sensor to make sure the circuit is dead. Hold the sensor's probe within ½" of the wires on either side of the switch. If the sensor beeps or lights up, then the switch is still live, and you'll need to trip the correct breaker to disconnect power to the switch. If the sensor does not beep or light up, the circuit is dead and you're safe to continue.

3 Remove the switch from the box by unscrewing the two long screws that hold the switch to the box, one at the top, the other at the bottom. Once the screws are free, gently pull the switch away from the box.

4 Inspect the screw connections. They should be tight and free of any scorch marks. If one of the connections is loose or scorched, the problem is probably a loose screw causing a short circuit. Reattach the wires, reassemble the switch and coverplate, and see if the switch works. If this isn't the problem, continue to the next step.

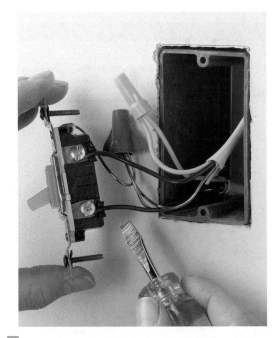

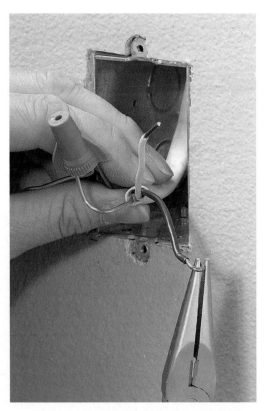

5 Loosen all the screw connections and detach the switch from the wires. (If there are three or four colored wires attached to the switch instead of just two, see the "WHAT IF" variation on the next page.) In many cases, there will also be two white wires connected with a wire connector in the box. You won't have to deal with these in your installation. Take the old switch to a hardware store or home center and purchase an identical replacement.

6 Before you begin to wire your new switch, clip of the ends of the wires and use your combination tool to strip away about ¾"of insulation. Then use your needlenose pliers to bend the stripped portion in a small clockwise hook.

WHAT IF...?

What if there is a white wire connected to the switch?

In certain installations, a switch is connected with one black wire and one white wire. (The pros call this installation a "switch loop.") If the electrician did a good job, the end of the white wire should have black tape, indicating that it carries current. Treat it just like a black wire when you install your new switch. If there is no tape on the end of the white wire, wrap a bit of electrical tape on the end. The next person who works on the circuit will thank you.

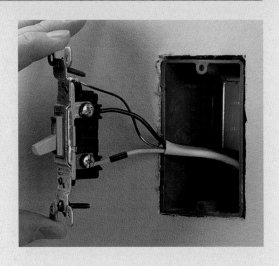

HOW TO FIX A BAD WALL SWITCH (CONTINUED)

WHAT IF...?

What if there are more than two colored wires connected to the switch? If this is the case, you're dealing with a three-way switch (if there are three colored wires) or a four-way switch (if there are four colored wires). Before removing a three- or four-way switch, use masking tape to label the wires to identify which screw terminals they are attached to.

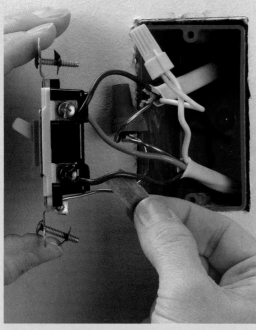

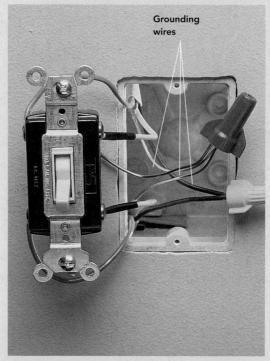

Grounding wires

For a three-way switch, one screw terminal is labeled "common," and is almost always darker in color than the other two. Make sure the wire that was attached to the common screw terminal on the old switch is connected to the common screw terminal on the new switch. The other two wires aren't critical; they can be attached to either of the remaining screw terminals.

Four-way switches are a little trickier. In most cases, you'll be attaching the pair of wires attached to the top two screw terminals on the old switch to the same screws on the new switch. Then you'll attach the other pair of wires to the bottom pair of screws. Some manufacturers, though, use a different pairing system, with one screw terminal pair on the right side of the switch, the other on the left. A good way to avoid problems is by buying a replacement made by the same manufacturer that made the old switch.

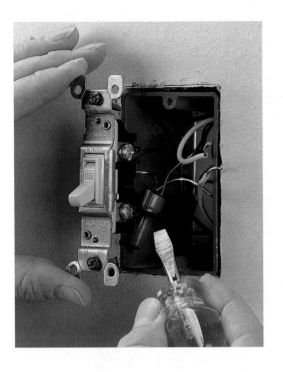

7 Position the switch so the ON/OFF markings read correctly. Take one of the colored circuit wires and wrap the end of the wire clockwise around one of the two screw terminals on the side of the switch. Tighten the screw so it's snug. Wrap the second colored wire around the other screw in the same way. If there was a bare copper wire connected to the old switch, connect it to the green-colored screw on the switch in the same way you connected the two black wires. (If you're installing a three-way or four-way, see the information on the opposite page.) Then connect the rest of the wires as described above. The other two screws are interchangeable, so it doesn't matter which of the remaining colored wires connects to which screw.

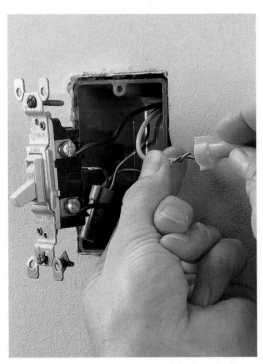

8 Check to make sure the white circuit wires (they're called the neutrals) are snugly connected. If not, then use a wire nut to join them.

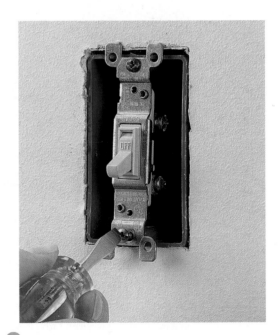

9 Once the connections are made, gently tuck the wires and the switch into the box so the holes in the top and bottom of the switch align with the holes in the box. Use a screwdriver to drive the two long mounting screws that hold the switch to the box. Replace the coverplate. Restore the power and test your switch.

Installing a Dimmer

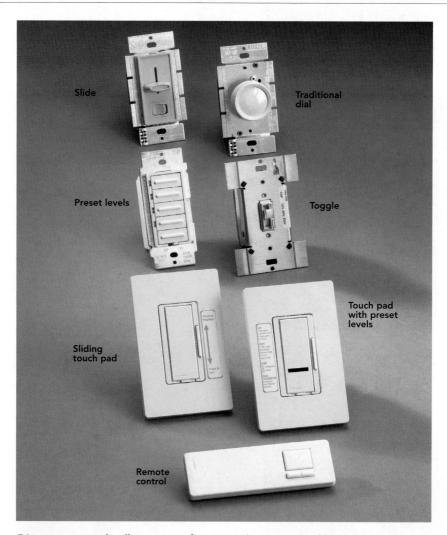

Slide

Traditional dial

Preset levels

Toggle

Touch pad with preset levels

Sliding touch pad

Remote control

Dimmers not only allow you to fine-tune the amount of light in a room, but also they save energy and extend lightbulb life. There is a wide variety of dimmer switches available to replace almost any standard ON/OFF switch. Whether you flip, turn, slide, or touch them, they all work the same. The one exception is an automatic dimmer, which has an electronic sensor that adjusts the light fixture to compensate for the changing levels of natural light. An automatic dimmer also can be operated manually.

DIMMER SWITCHES ARE SIMPLY LIGHT SWITCHES that allow you to control the intensity of light that comes from a fixture. The control may be a dial, a touch pad, a slider, or a faux-toggle switch, but they all function in basically the same way.

Installing a dimmer is no more difficult than installing a light switch. The only possible obstacles are the size of the electrical box and the type of light in the fixture. In some older homes, the metal box that contains the old switch may not be large enough for a dimmer. If the fixture uses fluorescent lightbulbs, you will not be able to use a standard dimmer.

DIMMER SWITCHES 101

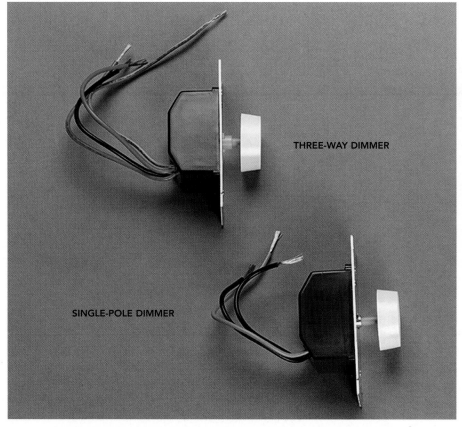

THREE-WAY DIMMER

SINGLE-POLE DIMMER

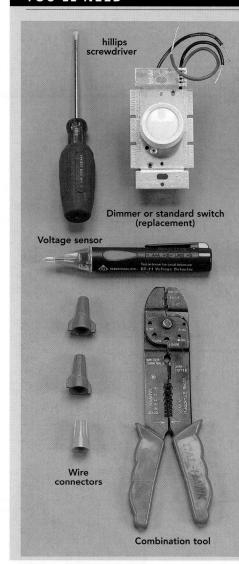

TOOLS & SUPPLIES YOU'LL NEED

hillips
screwdriver

Dimmer or standard switch
(replacement)

Voltage sensor

Wire
connectors

Combination tool

Unlike standard light switches, dimmers are connected to the household electrical wires by short lengths of wire called "leads." Leads come pre-attached to the dimmer. You attach them to the household wiring with wire connectors. Single-pole dimmers have two wire leads (plus a green grounding lead). Use this type for switches where the light fixture is controlled from a single wall location. Three-way dimmers have three black and red wire leads, and are used when a light fixture is controlled from two wall locations.

SKILLS YOU'LL NEED

- Turning off the power (page 12)
- Testing for current (page 13)
- Making wire connections (pages 14-16)

TERMS YOU NEED TO KNOW

COMMON WIRE—On a three-way wall switch or dimmer, one of the screw termi-nals or wire leads is designated as "common." Depending on where the switch is in the circuit, the common wire receives electrical current from the power source, or sends current to the light fixture. The common screw terminal or wire lead is the one that is a different color from the other two screws or wire leads.

TRAVELER WIRE—On three way switches and dimmers, the travelers are the two wires other than the common (see above). The traveler wires run between the two switches, providing alternative paths for electrical current.

DIFFICULTY LEVEL

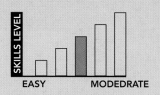

SKILLS LEVEL

EASY   MODEDRATE

Allow 1 to 2 hours for this job.

HOW TO INSTALL A DIMMER SWITCH

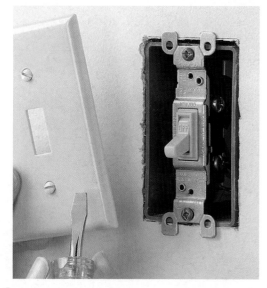

1 First shut off the power to the switch. Remove the decorative coverplate from the switch by unscrewing the two screws that hold the plate to the switch box. Set the screws and the plate aside. With the coverplate off, you will be able to see the switch and the electrical box it is attached to.

2 Use a voltage sensor to make sure that the circuit is dead. Hold your voltage sensor's probe within ½" of the wires on either side of the switch. If the sensor beeps or lights up, then the switch is still live, and you'll need to trip the correct breaker to disconnect power to the switch. If the sensor does not beep or light up, the circuit is dead and you are safe to continue.

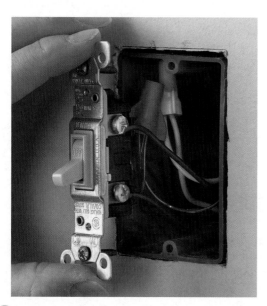

3 Remove the switch from the box by unscrewing the two long screws that hold it. One is at the top and another at the bottom. Once the screws are out, hold the top and bottom of the switch, and gently pull the switch away from the box.

WHAT IF...?

What if my electrical box seems too small to hold the dimmer switch? Dimmer switches have much bigger bodies than standard switches, and they are connected with twist wire con-

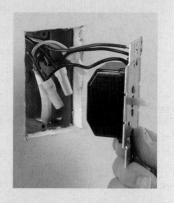

nectors rather than screw terminal connections. This means that the electrical box might be too small to hold the switch and the connections. If so, don't try to force the switch into the box. Instead, see the Here's How feature on page 89.

4 Remove the switch completely by unscrewing the screws that hold the wires. There may be as many as four wires connected to the switch: black, white, bare copper, and red. Disconnect each one by turning the screws on the sides of the switch just enough to free the wires. In many cases, there will also be two white wires connected with a wire connector in the box. You won't have to deal with these in your installation.

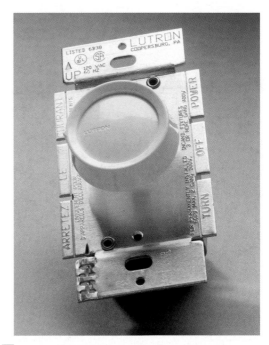

5 Buy a dimmer suited for your replacement. Choose a single-pole or three-way dimmer, as needed. Second, buy a dimmer rated for the maximum wattage of all light fixtures the switch will serve. For example, if the standard light switch you are replacing controls three recessed 60-watt lights, then the dimmer switch should be rated for 180 watts ($60 \times 3 = 180$).

WHAT IF...?

What if you find four colored wires attached to your switch?

This is a four-way switch, a type of switch used to control light fixtures from three or more different switch locations. A four-way switch can't be replaced with a dimmer, so if you run into this situation, you'll need to reassemble the switch. However, four-way switch installations are always installed in conjunction with three-way switches in the other switch locations. You will be able to replace one of the three-way switches at a different wall location with a three-way dimmer switch.

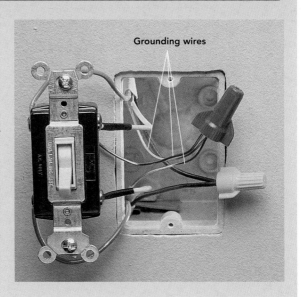

Grounding wires

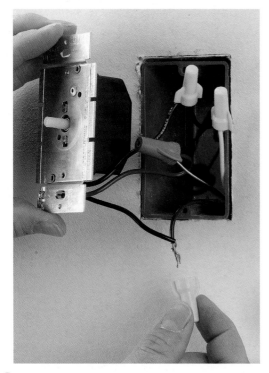

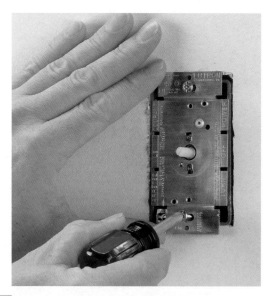

6 The dimmer will have two black wires, called leads, coming out of the dimmer's plastic body. The leads, like the two black wires coming out of the wall, are interchangeable, so you can't mix them up. Place the stripped end of one of the black leads and the end of one of the existing black wires into a wire connector (the dimmer will come with twist-on wire connectors). Twist the wire connector clockwise until it is tight. Hold the wires and tug gently on the connector to ensure that it is tight. Connect the other lead to the other wire from the wall in the same way. (If you are installing a three-way dimmer, see "WHAT IF...?" at right.)

7 Once the wires are firmly connected, you can attach the switch to the box. Tuck the new switch and wires neatly back into the box. Then drive the two long screws that are attached to the new switch into the two holes in the electrical box. These screws are typically long, so an electric screwdriver is handy. Reattach the coverplate. Then, turn the power back on at the main panel and test the switch for operation.

WHAT IF...?

If you're installing a three-way dimmer, attach the wire lead identified as the common to the circuit wire you tagged as the common in step 4. Now attach the other two wire leads to the other two colored circuit wires, using wire connectors. These wires, called the travelers, are interchangeable. It doesn't make any difference which of the two remaining circuit wires they get attached to.

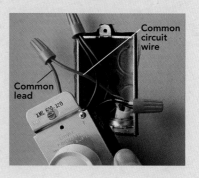

Common circuit wire

Common lead

Dimmer switches have larger bodies than traditional toggle switches, so you may find that the existing electrical box is too small to comfortably hold the new dimmer switch. Shallow, 2"-deep electrical boxes will not easily accommodate dimmer switches, especially if there are more than one set of wires inside the electrical box. If you purchase a dimmer and can't seem to get it to fit, don't force it. Dimmers produce more heat than standard switches, and it is a potential fire hazard to crowd the electrical box. You may be able to find a dimmer with a smaller body that will fit. Or, you can install a new, larger wall box.

Installing a new wall box is a somewhat advanced project, so you may want to hire a professional to do this work. But if you're up to the task, you can do it yourself by following the directions below. Allow yourself a full afternoon for this graduate school project.

1 Remove the old switch, following steps 1 through 5 on pages 88 and 89. To remove the old box, identify the location of the nails holding the electrical box to the wall studs. Use a reciprocating saw or jigsaw equipped with a metal-cutting blade to cut through the nails holding the box.

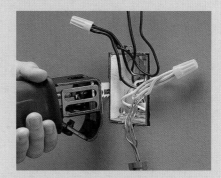

2 Bind the cable ends together and attach them to strings so they don't fall into the wall cavity when the old box is removed. Disconnect the cable clamps and slide the old box out.

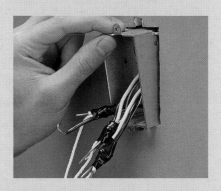

3 Feed the cable into the new box, tighten the cable clamps, and secure the box in the opening. The retrofit box shown here uses bracket arms that are inserted into the sides of the box, then bent around the front edges to secure the box in the opening. Other styles of retrofit boxes have other means of attachment. Attach the new dimmer, following steps 6 and 7 on the preceding page.

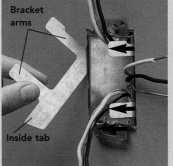

Bracket arms

Inside tab

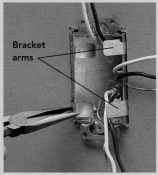

Bracket arms

Installing a Timer Switch

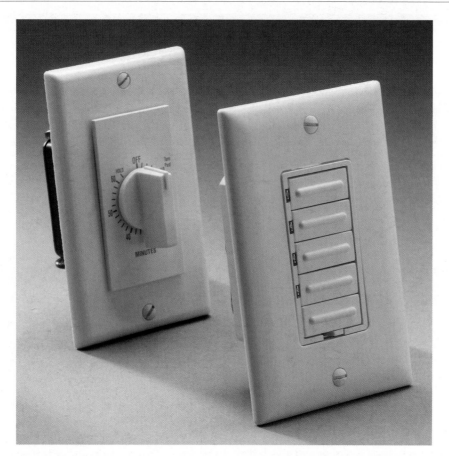

There are two common types of timer switch. Dial-type timers are commonly used to control bathroom vents and outdoor lights. To turn on the light and set the timer, simply twist the dial to the desired setting. When the dial winds down, the light or fan goes off. Push-button timers are commonly used to control lights. They have three or four switches, each with a preset time setting.

TIMER SWITCHES ARE SIMPLY SWITCHES THAT TURN ON OR OFF after a determined amount of time. This is useful for controlling some types of exterior lights and for controlling bathroom vent fans. With outdoor lights, you can use a timer to turn on landscape and security lighting at preset times. In the bathroom, the timer can vastly increase the efficacy of your vent fan by making sure it runs long enough to completely evacuate moist air. You can also use push-button-type timer switches to control room lights, thus assuring that no light is left burning indefinitely.

Installing a timer is no more difficult than installing a light switch. As with dimmers, the size of the box holding the switch in the wall is a consideration. In some older homes, the metal box that contains the old switch may not be large enough for a timer. If so, see page 89 for information on changing the box.

TIMER SWITCHES 101

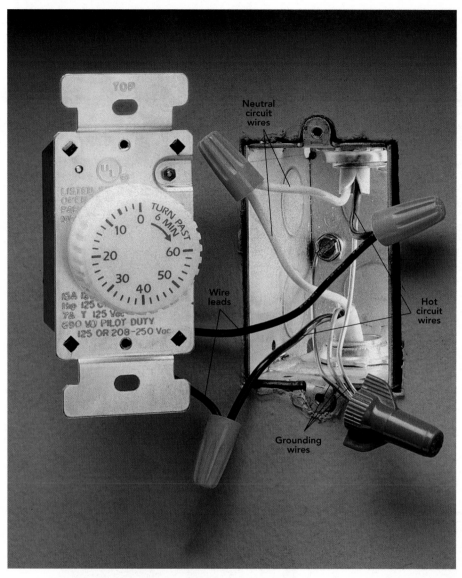

Neutral circuit wires

Wire leads

Grounding wires

Hot circuit wires

Unlike standard light switches and like dimmers, most timers are connected to the household electrical wires by short lengths of wire called leads. Leads come preattached to the timer. You attach them to the household wiring with wire connectors.

TERMS YOU NEED TO KNOW

LEADS—The preattached black wires attached to a timer switch.

GROUNDING WIRES—The bare copper circuit wires in an electrical box.

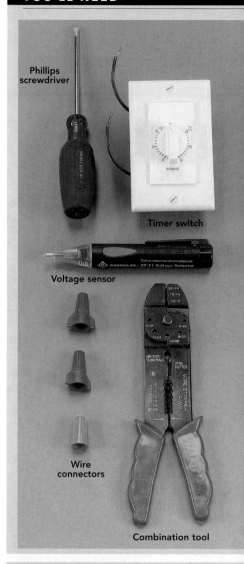

HOW TO INSTALL A TIMER SWITCH

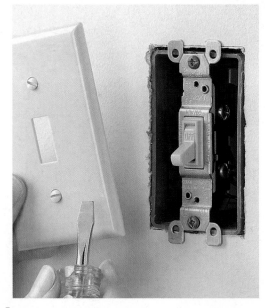

1 First shut off the power to the switch. Remove the decorative coverplate from the switch by unscrewing the two screws that hold the plate to the switch box. Set the screws and the plate aside.

2 Use a voltage sensor to make sure the circuit is dead. Hold your voltage sensor's probe within ½" of the wires on either side of the switch. If the sensor beeps or lights up, then the switch is still live, and you'll need to trip the correct breaker to disconnect power to the switch. If the sensor does not beep or light up, the circuit is dead and you're safe to continue.

3 Remove the switch from the box by unscrewing the two long screws that hold the switch to the box at the top and at the bottom. Once the screws are out, hold the top and bottom of the switch, and carefully pull the switch away from the box.

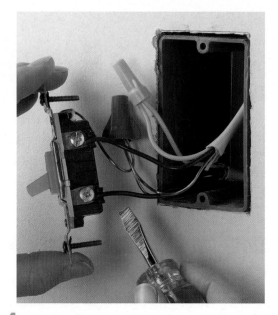

4 Remove the switch completely by unscrewing the screws that hold the two wires to the switch. In most cases, there will also be two white wires connected with a wire connector in the box. You won't have to deal with these in your installation.

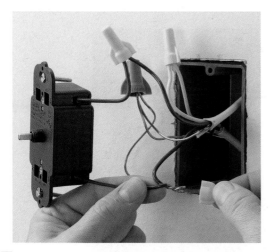

5 The timer will have two black wires, called leads, coming out of the timer's plastic body. The leads, like the two black wires coming out of the wall, are interchangeable, so you can't mix them up. Place the stripped end of one of the black leads and the end of one of the existing black wires into a wire connector (the dimmer will come with twist-on wire connectors). Twist the wire connector clockwise until it is tight. Hold the wires and tug gently on the connector to ensure that it is tight. Connect the other lead to the other wire from the wall in the same way.

6 Once the wires are firmly connected, you can attach the switch to the box. Tuck the new timer switch and wires neatly back into the box. Then drive the two long screws that are attached to the new switch into the two holes in the electrical box. These screws are typically long, so an electric screwdriver is handy. Pull the dial off the timer so the coverplate will fit over it. Reattach the coverplate and push the dial back onto the timer stem. Then, turn the power back on at the main panel and test the switch.

WHAT IF...?

What if there's a light switch right next to the fan switch?

This is a common arrangement. You might even find a group of three switches together. Behind the single coverplate, you'll find one large electrical box, called a "double-gang" box if there are two switches, that contains all the connections. This won't affect your installation except in one way: the coverplate. The coverplate that comes with your timer will be for a single switch. You'll need to buy a double-gang coverplate with a cutout for your timer (a small hole in the center) and one for a standard light switch.

18 Installing Low-voltage Cable Lights

Low-voltage cable lights are a flexible and attractive way to update a lighting design. It doesn't take more than a couple of hours to replace a standard ceiling fixture with a low-voltage cable system.

LOW-VOLTAGE CABLE LIGHTS are one of the newest developments in lighting. They offer many of the advantages of track lighting, but are even easier to install and often less expensive. The light fixtures can be moved along the cable and aimed individually to achieve the desired mood or task lighting, making them an ideal replacement for a central fixture that casts too many shadows. Replacing an old ceiling-mounted light fixture with a low-voltage cable light is a fairly simple project.

Before you begin, it's important to spend some time planning the location of the cables and lights. Investigate the area you would like to light. You can use a yardstick or tape measure to identify the length, the placement of cables, and the number of lights that you will need to achieve the effect you're looking for.

LOW-VOLTAGE LIGHTS 101

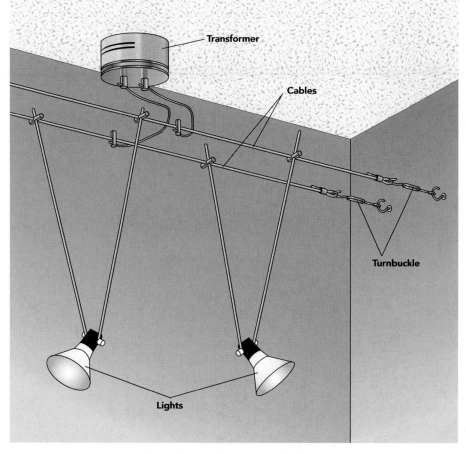

Transformer

Cables

Turnbuckle

Lights

Low-voltage cable lights run off a transformer that reduces 120-volt current to 12 volts. Current runs along the cables to the hanging light fixtures. This means that there is low risk of electrical shock from the cables as long as the location is dry. The low-voltage system includes a transformer, cables, and lights. The cables are secured in the walls using a turnbuckle system that allows you to pull the wires between the walls and tighten.

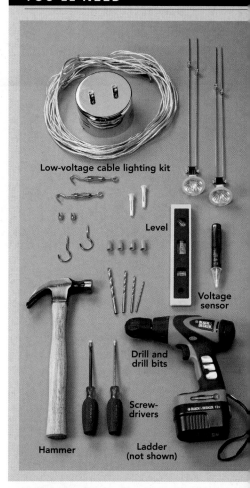

Low-voltage cable lighting kit

Level

Voltage sensor

Drill and drill bits

Screw-drivers

Hammer

Ladder (not shown)

SKILLS YOU'LL NEED

- Turning off power (page 12)
- Testing for current (page 13)
- Making wire connections (pages 14-16)
- Light carpentry tool skills

TERMS YOU NEED TO KNOW

LOW-VOLTAGE LIGHTING—For indoor lighting purposes, low voltage means 12 volts or, rarely, 24 volts. Normal voltage is 120 volts.

TRANSFORMER—An electrical device that steps up voltage and steps down current proportionally (or vice versa). In lighting applications, transformers take 120 volts down to 12.

HALOGEN—Low-voltage systems use small halogen bulbs. Halogen bulbs work like regular incandescent lightbulbs, except the bulbs are filled with halogen gas, making the bulbs burn brighter at a lower voltage.

DIFFICULTY LEVEL

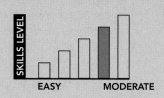

SKILLS LEVEL

EASY   MODERATE

This job takes about two hours, and is easier with two people.

1 Locate the circuit breaker that controls the existing ceiling-mounted light that you are working on, and switch that breaker into the OFF position. Close the cover of the breaker or fuse cabinet.

2 Remove the globe (many are held in place by a decorative nut in the center), and remove the lightbulbs from the fixture. Detach the old light from the ceiling electrical box. Most traditional fixtures use two long screws to secure the fixture base to the metal electrical box in the ceiling. Have a helper hold the fixture with one hand so it doesn't fall, while you use a screwdriver to remove the two screws. Gently pull the light straight down, exposing the wiring that powers the fixture.

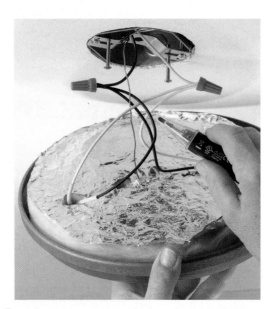

3 Before you touch the wires that feed the existing light, use a voltage sensor to verify that the circuit is now dead. Insert the sensor's probe into the electrical box and hold the probe within ½" of the black wires inside. If the sensor beeps or lights up, then the circuit is still live, and you'll need to trip the correct breaker to disconnect power to the fixture. If the sensor does not beep or light up, the circuit is dead and you're safe to continue.

4 Now remove the fixture by disconnecting the wires. Use your hands to unscrew the wire connectors by turning them counterclockwise. After removing the wire connectors, pull the fixture completely away from the box (you can recycle it or save it). If you need to stop working and restore the power, first separate the wires coming from the ceiling box and cap them each with a wire connector.

5 Plan a path for the parallel cables. The path should pass under (within a foot or so, at least) of the old fixture. Installation of the wall-anchoring system varies somewhat by manufacturer, so read and follow the specific instructions for your kit. The simplest systems use hooks and turnbuckles to tension the cables. To install, mark holes 6 to 10" apart on opposite walls at the ends of the planned cable runs.

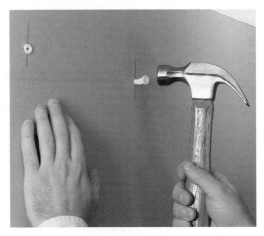

6 Unless you know your holes go into the studs behind the walls, you'll need to anchor the hooks in the drywall with hollow wall anchors. These are simply plastic tubes that ensure the hooks will be secure in the walls. Most kits include wall anchors appropriate for the supplied hooks. Use a drill and a ¼" drill bit to make holes on your marks. Tap a plastic wall anchor into the hole with a hammer so the anchor's top is nearly level with the surface. Do this for each of the holes unless you know the hole goes into a stud.

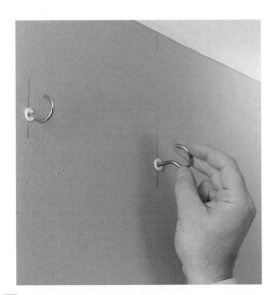

7 Now you can screw the hooks into the anchors. Screw the hooks in by hand. When they become too difficult to turn, use a pair of pliers to turn the hooks until all the threads have disappeared into the anchors.

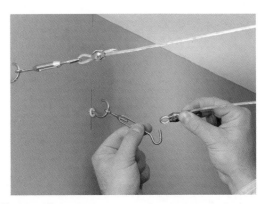

8 Measure the distance between opposite hooks, and then cut two lengths of the supplied cable to that length plus an extra 12". Use your lineman's pliers to cut the cable. Follow the manufacturer's instructions for attaching a loop to one end of each cable and a turnbuckle to the other. Then, place the loop of a cable on one hook and the turnbuckle on the opposite wall's hook. Tighten the turnbuckle to take up the slack until the cable is tight. Install the other cable in the same way. Cut away any extra cable for a clean look.

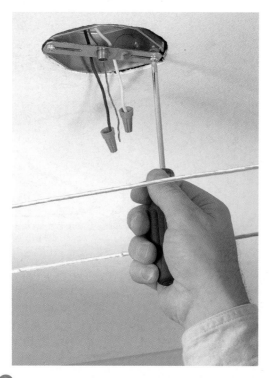

9 Make sure the power is off to the wires in the electrical box before you touch the wires or begin to install the transformer. Install the transformer crossbar to the electrical box using the two screws provided with the fixture.

11 Connect the transformer and its decorative cover to the crossbar you installed in step 9.

10 Have a helper hold the transformer or rest it on top of a ladder while you make the electrical connections. Place the stripped end of one of the black wires from the transformer and the end of one of the black wires coming from the ceiling into a wire connector (supplied with the lighting kit). Twist the wire connector clockwise until it is tight. Connect the white wire from the transformer to the white wire coming from the electrical box. Connect the bare copper wire from the transformer to the bare copper wire coming from the electrical box.

HERE'S HOW

Here's how to purchase the right cable light kit. Aside from purchasing a kit that looks right for your space, you'll need one with the appropriate transformer. This project shows a "hard-wired" transformer—one that's connected directly to the household wiring. Some inexpensive kits use plug-in transformers that connect to a regular wall receptacle. They work fine, but they don't look as polished. You'll also need a transformer that supplies the right amount of power in watts. You can figure out the maximum number of watts simply by looking on the sides of the sockets of the old fixture. It should have a rating for maximum watts. Multiply this number by the number of bulb sockets. You can use a transformer that has up to this many watts.

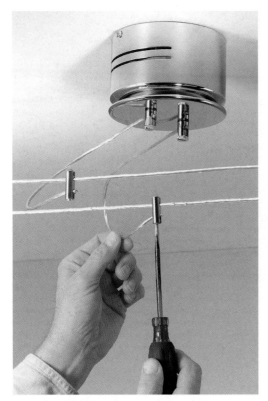

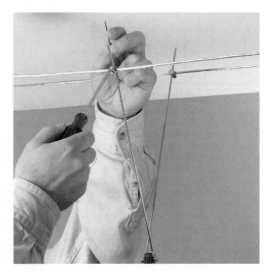

12 Now you can begin to connect the transformer to the two parallel cables you already installed. The transformer has two screw terminals somewhere on its cover. Cut two lengths of the supplied cable to reach from the screw terminals to the parallel cables. Insert one end of the cable into the screw terminal on the transformer and tighten the screw until you feel its tip pierce the insulation. Connect the other lead to the transformer in the same way.

13 Using the connector supplied with the kit, connect the other end of one of the short cables to one of the two parallel cables. The key is to make sure all the screws are tight enough so their tips pierce the cable's insulation and provide a good electrical connection. Connect the other short cable to the other parallel cable in the same way.

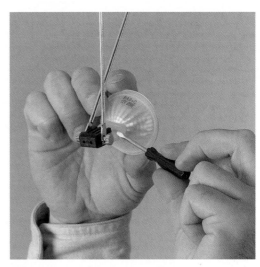

14 At this point, it's a good idea to restore power and turn the light switch on. 12 volts won't hurt you (if you can even feel it) and it's easier to adjust the lights when they're on. The hardware used to connect the fixtures to the cables varies considerably from manufacturer to manufacturer, but most rely on some sort of setscrew to pierce each cable's insulation so current can flow to the lightbulbs. The key is to get those screws (which are often small) tight. A small, short screwdriver is very helpful.

15 Once the fixtures are connected, install and adjust the bulbs so they're aimed as you like. The bulbs have two short prongs coming out of their bases. These provide the electrical connection. Typically, the prongs slide into two holes in the fixtures base and are secured by two small screws. Tightening these can be tricky. Use a small screwdriver and don't overtighten the screws. Get them just tight enough to hold the bulbs.

19 Replacing a Ceiling-mounted Fixture

Installing a new ceiling fixture can provide more light to a space, not to mention an aesthetic lift. It's one of the easiest upgrades you can do.

CEILING FIXTURES DON'T HAVE ANY MOVING PARTS and their wiring is very simple, so, other than changing bulbs, you're likely to get decades of trouble-free service from a fixture. This sounds like a good thing, but it also means that the fixture probably won't fail and give you an excuse to update a room's look with a new one. Fortunately, you can don't need an excuse. Upgrading a fixture is easy and can make a dramatic impact on a room. You can substantially increase the light in a room by replacing a globe-style fixture by one with separate spot lights, or you can simply install a new fixture that matches the room's décor.

CEILING FIXTURES 101

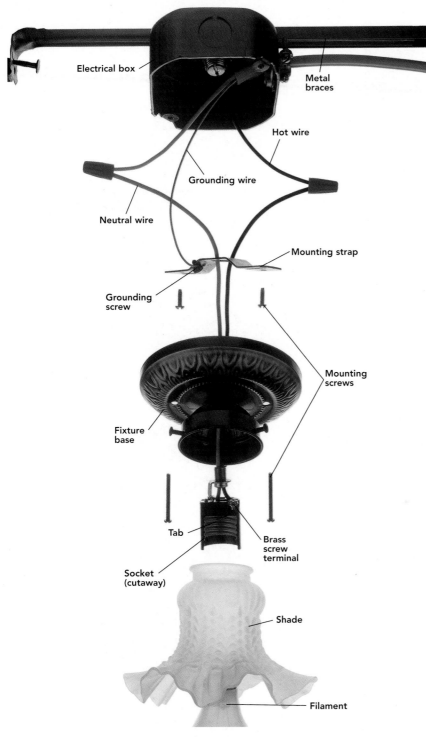

Electrical box

Metal braces

Hot wire

Grounding wire

Neutral wire

Mounting strap

Grounding screw

Mounting screws

Fixture base

Tab

Brass screw terminal

Socket (cutaway)

Shade

Filament

No matter what a ceiling light fixture looks like on the outside, they all attach in basically the same way. An electrical box in the ceiling is fitted with a mounting strap, which holds the fixture in place. The bare wire from the ceiling typically connects to the mounting strap. The two wires coming from the fixture connect to the black and white wires from the ceiling.

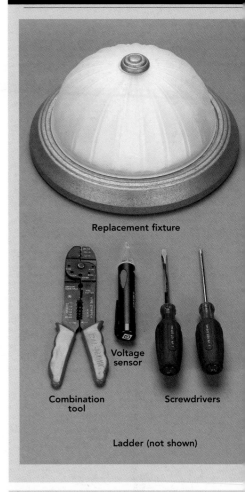

Replacement fixture

Voltage sensor

Combination tool

Screwdrivers

Ladder (not shown)

SKILLS YOU'LL NEED

- Turning off the power (page 12)
- Testing for current (page 13)
- Making wire connections (pages 14-16)

DIFFICULTY LEVEL

SKILL LEVEL

EASY   MODERATE

This project should take you 2 hours or less, and will be easier if you have a helper.

HOW TO REPLACE A CEILING-MOUNTED LIGHT FIXTURE

1 Begin by turning off the power to the fixture. Remove the globe by unthreading the globe (turning it counterclockwise) or by loosening the three screws that pinch the globe in place (the screws usually go through a collar around the base of the globe). Next, remove the lightbulbs from the fixture.

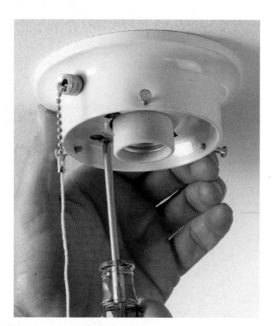

2 Detach the old light from the ceiling electrical box. Most traditional fixtures use two long screws to secure the fixture base to the metal electrical box in the ceiling. Have a helper hold the fixture with one hand so it doesn't fall, while you use a screwdriver to remove the two screws. Gently pull the light straight down, exposing the wiring that powers the fixture.

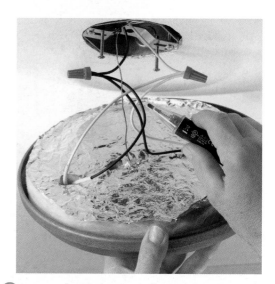

3 Before you touch the wires that feed the existing light, use a voltage sensor to verify that the circuit is now dead. With the fixture's switch in the ON position, insert the sensor's probe into the electrical box and hold the probe within ½" of the black wires inside. If the sensor beeps or lights up, then the circuit is still live, and you'll need to trip the correct breaker to disconnect power to the fixture. If the sensor does not beep or light up, the circuit is dead and you can proceed safely.

4 Once you have verified that the power to the light is off at the main panel, remove the fixture by disconnecting the wires. Use your hands to unscrew the wire connectors by turning them counterclockwise. After removing the wire connectors, pull the fixture completely away from the box (you can recycle it or save it). If you need to stop working and restore the power, first separate the wires coming from the ceiling box and cap them each with a wire connector.

WHAT IF...?

What if there are no wire connectors?

If the fixture is small, the wires from the box may be connected directly to the fixture. To disconnect them, simply loosen the screws enough to free the wires.

5 Before you install the new fixture, check the ends of the wires coming from the ceiling electrical box. They should be clean and free of nicks or scorch marks. If they're dirty or worn, clip off the stripped portion with your combination tool. Then, strip away about ¾" of insulation from the end of each wire.

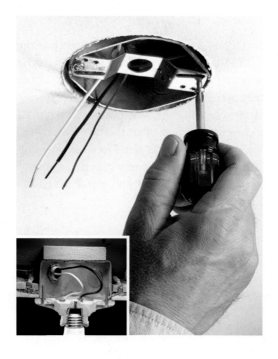

6 Now, take a look at the electrical box. Most fixtures installed in the last few decades are attached to a mounting strap, a strip of metal reaching from one side of the electrical box to another and attached with two screws. Older light fixtures were often mounted directly to the holes in the box (inset), a less safe installation that doesn't meet current electrical codes.

7 If the box doesn't have a mounting strap, attach one. One might be included with your new fixture; otherwise, you can buy one at any hardware store or home center.

8 You will probably find a bare copper wire in the box. Connect this wire to the screw near the center of the mounting strap. Wrap the wire clockwise around the screw and turn the screw until it is snug.

9 Set the new fixture on top of a ladder or have a helper support it. You'll find two short wires—called leads—coming from the fixture, one white and one black. If the ends of the leads are not already stripped, remove about ¾" of insulation from each wire end. Hold the white lead from the fixture next to the white wire from the ceiling. Push the ends into a wire connector, and twist the connector clockwise until it is snug.

10 Now connect the black wire to the black lead with a wire connector in the same way. Give both connections a gentle tug to make sure the connectors are tight.

11 Tuck the wire connections into the ceiling box on either side of the mounting strap. Hold the fixture over the electrical box so its two mounting holes line up with the holes on the mounting strap. Secure the light to the ceiling box by driving the fixture's mounting screws through the holes in the fixture base and into the strap. These screws are typically quite long, so an electric screwdriver is helpful.

12 With the fixture secured to the box, you can install the lightbulbs and shades. Each fixture is a little different; follow the manufacturer's instructions. Once the bulbs are in, restore power to the fixture and test it.

20 Replace a Hanging Light Fixture

Replacing an old chandelier is a quick and easy way to make a big change to a room's character, not to mention the quality of its light.

CHANDELIERS AND OTHER HANGING FIXTURES EXIST IN A HUGE VARIETY OF STYLES, so chances are good that you might acquire a house with a chandelier you find less than attractive. Of course, you might also have a chandelier stop working for some reason. Either way, they're easy enough to replace.

A properly installed chandelier has more bracing behind it than a standard ceiling fixture, so don't try to replace a simple ceiling globe with a 50-pound chandelier. You'll likely find a broken chandelier on your dining room table if you do.

CHANDELIERS 101

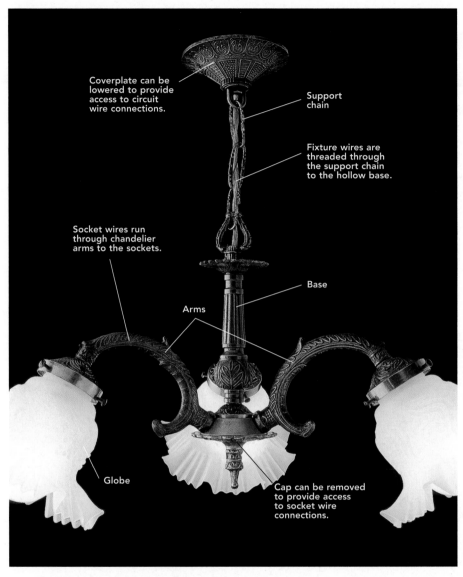

Coverplate can be lowered to provide access to circuit wire connections.

Support chain

Fixture wires are threaded through the support chain to the hollow base.

Socket wires run through chandelier arms to the sockets.

Base

Arms

Globe

Cap can be removed to provide access to socket wire connections.

Chandeliers can be a maze of wires, but fortunately, to install one, you only need to deal with the two fixture wires that snake up the chain.

TOOLS & SUPPLIES YOU'LL NEED

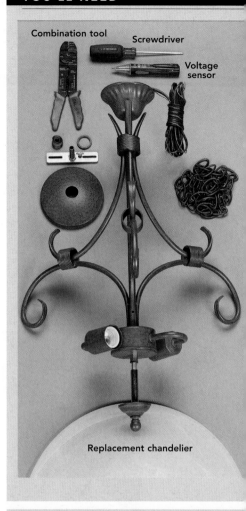

Combination tool

Screwdriver

Voltage sensor

Replacement chandelier

SKILLS YOU'LL NEED

- Making wire connections (pages 14-16)

Note: This job is easier with two people.

HERE'S HOW

Heavy chandeliers and ceiling fans are suspended from electrical boxes that are secured between ceiling joists with heavy-duty braces.

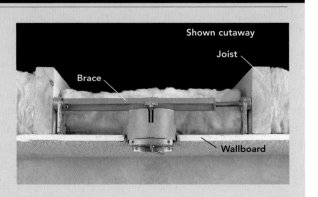

Shown cutaway

Joist

Brace

Wallboard

DIFFICULTY LEVEL

SKILLS LEVEL

EASY   MODERATE

Allow about 2 hours for this project.

HOW TO INSTALL A NEW CHANDELIER

Chandeliers are heavy, as you will learn very quickly when you're removing or installing one. It's better to rig up some means of temporary support for the fixture than to rely on a helper to hold it or—worse still—try to hold it yourself (you will need both hands to make the connections). One solution is to position a tall stepladder directly below the work area so you can rest the fixture on the top platform. And just in case the fixture falls, remove all the bulbs and globes before you do any of the work.

Retainer nut with integral chain loop

1 Remove the old light fixture. To gain access to the wiring connections, unfasten the retainer nut that secures the coverplate for the electrical box. On some chandeliers (such as the one above), the ring that holds the support chain for the chandelier is integral to the retainer nut, so unfastening it will mean the fixture is being supported only by the electrical wires.

2 Turn off the power to the old fixture at the main service panel. Use a voltage sensor to verify that the circuit is dead. With the light switch turned on, insert the sensor's probe into the electrical box within ½" of the wires inside. If the sensor beeps or lights up, then the circuit is live and you've shut off the wrong circuit. Shut off additional circuits until the probe confirms that you've shut off the correct one.

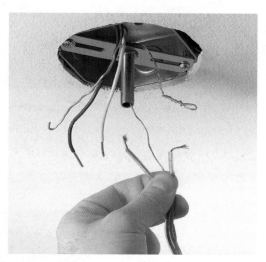

3 Remove the wire connectors from all the wires in the box and separate the wires. If the support chain is still attached, unscrew the mounting nut from the end of the threaded nipple inside the box. Disconnect the bare copper wire from the screw near the center of the mounting strap. Pull the old wires down through the threaded nipple.

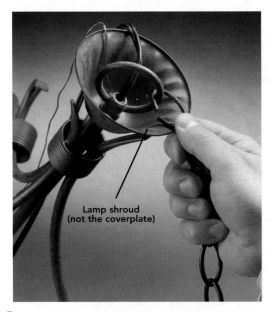

Lamp shroud
(not the coverplate)

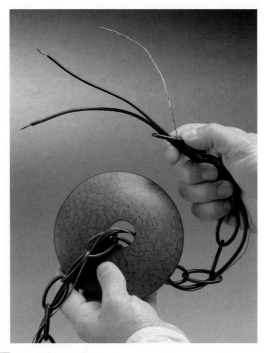

4 Adjust the length of the support chain on the new chandelier (if necessary) so it will hang at the desired height when mounted. This is normally done by disconnecting the chain from the support ring on the fixture, removing the required number of links and then reattaching the chain.

5 There will be two insulated wires and a bare copper ground woven in with the chain on your new fixture. There should be 6" to 12" of extra wire at the top of the chain. If the ends of these wires aren't stripped, use your combination tool to strip away ¾" of insulation.

6 Hang the new fixture from the threaded nipple (unless the chain support nut is integral to the coverplate retainer, as in step 1). You may need to screw the threaded nipple farther into the mounting plate so it does not extend past the coverplate. Or, you may need to replace the mounting strap and nipple with correctly sized hardware (usually provided with the new fixture). Make the wire connections, including attaching the bare copper wire to the grounding screw on the mounting strap.

7 Carefully tuck the wires into the electrical box and then tighten the retainer for the coverplate so it is snug against the ceiling. Restore power and test the fixture.

If you currently have a ceiling-mounted light fixture that is not meeting your lighting needs, it's simple to replace it with a track-lighting fixture. With track lighting you can easily change the type and number of lights, their position on the track, and the direction they aim. These fixtures come in many different styles, including short three-foot track systems with just one or two lights up to 12-foot systems with five or more lights.

TRACK LIGHTING OFFERS A BEAUTIFUL AND FUNCTIONAL WAY TO INCREASE THE AMOUNT OF LIGHT in a room or simply to update its look. A variety of fixture and lamp options lets you control the shape, color, and intensity of the light. Installing track lighting in place of an existing ceiling-mounted light fixture involves basic wiring and hand-tool skills, but the connections are even easier to make than with traditional light fixtures. Once installed, the system is very easy to upgrade or expand in the future.

TRACK LIGHTING 101

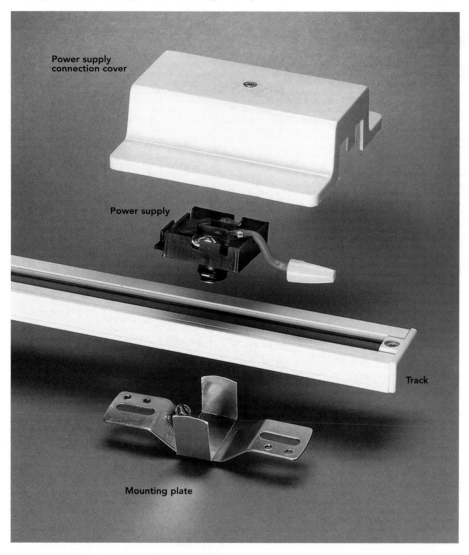

Power supply
connection cover

Power supply

Track

Mounting plate

Track systems include a lot of components, but fortunately you can buy all-inclusive starter kits containing everything you need for a basic installation, as well as a foundation for later upgrades if you wish.

TERMS YOU NEED TO KNOW

POWER SUPPLY—This little piece of hardware varies in appearance from kit to kit, but in all cases, it feeds power from the household wiring to the electrified pathways inside the track (and this powers the lights).

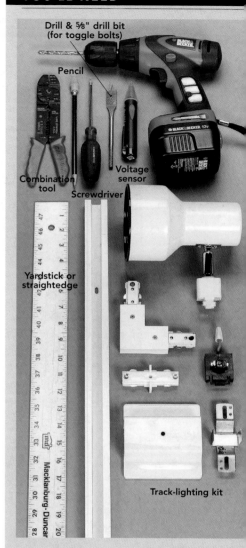

1 Locate the breaker for the light circuit you're working on and switch that breaker into the OFF position. If you have an older electrical service panel, you may have glass fuses instead of breakers. If so, pull the fuse for that circuit. Close the cover of the breaker or fuse cabinet.

2 Remove the globe and the lightbulbs from the fixture. Detach the old light from the ceiling electrical box. Most fixtures use two long screws to secure the fixture base to the electrical box in the ceiling. Hold the fixture with one hand while you use a screwdriver to remove the two screws. Gently pull the light straight down, exposing the wiring.

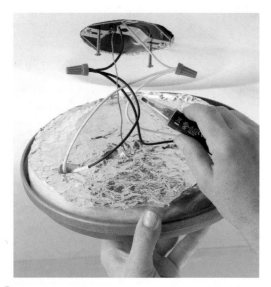

3 Use a voltage sensor to verify that the circuit is dead. Insert the sensor's probe into the electrical box within ½" of the black wires inside. If the sensor beeps or lights up, then the circuit is still live, and you'll need to trip the correct breaker to disconnect power to the fixture. If the sensor does not beep or light up, the circuit is dead and you can proceed safely.

4 Remove the fixture by disconnecting the wires. Use your hands to unscrew the wire connectors by turning them counterclockwise. After removing the wire connectors, pull the fixture completely away from the box (you can recycle it or save it). If you need to stop working and restore the power, first separate the wires coming from the ceiling box and cap them each with a wire connector.

HOW TO INSTALL TRACK LIGHTING

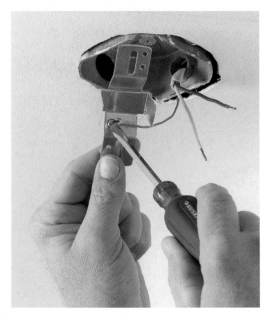

1 Turn off power (step 1, opposite page). Thread the three wires from the power supply hardware through the hole in the center of the mounting plate. Connect the power supply wires using wire connectors (the kit will come with them). The green wire on the power supply is connected to the bare copper wire coming out of the electrical box. Connect the white and black wires from the power supply to the white wire and black wires coming from the electrical box in the same way.

WHAT IF...?

What if the track is too long? Most types of track can be cut to length easily with a hacksaw. Use a saw fitted with a sharp blade and make a straight cut.

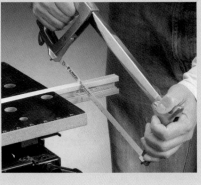

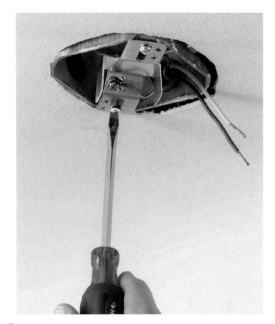

2 Carefully tuck the wires back up into the ceiling box and attach the mounting plate using the screws provided with the kit. The power supply can simply hang by its wires for the time being.

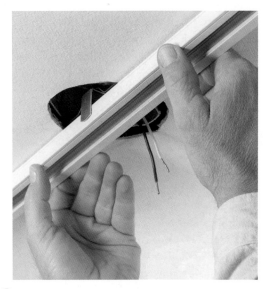

3 Draw a reference line on the ceiling to mark the track's path from the mounting plate to the end of the track. If possible, position the track directly underneath a ceiling joist so you can screw it to the joists. Otherwise, you will need to use toggle bolts to hold the tracks in the ceiling. Snap the track temporarily onto the mounting plate so it follows the reference line.

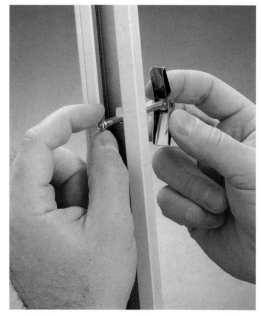

4 Mark the screw hole locations on the ceiling by making a dot through each hole in the track. After you mark the screw locations, remove the track and drill holes in the ceiling for the mounting screws. Begin by threading the bolts onto the track. First, unscrew the toggle bolt from the spring-loaded wings. Insert the toggle bolts through the holes in the track. Hold the wing on the ceiling-side of the track, then screw the bolt back into the toggle wings with two or three turns of the bolt.

5 Drill holes slightly larger then the thickness of the closed toggle wings. Pinch the wings of one toggle together and push it into the hole in the ceiling. The wings will snap open once they enter the cavity and hold the bolt in place. Push the other toggle bolts into their holes in the same way. Once all the bolts for a track section are in their holes, fit the track end to the mounting plate, and then tighten all the toggle bolts. Tighten the two screws on the mounting plate.

HERE'S HOW

Here's how to add another section of track. You can link sections of track together with connectors (your kit may include some or you can buy them separately, along with additional track sections). Connector pieces will also allow you to make 90-degree turns or T's on your track path. The connectors snap into the end of the track and are secured with screws.

6 Now you can connect the power supply to the track. Insert the power supply into the track and twist the connector until it snaps securely into place (connector installation may vary by manufacturer). The connector is made so that it cannot be snapped in the wrong way, so you'll know when it's in correctly. Attach the white and black wires to the screw terminals on the power supply.

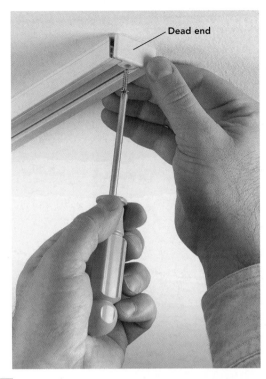

Dead end

7 Most kits will require you to cap the open ends of track dead ends. Snap them onto the ends of track pieces and secure them with screws.

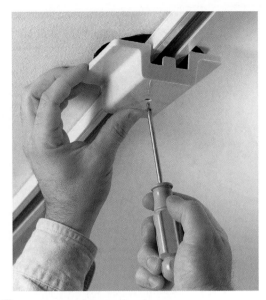

8 Now you can fit the decorative cover over the mounting plate. It may snap in place or be secured with screws. This will cover up the mounting plate completely.

9 You can begin inserting the light heads into the track at this point. These should simply twist-lock into place. Turn on power and test the light head.

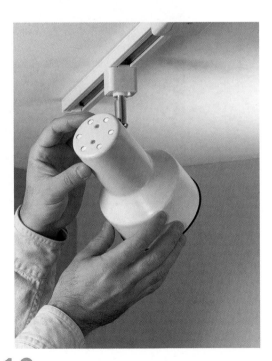

10 If the light works, locate a position you like and push down the locking tab on the side of the fixture to secure the light in this location. Install appropriate bulbs in the light sockets, according to the manufacturer's instructions. Install the remaining heads.

Installing a Motion-sensing Floodlight

An exterior floodlight with a motion sensor is an effective security measure. Make sure you keep the motion sensor adjusted so it doesn't give false alarms.

MOST HOUSES AND GARAGES HAVE FLOODLIGHTS ON THEIR EXTERIORS. You can easily upgrade these fixtures so that they provide additional security by replacing them with motion-sensing floodlights. Motion-sensing floods can be set up to detect motion in a specific area—like a walkway or driveway—and then cast light into that area. And there are few things intruders like less than the spotlight. These lights typically have timers that allow you to control how long the light stays on and photosensors that prevent the light from coming on during the day.

FLOODLIGHTS 101

A motion-sensing light fixture provides inexpensive and effective protection against intruders. It has an infrared eye that triggers the light fixture when a moving object crosses its path. Choose a light fixture with: a photo cell (A) to prevent the light from turning on in daylight; an adjustable timer (B) to control how long the light stays on; and range control (C) to adjust the reach of the motion-sensor eye.

TOOLS & SUPPLIES YOU'LL NEED

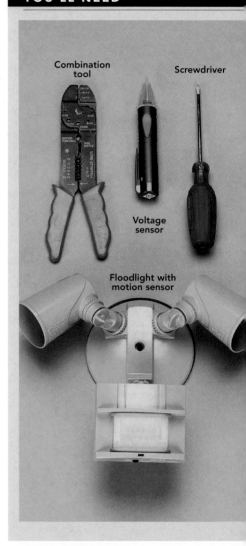

Combination tool

Screwdriver

Voltage sensor

Floodlight with motion sensor

SKILLS YOU'LL NEED

- Turning off the power (page 12)
- Testing for current (page 13)
- Making wire connections (pages 14-16)

HERE'S HOW

Here's how to make sure no one accidentally turns off your security lights—or any other light you don't want turned off. Switch locks are inexpensive plastic covers that lock a switch in the ON or OFF position. You can find them at any hardware store or home center.

DIFFICULTY LEVEL

SKILLS LEVEL

EASY   MODERATE

This project will take about 1 hour.

HOW TO INSTALL A MOTION-SENSING FLOODLIGHT

1 Turn off power to the old fixture. To remove it, unscrew the mounting screws on the part of the fixture attached to the wall. There will probably be four of them. Carefully pull the fixture away from the wall, exposing the wires. Don't touch the wires yet.

2 Before you touch any wires, use a voltage sensor to verify that the circuit is dead. With the light switch turned ON, insert the sensor's probe into the electrical box and hold the probe within ½" of the wires inside to confirm that there is no voltage flow. Disconnect the wire connectors and remove the old fixture.

Grounding clip

4 If the electrical box is nonmetallic and does not have a metal grounding clip, install a grounding clip or replace the box with one that does have a clip and make sure the ground wire is attached to it securely. Some light fixtures have a grounding terminal on the base. If yours has one, attach the grounding wire from the house directly to the terminal.

3 Examine the ends of the three wires coming from the box (one white, one black, and one bare copper). They should be clean and free of corrosion. If the ends are in poor condition, clip them off and then strip ¾" of wire insulation with a combination tool.

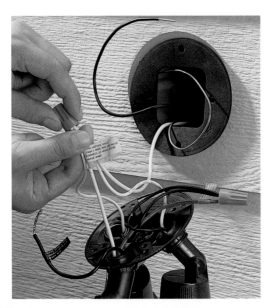

5 Now you can attach the new fixture. Begin by sliding a rubber or foam gasket (usually provided with the fixture) over the wires and onto the flange of the electrical box. Set the new fixture on top of a ladder or have a helper hold it while you make the wiring connections. There may be as many as three white wires coming from the fixture. Join all white wires, including the feed wire from the house, using a wire connector.

6 Next, join the black wire from the box and the single black wire from the fixture with a wire connector. You may see a couple of black wires and a red wire already joined on the fixture. You can ignore these in your installation.

7 Neatly tuck all the wires into the box so they are behind the gasket. Align the holes in the gasket with the holes in the box, and then position the fixture over the gasket so its mounting holes are also aligned with the gasket. Press the fixture against the gasket and drive the four mounting screws into the box. Install floodlight bulbs (exterior rated) and restore power.

8 Test the fixture. You will still be able to turn it on and off with the light switch inside. Flip the switch to ON and pass your hand in front of the motion sensor. The light should come on. Adjust the motion sensor to cover the traffic areas and pivot the light head to illuminate the intended area.

23 Repairing Fluorescent Light Fixtures

Troubleshooting a fluorescent light that's flickering or won't work is a process of testing and checking that begins with inspecting the fluorescent tubes to make sure they're making good contact with the fixture sockets and are in good condition.

FLUORESCENT FIXTURES ARE GREAT LIGHTING CHOICES because they save energy and offer many different quality-of-light options, from the hue and color of the light to its brightness. And fluorescent lamps have a much longer life than regular incandescent lamps. But as fluorescent fixtures age, small parts begin to fail. Replacing the tubes is easy, and replacing the ballast (a transformer-type part that distributes power to the sockets) is only slightly more difficult. But if the fixture is old it may make more sense to replace the entire fixture with a newer (and probably quieter) model.

FLUORESCENT LIGHTS 101

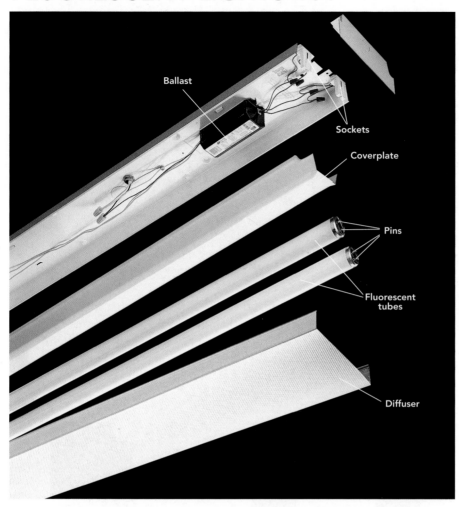

Ballast

Sockets

Coverplate

Pins

Fluorescent tubes

Diffuser

Fluorescent fixtures come in lots of different lengths, from 6 inches to 6 feet. They all work basically the same. The fixture consists of a diffuser and a coverplate and housing that contain a ballast that connects to the sockets that hold the tubes.

BUYER'S TIP

Here's how to buy a fluorescent tube: You'll need three pieces of information: the length of the tube, the end type, and the wattage. There are a couple different styles of pin configuration for the ends of tubes. The two-pin style shown here is most common, but there are others. If yours looks different, take it with you to the hardware store to find an exact match. The wattage of the fluorescent tube will be printed somewhere along its length. Buy a new tube with the same watt rating. For best value, buy fluorescent tubes in multiple tube packs, as you would with other types of lightbulbs.

TOOLS & SUPPLIES YOU'LL NEED

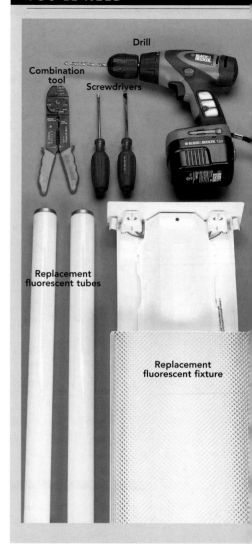

Drill

Combination tool

Screwdrivers

Replacement fluorescent tubes

Replacement fluorescent fixture

SKILLS YOU'LL NEED

- Turning off power (page 12)
- Testing for current (page 13)
- Making wire connections (pages 14-16)

Note: This may be easier with two people.

DIFFICULTY LEVEL

SKILLS LEVEL

EASY   MODERATE

Allow about 2 hours for this project.

HOW TO REPLACE A FLUORESCENT TUBE

1 If your fluorescent light is flickering or not working, check the tubes first. Start by removing the plastic diffuser that covers the light so you can access the florescent tubes. The diffuser normally snaps into place. Squeeze it slightly at its sides to remove it.

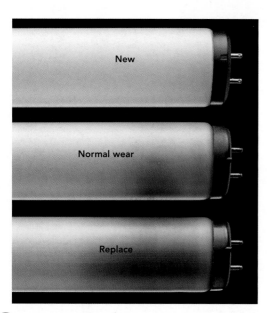

3 Take a look at the ends of the bulb. A little light gray coloring at the ends of a used fluorescent bulb is normal. But if one or more of the tube ends is blackened, the tube should be replaced.

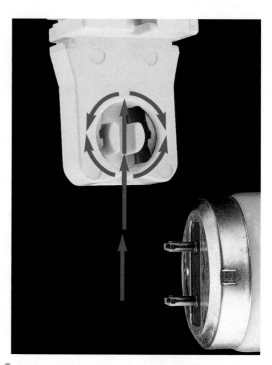

2 Twist the tubes to confirm that they are seated correctly in the sockets. If they are securely in the sockets but the light won't light, remove the tubes by rotating them a quarter turn in each direction and pulling down.

4 Purchase a replacement tube (see page 123) and install the new tubes by holding the tube so the pins are vertical. Slide the pins into the grooves in the sockets and push up. Then, turn the tube a quarter turn in each direction. Replace the diffuser and test the fixture.

HOW TO REPLACE A BALLAST

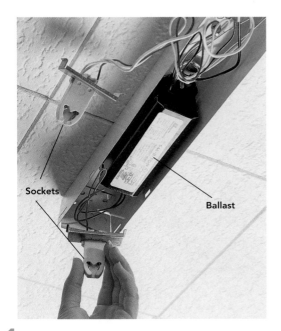

Sockets

Ballast

1 Turn off the power at the main service panel, then remove the diffuser, fluorescent tube, and coverplate. Test for power. Remove the sockets from the fixture housing by sliding them out, or by removing the mounting screws and lifting the sockets out.

2 Disconnect the wires that lead from the ballast to the sockets by pushing a small screwdriver into the release openings (as seen above) or loosening the screw terminals. On some socket styles you'll need to cut the wires to within 2" of the socket to remove the ballast.

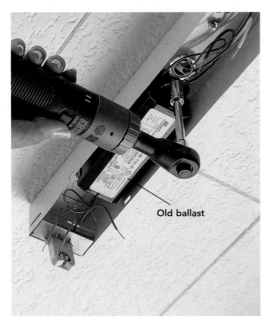

Old ballast

3 Remove the old ballast, using a ratchet wrench or screwdriver. Make sure to support the ballast so it does not fall (a little duct tape will do the job).

New ballast

4 Install a new ballast that has the same ratings as the old ballast. Attach the ballast wires to the socket wires and reinstall the coverplate, fluorescent tube, and diffuser. Turn on power to the light fixture at the main service panel.

1 If replacing the tube or ballast doesn't fix the problem, it's best to replace the whole light fixture. Start by removing the diffuser and the tubes. Then, turn off the power to the fixture at the service panel and test with a voltage tester.

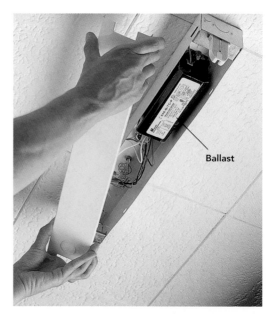

Ballast

2 Loosen the screws at each end of the metal coverplate on the fixture. If there are no screws, you may be able to remove the cover by pinching its ends and pulling down. Pull the coverplate free and set it aside.

BUYER'S TIP

How to buy a new fluorescent fixture: Look for a fixture of the same length and with the same number of tubes as the one you're replacing. You'll also want one rated for the same number of watts as your old one. The watt rating will be printed somewhere on the inside of the fixture.

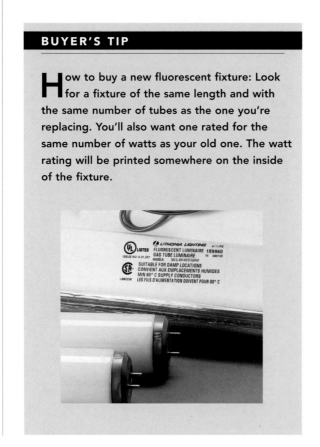

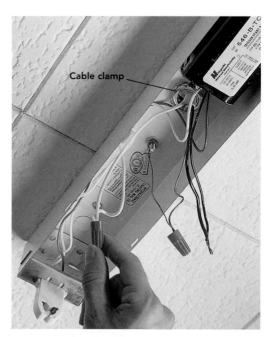

Cable clamp

3 Disconnect the fixture by unscrewing the wire connectors inside the fixture housing. Straighten out the three wires feeding into the fixture through the cable clamp and then unscrew the cable clamp.

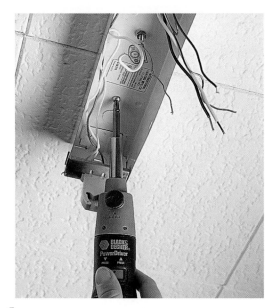

4 You can now completely remove the fixture by unscrewing the mounting screws. It's a good idea to have a helper support the fixture as you undo the screws. Move the fixture away from the ceiling, pulling the three wires through the hole.

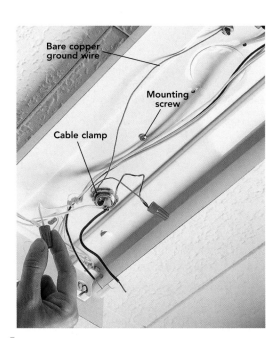

Bare copper ground wire

Mounting screw

Cable clamp

6 Attach the fixture to the ceiling with screws or toggle bolts driven up through mounting screw holes in the top of the fixture, and then tighten a retaining nut around the cable clamp. Make the wire connections (white to white, black to black, bare copper ground to grounding screw on fixture).

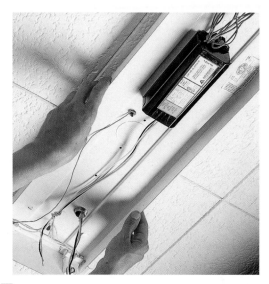

5 Remove the coverplate from the new fixture. On the bottom of the new fixture, you'll find several knockout holes. Remove a knockout that will fall under the electrical box in the ceiling when the fixture is installed (drive a screwdriver through the knockout to remove it). Attach a cable clamp in the knockout hole and feed the three wires from the ceiling box through the cable clamp as you raise the fixture up against the ceiling.

7 Reattach the coverplate on the new fixture, install the fluorescent tubes and snap in the diffuser. Restore power and test the fixture.

Fixing a Ceiling Fan

24

Even ceiling fans that are operated only occasionally are prone to failure or problems like excess wobble. Following the steps in this chapter will help you diagnose and solve common ceiling fan maladies.

CEILING FANS THAT WORK PROPERLY WILL SAVE MONEY on heating and cooling costs and add to the comfort of your home. But over time ceiling fans can fail to work, become noisy, the blades may wobble, or the pull-chain switch may become unreliable or just plain faulty. Before putting many hours of time and hard labor—not to mention the expense—into a new fan installation, diagnose the old fan to see if it can be easily repaired using these steps. Keep in mind that most consumer-level ceiling fans will never be completely silent when the fan is operating— moving air does make some noise, after all.

CEILING FANS 101

Mounting bracket

Canopy

Motor

Fan blades

Switch housing

Pull chain

Bottom cap

A ceiling fan is suspended from a sturdy mounting bracket and the connection is concealed by a decorative canopy.

FAN NOT WORKING? TRY THIS FIRST:

1 Make sure that the wall switch that controls the ceiling fan is in the ON position. Reach up to the fan and move the fan direction switch back and forth to confirm that it is fully engaged in one of the two positions (clockwise blade movement for summer, counterclockwise for winter). If the fan blades do not start rotating, even though the switch feels secure in one of the two positions, go to step 2.

2 Put your hand on the switch housing to feel for vibration. If a vibration or humming is present, the fan motor is malfunctioning and you should consider replacing the entire unit. No hum or vibration? Proceed to the further diagnostics beginning on page 128.

Fan direction switch

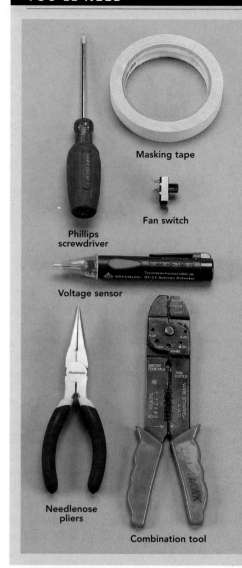

Masking tape

Fan switch

Phillips screwdriver

Voltage sensor

Needlenose pliers

Combination tool

SKILLS YOU'LL NEED

- Turning off power (page 12)
- Testing for current (page 13)
- Making wire connections (pages 14-16)

DIFFICULTY LEVEL

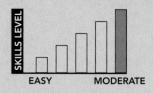

SKILLS LEVEL

EASY   MODERATE

Allow 2 to 4 hours, and work with a helper

HOW TO FIX A CEILING FAN

1 A leading cause of fan failure is loose wire connections. To inspect these connections, first shut off the power to the fan. Remove the fan blades to gain access, then remove the canopy that covers the ceiling box and fan mounting bracket. Most canopies are secured with screws on the outside shell. Have a helper hold the fan while you remove the screws so it won't fall.

2 Once the canopy is lowered, you'll see black, white, green, copper, and possibly blue wires. Hold a voltage sensor within ½" of these wires with the wall switch that controls the fan in the ON position. The black and blue wires should cause the sensor to beep if power is present.

HERE'S HOW

One common problem with older ceiling fans is that over time or due to incorrect initial installation, the blades begin to wobble as they spin. If you're within earshot, the vibration from wobbling is irritating, but it can also damage the fan and shorten its life. Wobbling has three main causes: (1) the fan blades may not be balanced properly, (2) the fan may not be tightly secured to the ceiling fan box, or (3) one or more of the fan blades may have become warped. Fixing any of these situations requires minimal effort and time.

1 Start by checking and tightening all hardware used to attach the blades to the mounting arms and the mounting arms to the motor. Hardware tends to loosen over time and this is frequently the cause of wobble.

2 If wobble persists, try switching around two of the blades. Often, this is all it takes to get the fan back into balance. If a blade is damaged or warped, try to locate a replacement blade.

3 If you still have wobble, turn the power off at the panel, remove the fan canopy, and inspect the mounting brace and the connection between the mounting pole and the fan motor. Tighten any loose connections and replace the canopy.

3 When you have confirmed that there is no power, check all the wire connections to make certain each is tight and making good contact. You may be able to see that a connection has come apart and needs to be remade. But even if you see one bad connection, check them all by gently tugging on the wire connectors. If the wires pull out of the wire connector or the connection feels loose, unscrew the wire connector from the wires.

4 Twist the wires back together the same way you found them, making sure the bare wires are making good contact with each other. Secure them with a new wire twist connector.

HERE'S HOW

Bad wiring connections often are caused by failed wire connectors. Inspect connections for signs of burning, corrosion, or rust. If the inside of any wire connector does not look clean and shiny, replace it with a new connector of the same size.

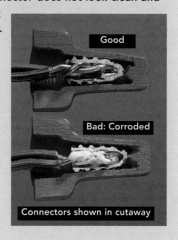

Good

Bad: Corroded

Connectors shown in cutaway

5 If everything works, reinstall the canopy by replacing the screws that were holding it in place. Reattach the fan blades and then restore power. If all connections are secure but the fan still doesn't work, try replacing the pull chain to resolve the problem (see next page).

HOW TO REPLACE A PULL-CHAIN SWITCH

1 Turn off the power at the main service panel. Use a screwdriver to remove the three to four screws that secure the bottom cap on the fan switch housing. Lower the cap to expose the wires that supply power to the pull-chain switch.

2 Test the wires by placing a voltage sensor within ½" of the wires. If the sensor beeps or lights up, then the circuit is still live, and is not safe to work. When the sensor does not beep or light up, the circuit is dead and may be worked upon.

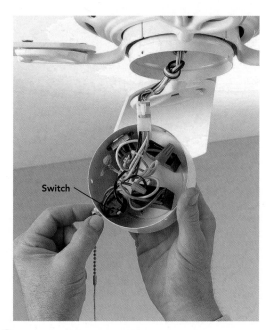

Switch

3 Locate the switch unit (the part that the pull chain used to be attached to if it broke off); it's probably made of plastic. You'll need to replace the whole switch. Fan switches are connected with from three to eight wires, depending on the number of speed settings.

4 Attach a small piece of tape to each wire that enters the switch and write an identifying number on the tape. Start at one side of the switch and label the wires in the order they're attached.

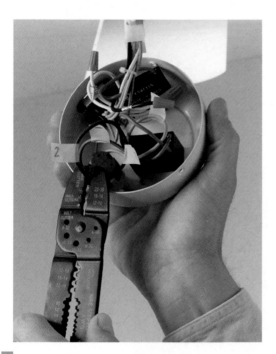

BUYER'S TIP

Here's how to buy a new switch. Bring the old switch to the hardware store or home center, and find an identical new switch—one with the same number and color of wires. It should also attach to the fan motor wires in the same way (slots or screw terminals or with integral wires and wire connectors) and that attaches to the fan in the same way. If you are unable to locate an identical switch, find the owners manual for your ceiling fan and contact the manufacturer. Or, find the brand and model number of the fan and order a switch from a ceiling fan dealer or electronics supply store.

5 Disconnect the old switch wires, in most cases by cutting the wires off as close to the old switch as possible. Unscrew the retaining nut that secures the switch to the switch housing.

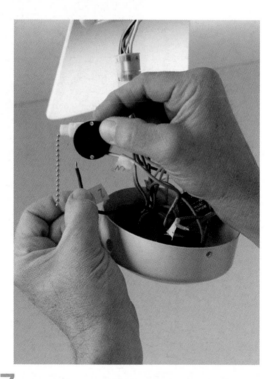

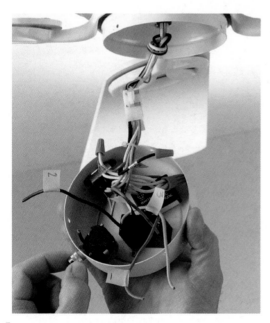

6 Remove the switch. There may be one or two screws that hold it in place or it may be secured to the outside of the fan with a small, knurled nut, which you can loosen with needlenose pliers. Purchase an identical new switch.

7 Connect the new switch using the same wiring configuration as on the old model. To make connections, first use a wire stripper to strip ¾" of insulation from the ends of each of the wires coming from the fan motor (the ones you cut in step 5). Attach the wires to the new switch in the same order and configuraion as they were attached to the old switch. Secure the new switch in the housing and make sure all wires are tucked neatly inside. Reattach the bottom cap. Test all the fan's speeds to make sure all the connections are good.

Welcome to Plumbing
101

LET'S FACE IT, PLUMBERS SPEND A LOT OF TIME FISHING SOCKS OUT OF TOI-LETS AND REPLACING 5-CENT WASHERS ON DRIPPY FAUCETS. NOTHING WRONG WITH THAT, EXCEPT THEY CHARGE $100 AN HOUR AND PROMISE TO MEET YOU AT THE DOOR "OH, SOMETIME BETWEEN 10 AND 3 O'CLOCK." WE THINK YOU HAVE BETTER WAYS TO SPEND YOUR TIME AND MONEY.

Look at the Table of Contents of *Plumbing 101*, and you'll find salt-of-the earth repairs and replacements—the kind of projects you need to keep your house running smoothly and looking good. Most important, they're doable.

Plumbing 101 is part of a new series of Black & Decker books that starts at square one. Unlike legions of other books on the trades, we present step-by-step repair and replacement instructions that assume no prior how-to knowledge. In *Plumbing 101*, we won't expect you to know where your water turns off or even what a water pipe looks like. We'll tell you. Period. If it's old news, skip ahead.

The 25 repair and replacement projects covered in this book involve a few basic tools and the ability to follow directions. If you skipped Vocational Ed. in high school, no problem, you're forgiven. We're replacing a toilet, not plumbing the *Queen Mary*.

The trick with any successful do-it-yourself project lies in identifying those jobs that you can complete without resorting to professional help (mechanical or psychiatric). Again, the 101 Series to the rescue. We've pre-screened projects to minimize chance of failure, property damage, and injury.

The *Plumbing 101* book will not ask you to use a torch. You will not need to smear molten metals on pipes hot enough to brand cattle. You will not be encouraged to re-plumb your bathroom, build a granite island sink in your kitchen, or install a multi-zone irrigation system in your backyard.

Hey, those are all wonderful projects, but they don't fit into the mission of this book. Here, we aim to provide practical information for practical people who don't have the time or inclination to take up plumbing as a second career.

On the following pages, we'll walk you through projects you can do. We'll let you know when a job might get hairy. And we'll show you, in photographs, what each step in a project looks like.

HERE'S HOW TO USE THIS BOOK:

The first two pages of most projects give necessary background information. You'll examine how things fit together and work, learn techniques, get an idea of how long the project might take, and see all the tools and materials you'll need to do a project.

Then, turn the page and begin. Virtually every step is photographed so you'll see exactly how to do the work, and along the way you'll find helpful sidebars that show you what to do if something unexpected happens, tips for using tools correctly, safety recommendations, and more. Before you know it, you'll notch up another home repair success.

The Home Plumbing System

A TYPICAL HOME PLUMBING SYSTEM INCLUDES THREE BASIC PARTS: a water supply system, a fixture and appliance set, and a drain system. These three parts can be seen clearly in the photograph of the cut-away house on the opposite page.

Fresh water enters a home through a main supply line (1). This fresh water source is provided by either a municipal water company or a private underground well. If the source is a municipal supplier, the water passes through a meter (2) that registers the amount of water used. A family of four uses about 400 gallons of water each day.

Immediately after the main supply enters the house, a branch line splits off (3) and is joined to a water heater (4). From the water heater, a hot water line runs parallel to the cold water line to bring the water supply to fixtures and appliances throughout the house. Fixtures include sinks, bathtubs, showers, and laundry tubs. Appliances include water heaters, dishwashers, clothes washers, and water softeners. Toilets and exterior sillcocks are examples of fixtures that require only a cold water line.

The water supply to fixtures and appliances is controlled with faucets and valves. Faucets and valves have moving parts and seals that eventually may wear out or break, but they are easily repaired or replaced.

Waste water then enters the drain system. It first must flow past a trap (5), a U-shaped piece of pipe that holds standing water and prevents sewer gases from entering the home. Every fixture must have a drain trap.

The drain system works entirely by gravity, allowing waste water to flow downhill through a series of large-diameter pipes. These drain pipes are attached to a system of vent pipes. Vent pipes (6) bring fresh air to the drain system, preventing suction that would slow or stop drain water from flowing freely. Vent pipes usually exit the house at a roof vent (7).

All waste water eventually reaches a main waste and vent stack (8). The main stack curves to become a sewer line (9) that exits the house near the foundation. In a municipal system, this sewer line joins a main sewer line located near the street. Where sewer service is not available, waste water empties into a septic system.

Water meter and main shutoff valves are located where the main water supply pipe enters the house. The water meter is the property of your local municipal water company. If the water meter leaks, or if you suspect it is not functioning properly, call your water company for repairs.

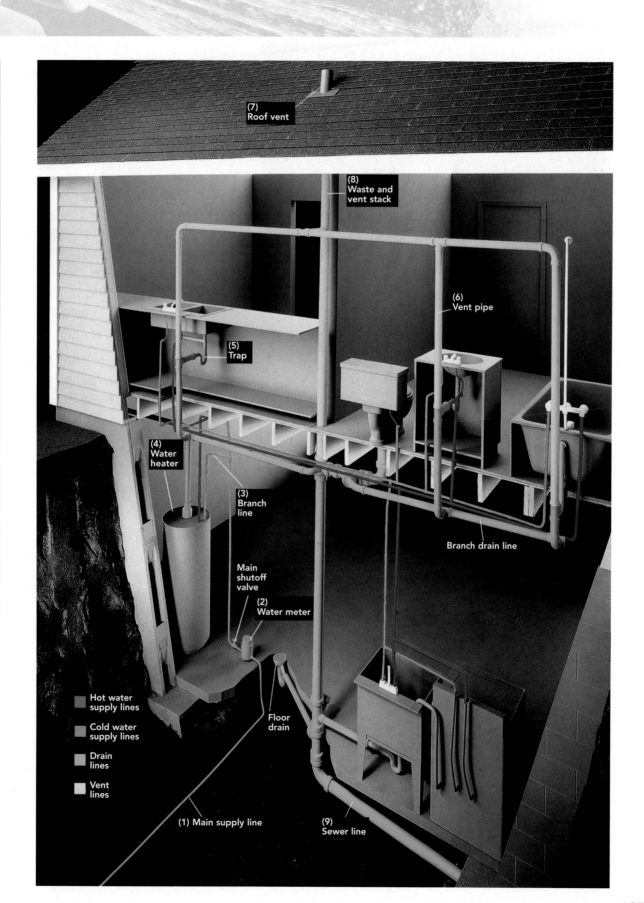

(7) Roof vent

(8) Waste and vent stack

(6) Vent pipe

(5) Trap

(4) Water heater

(3) Branch line

Main shutoff valve

(2) Water meter

Branch drain line

Floor drain

Hot water supply lines

Cold water supply lines

Drain lines

Vent lines

(1) Main supply line

(9) Sewer line

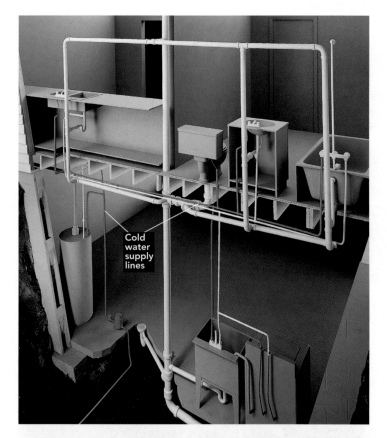

Cold water supply lines

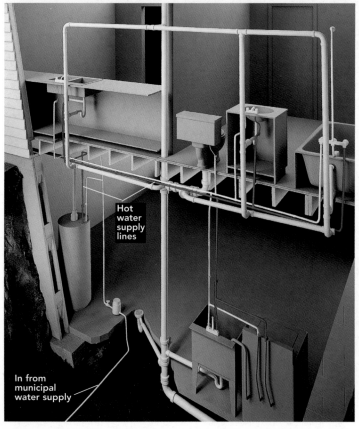

Hot water supply lines

In from municipal water supply

WATER SUPPLY SYSTEM

Water supply pipes carry hot and cold water throughout a house. In homes built before 1960, the original supply pipes are usually made of galvanized iron. Newer homes have supply pipes made of copper. In most areas of the country, supply pipes made of rigid plastic or PEX are accepted by local plumbing codes. Water supply pipes are made to withstand the high pressures of the water supply system. They have small diameters, usually ½" to ¾", and are joined with strong, watertight fittings. The hot and cold lines run in tandem to all parts of the house. Usually, the supply pipes run inside wall cavities or are strapped to the undersides of floor joists.

Hot and cold water supply pipes are connected to fixtures or appliances. Fixtures include sinks, tubs, and showers. Some fixtures, such as toilets or hose bibs, are supplied only by cold water. Appliances include dishwashers and clothes washers. Tradition says that hot water supply pipes and faucet handles are found on the left-hand side of a fixture, with cold water on the right.

Because it is pressurized, the water supply system is prone to leaks. This is especially true of galvanized iron pipe, which has limited resistance to corrosion.

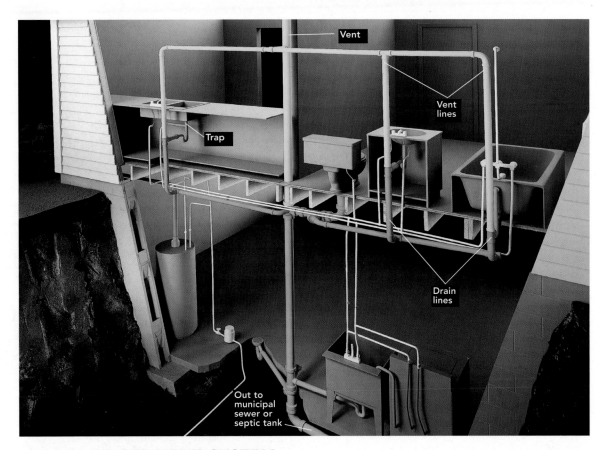

Vent

Vent lines

Trap

Drain lines

Out to municipal sewer or septic tank

DRAIN-WASTE-VENT SYSTEM

Drain pipes use gravity to carry waste water away from fixtures, appliances, and other drains. This waste water is carried out of the house to a municipal sewer system or septic tank.

Drain pipes are usually plastic or cast iron. In some older homes, drain pipes may be made of copper or lead. Because they are not part of the supply system, lead drain pipes pose no health hazard. However, lead pipes are no longer manufactured for home plumbing systems.

Drain pipes have diameters ranging from 1½" to 4". These large diameters allow waste water to pass through easily.

Traps are an important part of the drain system. These curved sections of drain pipe hold standing water, and they are usually found near any drain opening. The standing water of a trap prevents sewer gases from backing up into the home. Each time a drain is used, the standing trap water is flushed away and is replaced by new water.

In order to work properly, the drain system requires air. Air allows waste water to flow freely down drain pipes.

To allow air into the drain system, drain pipes are connected to vent pipes. All drain systems must include vents, and the entire system is called the drain-waste-vent (DWV) system. One or more vent stacks, located on the roof, provide the air needed for the DWV system to work.

Plumbing Tools

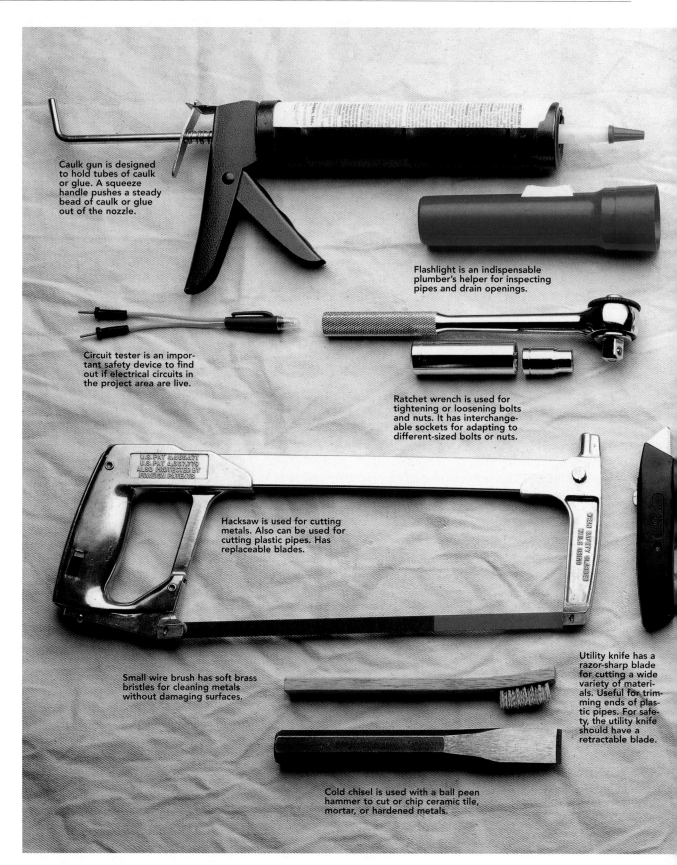

Caulk gun is designed to hold tubes of caulk or glue. A squeeze handle pushes a steady bead of caulk or glue out of the nozzle.

Flashlight is an indispensable plumber's helper for inspecting pipes and drain openings.

Circuit tester is an important safety device to find out if electrical circuits in the project area are live.

Ratchet wrench is used for tightening or loosening bolts and nuts. It has interchangeable sockets for adapting to different-sized bolts or nuts.

Hacksaw is used for cutting metals. Also can be used for cutting plastic pipes. Has replaceable blades.

Small wire brush has soft brass bristles for cleaning metals without damaging surfaces.

Utility knife has a razor-sharp blade for cutting a wide variety of materials. Useful for trimming ends of plastic pipes. For safety, the utility knife should have a retractable blade.

Cold chisel is used with a ball peen hammer to cut or chip ceramic tile, mortar, or hardened metals.

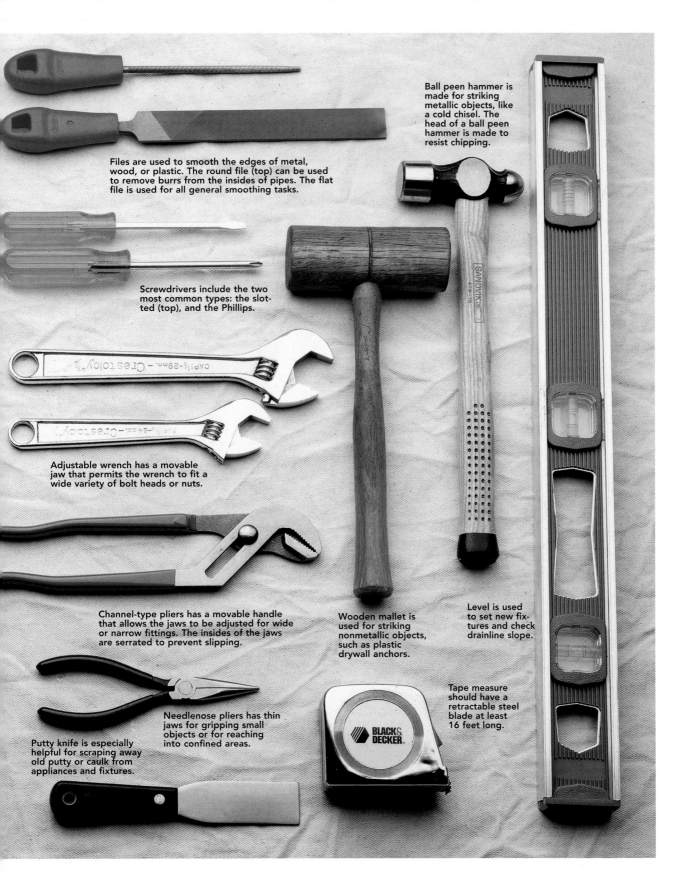

Files are used to smooth the edges of metal, wood, or plastic. The round file (top) can be used to remove burrs from the insides of pipes. The flat file is used for all general smoothing tasks.

Ball peen hammer is made for striking metallic objects, like a cold chisel. The head of a ball peen hammer is made to resist chipping.

Screwdrivers include the two most common types: the slotted (top), and the Phillips.

Adjustable wrench has a movable jaw that permits the wrench to fit a wide variety of bolt heads or nuts.

Channel-type pliers has a movable handle that allows the jaws to be adjusted for wide or narrow fittings. The insides of the jaws are serrated to prevent slipping.

Wooden mallet is used for striking nonmetallic objects, such as plastic drywall anchors.

Level is used to set new fixtures and check drainline slope.

Needlenose pliers has thin jaws for gripping small objects or for reaching into confined areas.

Putty knife is especially helpful for scraping away old putty or caulk from appliances and fixtures.

Tape measure should have a retractable steel blade at least 16 feet long.

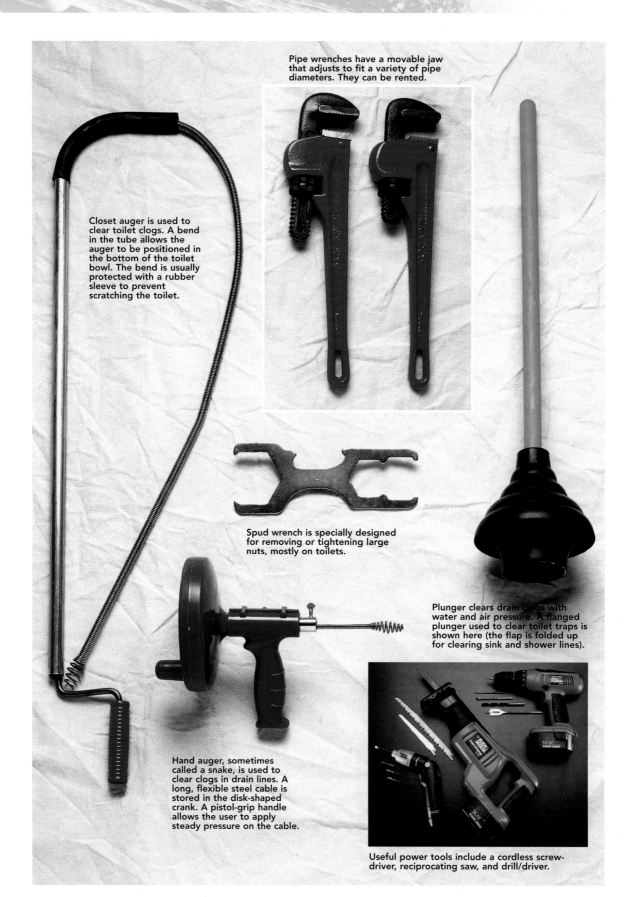

Pipe wrenches have a movable jaw that adjusts to fit a variety of pipe diameters. They can be rented.

Closet auger is used to clear toilet clogs. A bend in the tube allows the auger to be positioned in the bottom of the toilet bowl. The bend is usually protected with a rubber sleeve to prevent scratching the toilet.

Spud wrench is specially designed for removing or tightening large nuts, mostly on toilets.

Plunger clears drain clogs with water and air pressure. A flanged plunger used to clear toilet traps is shown here (the flap is folded up for clearing sink and shower lines).

Hand auger, sometimes called a snake, is used to clear clogs in drain lines. A long, flexible steel cable is stored in the disk-shaped crank. A pistol-grip handle allows the user to apply steady pressure on the cable.

Useful power tools include a cordless screwdriver, reciprocating saw, and drill/driver.

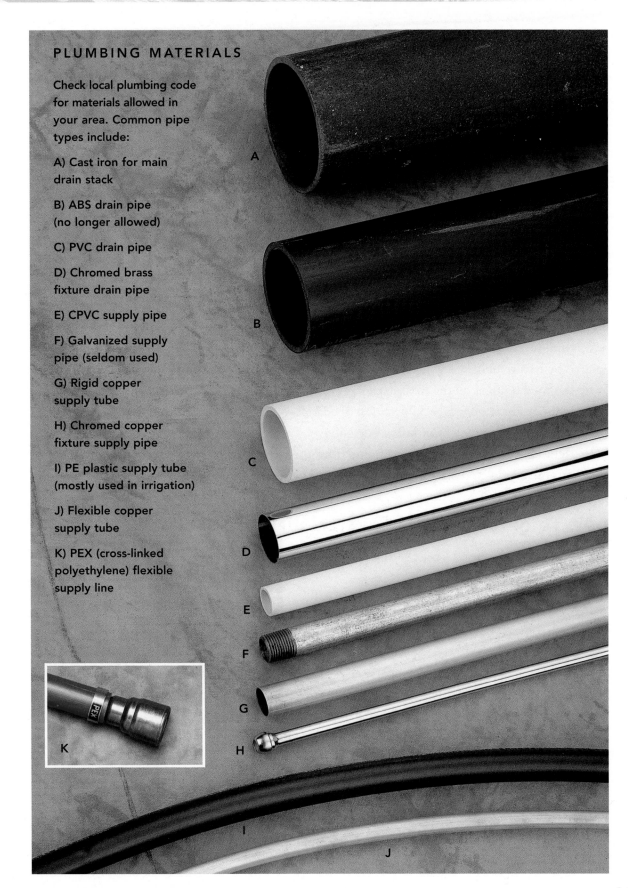

PLUMBING MATERIALS

Check local plumbing code for materials allowed in your area. Common pipe types include:

A) Cast iron for main drain stack

B) ABS drain pipe (no longer allowed)

C) PVC drain pipe

D) Chromed brass fixture drain pipe

E) CPVC supply pipe

F) Galvanized supply pipe (seldom used)

G) Rigid copper supply tube

H) Chromed copper fixture supply pipe

I) PE plastic supply tube (mostly used in irrigation)

J) Flexible copper supply tube

K) PEX (cross-linked polyethylene) flexible supply line

Evaluating Your Plumbing

You don't have to possess the knowledge and experience of a journeyman plumber to do some basic evaluations of your plumbing system. Taking a few moments to examine the system helps you learn which parts are which and identify any parts of your system that may be in disrepair or hold the potential for future problems.

Fixture Units	Minimum Gallons per Minute (GPM)
10	8
15	11
20	14
25	17
30	20

The tips on the next page offer a bit of guidance on how to be a home plumbing sleuth. By following them you can quickly and accurately identify cold and hot supply lines, drain lines, the water main, and shutoff valve locations. And the tips below will help you test your water supply capacity to find out if the pressure and volume are adequate to meet your water needs.

Minimum recommended water capacity is based on total demand on the system, as measured by fixture units, a standard of measurement assigned by the plumbing code. First, add up the total units of all the fixtures in your plumbing system (see chart above). Then, perform the water supply capacity test described below. Finally, compare your water capacity with the recommended minimums listed above. If it falls below that recommended GPM, then the main water supply pipe running from the city water main to your home is inadequate and should be replaced with a larger pipe by a licensed contractor.

HOW TO DETERMINE YOUR WATER SUPPLY CAPACITY

1 Shut off the water at the valve on your main water meter, run a faucet on every floor to empty the supply lines, and then disconnect the pipe on the house side of the meter. You can do this by counter-rotating the large nuts on the line with two pipe wrenches (you can rent these if you don't want to invest in a pair).

2 Make a downspout like the one seen above from 2" PVC pipe sections and position it over the water line to direct water down into a garbage can. Open the main supply valve and let the water run for 30 seconds. Shut off the water, then measure the water in the container by bailing with a 1-gallon container. Multiply this figure by two to find your water capacity in gallons per minute (GPM).

HOW TO INSPECT YOUR PLUMBING

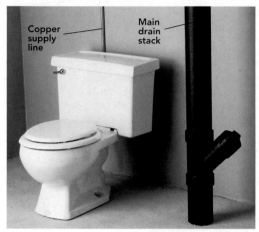

Copper supply line

Main drain stack

There are two basic kinds of pipes in a plumbing system: supply pipes and drain pipes. Supply pipes are always full of water under pressure and drain pipes (which include vent pipes that only move air) are empty when not in use. Supply pipes usually are ½" or ¾" in diameter and drain pipes are anywhere from 1½" to 4" or more. The largest drain pipes are the main drain stack (multi-level houses) and horizontal house drains fed by branch lines.

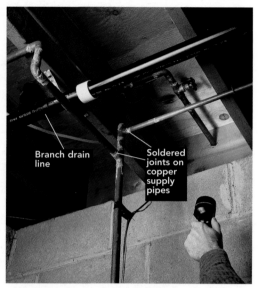

Branch drain line

Soldered joints on copper supply pipes

In your basement, branch drain lines run horizontally at a very low slope and ultimately feed into the main drain stack or house drain. They enter the basement through the floor, usually directly under walls. Look for moisture or discoloration around joints. On copper supply lines, visually inspect the soldered joints for pinholes or other signs of deterioration.

Trace hot water pipes from the water heater (the outlet side will be labeled "Hot" on the appliance). Hot supply lines will be hot to the touch when the fixture they connect to is in use.

Heat duct

To identify which supply pipes feed which fixture, you can sometimes measure from the fixture to a heating register. Then, locate the ductwork directly below the register and measure out from it and look for supply lines.

Shutting Off the Water

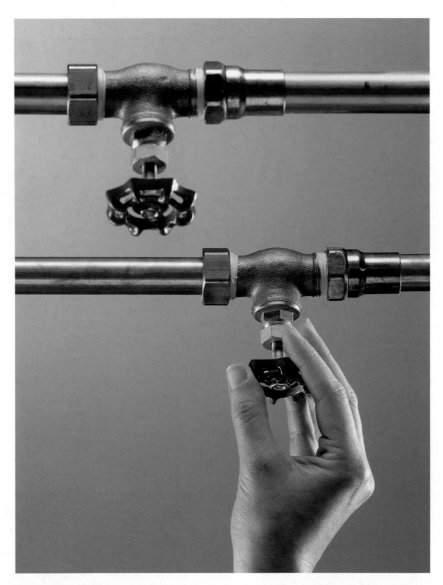

1

Just as the first step in any wiring project is to shut off the power at the main service panel, most plumbing projects begin with shutting off the water supply at one of the shutoff valves in the plumbing system.

USUALLY THERE ARE TWO OR THREE WAYS TO TURN OFF THE WATER. First, try to close the stop valves at the fixture or appliance that's broken. If these are damaged or absent, turn off the water at intermediate shutoff valves that control the hot and cold water to the part of the house with the problem. The whole hot water system usually can be turned off near the hot water heater. Finally, you can stop the water to the entire house at a main shut-off located near the water meter. As a last resort, your municipal water works can shut off your water before it gets to your house. If you have a well, find the shutoff on the pipe between the pressure tank and the rest of your plumbing.

WATER STOP VALVES 101

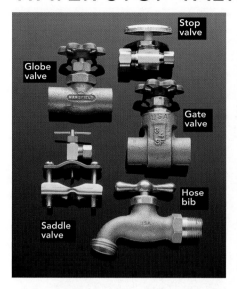

Globe valve
Stop valve
Gate valve
Hose bib
Saddle valve

Main shutoff
Water meter

Access panel with door opens to shutoffs for tub/shower

Water stop valves and shutoff valves function much like faucets, except most of them are left open all the time. Unfortunately, valves used on potable water (water for drinking and cooking) lines may be similar to valves used on natural gas lines, heating oil pipes, and hot water heating pipes. Finding the valves you need may require some careful tracing of pipes from a fixture back to the water meter. The photos here show common water shutoff valves.

TOOLS & SUPPLIES YOU'LL NEED

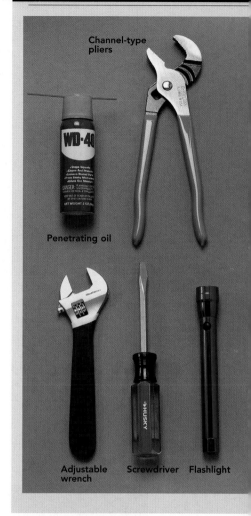

Channel-type pliers
Penetrating oil
Adjustable wrench
Screwdriver
Flashlight

SKILLS YOU'LL NEED

- Using locking pliers
- Loosening stuck valve handles

DIFFICULTY LEVEL

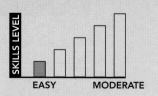

SKILLS LEVEL

EASY   MODERATE

Time: A few minutes to ½ hour

TERMS YOU NEED TO KNOW

VALVE—any device that regulates the flow of fluids or gases through a pipe.

STOP VALVE—a valve used to stop hot or cold water to a single faucet, toilet, or appliance.

INTERMEDIATE SHUTOFF VALVE—a valve on a pipe used to stop hot or cold water to part of a house or building; often a gate valve or globe valve.

HOT WATER SHUTOFF VALVE—a valve that shuts off cold water supply to the hot water tank.

MAIN SHUTOFF VALVE—a valve that shuts off all the water to a house or building.

HOW TO SHUT OFF HOT AND COLD WATER

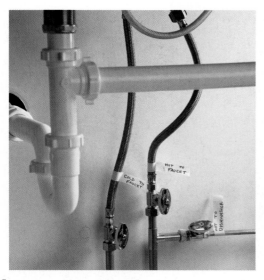

1 Try to shut off the water locally first. Toilets and sinks usually have stop valves under them. Tubs and showers may have hot and cold shutoffs on the faucet itself or through a wall access panel in a room adjoining the bathroom. Washing machines are connected to shutoff valves with hot and cold supply hoses. Dishwashers sometimes share a two-outlet shutoff with the hot water supply tube for the kitchen faucet.

2 If you can't locate or operate the stop valve, look for intermediate shutoffs that control multiple fixtures in a supply line. Finding the right intermediate shutoff(s) can require trial and error and detective work. Hot water pipes will always lead back to a hot water heater and cold water pipes will lead back to a water meter (below) or a well pressure tank.

3 The hot water shutoff is located at or near the water heater and lets you turn off all the hot water in the house. There will usually be a valve on the pipe supplying cold water to the heater, and there may also be a valve on the outgoing pipe from the heater. If your water is heated by gas, do not be confused by the gas pipe and gas shutoff. The gas pipe leads to the thermostat at the bottom of the water heater.

4 The main water shutoff will be located near the water meter, generally found in your basement. Do not confuse it with the gas meter shutoff, which has a disc shaped device associated with it and generally turns off with a wrench or lever, rather than by hand-spinning. In an emergency, your municipal water works may be contacted to shut off the water with a key (a special wrench) between the public water main on the street and your house. NOTE: Some municipal water works do not meter water use.

What if the valve is stuck?

1 Stop valves and shutoff valves may become fused by corrosion if they are not used regularly. If your valve won't operate, rap lightly on the valve body with a wrench handle or hammer and try again to turn the handle clockwise.

2 If rapping the valve doesn't work, try loosening the packing nut with your adjustable wrench until it leaks just a little bit of water. Then, retighten the nut and try the handle again.

3 If the valve handle won't turn the stem, remove it so you can grip the valve stem directly. Start by unscrewing the screw that secures the handle to the valve. Remove the screw and the handle.

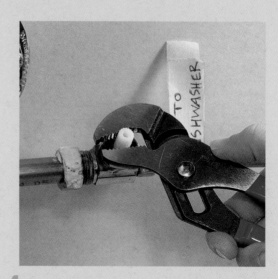

4 Grip the end of the handle stem with channel-type pliers or locking pliers and twist clockwise. Don't overdo it; you can break the valve and create a flood.

Lost Down the Drain?
Opening the Trap

2

Your wedding ring fell down the drain? Don't panic yet. Chances are good that the P-trap caught it.

EVERY PLUMBING FIXTURE IN YOUR HOUSE HAS A TRAP—a downward facing drainage loop that can collect small, heavy items (like wedding rings) that accidentally fall into the drain. The main function of a trap is not to catch rings, but to hold water. The water in a trap acts as a plug to keep sewer gases from rising into the house. Sink traps are located beneath the sink basin. Bathtub and shower traps are located near the drain and are sometimes accessible through a panel in an adjoining room. A toilet trap is an integral part of the fixture—the front part of the trap is the bowl itself. You can fish out an object from a toilet trap with coat-hanger wire since the bend only goes back a little way from the visible side before bending up again. But if an object is swept out of a trap, it has embarked on a journey through the sewer system, and you may be out of luck.

TRAPS 101

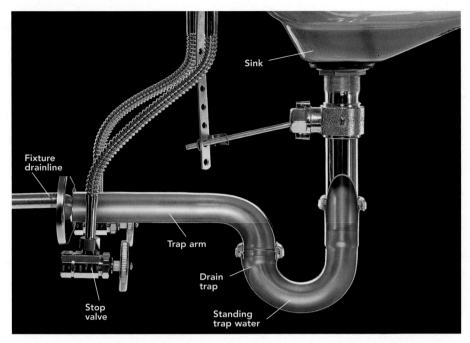

Sink

Fixture drainline

Stop valve

Trap arm

Drain trap

Standing trap water

A *drain trap* is a section of pipe attached near the top of a *fixture drain* that loops downward and then upward again. This creates a "trap" for water that blocks sewer gases from rising up though your drainlines and out the drain opening of a *fixture*. It also creates a blockage point for debris and a catch basin for small objects that find their way into the drain opening. Traps are designed to be easy to take apart for cleaning or retrieval.

TERMS YOU NEED TO KNOW

TRAP—downward bend in a drain in or near a fixture that can catch small objects. The standing water in a trap keeps sewer gases from rising into the house.

S-TRAP—The S-shaped trap is an older design used when the waste pipe comes out of the floor.

P-TRAP—Modern sink, tub, and shower traps are shaped like a P tipped on its face.

J-BEND—also called a "drain bend" or simply a "trap", this is the part that forms the low bend on a P-Trap or S-Trap.

TRAP ARM—also called a "wall tube," this extends from the J-bend to the trap adapter at the wall on a P-trap.

TRAP ADAPTER—also called a "drain pipe connector," this is a common transition fitting that lets you attach a light gauge chromed-brass or plastic trap arm to the larger heavy-gauge waste pipe coming out of the wall. It uses a washer and slip nut.

TOOLS & SUPPLIES YOU'LL NEED

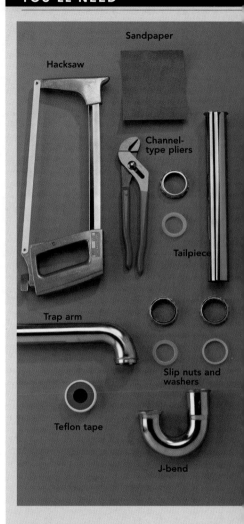

Sandpaper

Hacksaw

Channel-type pliers

Tailpiece

Trap arm

Slip nuts and washers

Teflon tape

J-bend

SKILLS YOU'LL NEED

- Unscrewing and retightening compression-style slip joints

DIFFICULTY LEVEL

SKILLS LEVEL

EASY   MODERATE

Time: ½ hour to 1 hour

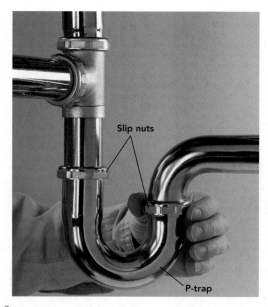

1 Before removing a sink trap, place a bucket under the trap to catch water that spills out. Loosen the slip nut at one end of the trap (a P-trap is seen here). Use channel-type pliers if the nut won't unscrew by hand.

2 Loosen the slip nut on the other end of the trap and pull both nuts away from the union. You will find a compression washer at each union. Slide these back as well and remove the trap by pulling down on it.

3 Keep track of slip nuts and washers and note their up/down orientation. Clean out debris within the trap and examine it. If the trap or the slip nuts and washers are in poor repair (very common), purchase replacement parts, making sure they are made from the same material and are the same size as the rest of the trap.

4 Reassemble the trap pieces just as they came off, or follow instructions on replacement parts. If the trap is made of plastic, hand tighten only. Wrap Teflon tape onto the male threads of metal tubes and then tighten a quarter turn beyond hand tight with channel-type pliers. Tighten joints that leak.

What if your trap looks like this?

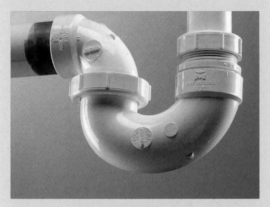

Some sink, tub, and shower traps are made out of the same heavy plastic (Schedule 40 PVC) or metal as the rest of your DWV plumbing and do not fit together like light plastic or chromed drain traps. But even if some parts are permanently fused together by a process called solvent-welding (these typically have a tell-tale purple band of color around the joint) you may still be able to access the trap by untwisting a union. Threaded joints are a sign that you've got a removable trap.

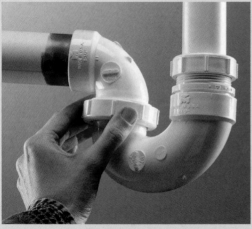

To access the trap, simply unscrew the joint fittings as on the previous page. Unlike a tubular trap, the nut at the DWV trap arm union unscrews counterclockwise from below. That's because the nut faces up instead of down. The slip nut on the fixture side of the trap is loosened like that of a tubular trap.

What if my trap is permanently solvent-welded to the drain and trap arm?

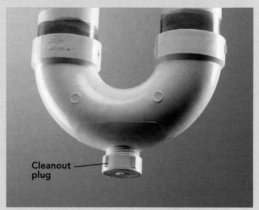

Cleanout plug

Often, bathtubs or showers have a drain trap system that is completely solvent-welded together, making it impossible to disassemble without cutting the pipes. But if you're lucky, the trap will have a cleanout plug at the bottom, like the one above.

The cleanout plug can be removed to clear the trap and retrieve lost items. Try hand-loosening the plug first, although unless your plumbing is virtually brand new you'll probably need an adjustable wrench to remove the plug. Fair warning—your hand is very likely to be drenched with fairly disgusting drain water, but hopefully, it will be worth it.

3

Maintaining Your Water Heater

A well-maintained water heater can last up to 20 years (if you're lucky as well as conscientious) and is also a much safer home appliance.

WATER HEATERS ARE THE SECOND BIGGEST CONSUMER OF ENERGY IN MOST HOMES (AFTER THE FURNACE). In fact, heating water is responsible for 4 percent of America's total energy consumption, according to the United States Geological Survey. It's easy to see that maintaining your water heater saves money, but it also protects your home and family. At their most basic, water heaters are containers filled with extremely hot water and fueled by gas burners or major amounts of electricity. It's worth taking the time to treat them with care.

WATER HEATERS 101

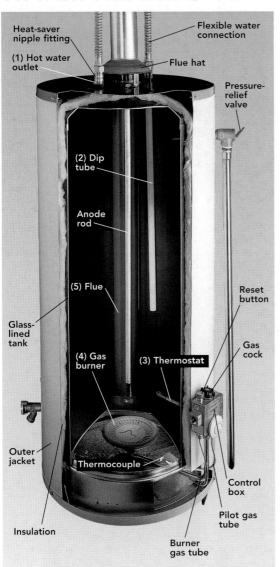

Heat-saver nipple fitting
(1) Hot water outlet
Flexible water connection
Flue hat
Pressure-relief valve
(2) Dip tube
Anode rod
(5) Flue
Reset button
Glass-lined tank
Gas cock
(4) Gas burner
(3) Thermostat
Thermocouple
Outer jacket
Control box
Insulation
Pilot gas tube
Burner gas tube

How a gas water heater works: Hot water leaves the tank through the *hot water outlet* (1) as fresh, cold water enters the water heater through the *dip tube* (2). As the water temperature drops, the *thermostat* (3) opens the gas valve, and the *gas burner* (4) is lighted by a pilot flame. Exhaust gases are vented through the *flue* (5). When the water temperature reaches a preset temperature, the thermostat closes the gas valve, extinguishing the burner. The *thermocouple* protects against gas leaks by automatically shutting off the gas if the pilot flame goes out. An *anode rod* protects the tank lining from rust by attracting corrosive elements in the water. A *pressure-relief valve* guards against ruptures caused by steam buildup in the tank.

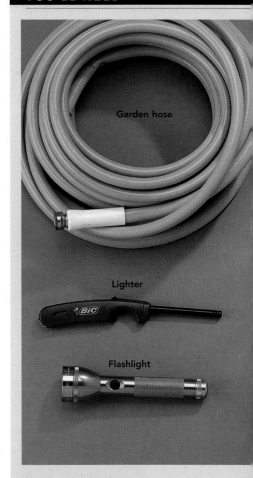
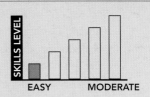
The best setting for a water heater is between 120° and 125°, or L for Low. If the thermostat's set too high, the water coming from your faucets can be hot enough to cause serious burns, especially on children or the elderly. To check the temperature, let the water run for a few minutes, then check it with a candy thermometer. Adjust the water heater's thermostat as necessary.

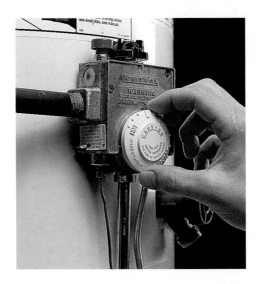

HOW TO FLUSH A WATER HEATER

1 First, turn off the heater. If you have a gas unit, set the gas valve on "Pilot." If it's electric, turn the circuit breaker to the Off position. Keep all children and pets away from the area.

2 Connect a garden hose to the drain valve at the bottom of the tank. Close the shutoff valve on the cold-water inlet. Open the temperature/pressure relief valve, and leave it open. Run the hose to a nearby sink or floor drain.

3 Open the drain valve at the bottom of the heater. Be careful: hot water will flow out. If the tank doesn't drain, sediment probably is clogging the drain valve. Close the pressure relief valve and turn on the cold water inlet valve. If it still doesn't drain, it's time to call a plumber. Keep an eye on the water coming out of the hose. When it runs clear, you've removed as much sediment as possible. Close the drain valve and disconnect the hose. Close the pressure relief valve and open up the cold-water inlet valve.

OPTION: If you have a water heater with a high enough tank drain valve, you may find it easier to simply drain the tank by opening the valve and letting the water run into a bucket.

HOW TO RE-LIGHT PILOT LIGHTS

1 If the pilot light on your gas water heater goes out, here is how to re-light it. Turn the gas cock on top of the water heater control box to the "Pilot" position.

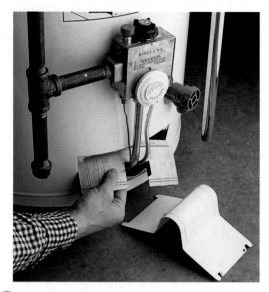

2 Remove the outer and inner access panels covering the burner chamber. With a flashlight, inspect inside the exposed chamber to make sure there are no cobwebs or other flammable debris. If you see anything that could catch fire, vacuum out the chamber with a shop vac.

3 Strike a flame (preferably a long fireplace match or lighter) and hold the flame next to the end of the pilot gas tube inside the burner chamber.

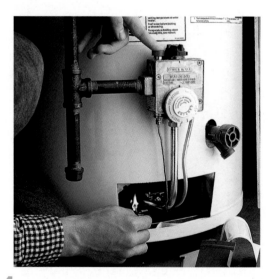

4 While holding the match next to the end of the gas tube, press the "Reset" button on top of the control box. When the pilot flame lights, continue to depress the "Reset" button for one minute. Then, turn the gas cock to the "On" position and replace the panels. If the pilot will not stay lit, your gas burner jets may need cleaning or the thermocouple might need to be replaced. Call a plumber or your public utility service and have a professional perform this job.

Fixing a Dripping Sink Faucet

4

Eventually, just about every faucet develops leaks and drips. Repairs can usually be accomplished simply by replacing the mechanical parts inside the faucet body (the main trick is figuring out which kind of parts your faucet has).

IT'S NOT SURPRISING THAT SINK FAUCETS LEAK AND DRIP. Any fitting that contains moving mechanical parts is susceptible to failure. But add to the equation the persistent force of water pressure working against the parts, and the real surprise is that faucets don't fail more quickly or often. It would be a bit unfair to say that the inner workings of a faucet are regarded as disposable by manufacturers, but it is safe to say that these parts have become more easy to remove and replace.

The most important aspect of sink faucet repair is identifying which type of faucet you own. In this chapter we show all of the common types and provide instructions on repairing them. In every case, the easiest and most reliable repair method is to purchase a replacement kit with brand new internal working parts for the model and brand of faucet you own.

SINK FAUCETS 101

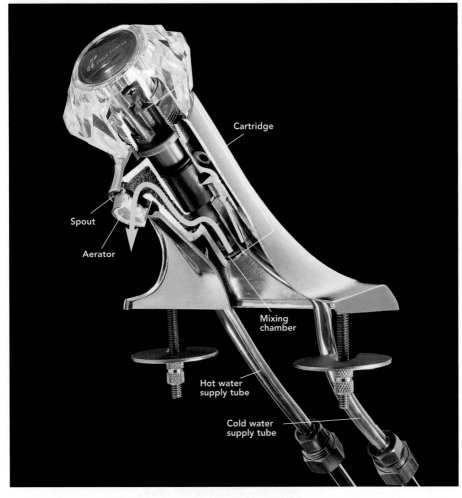

- Cartridge
- Spout
- Aerator
- Mixing chamber
- Hot water supply tube
- Cold water supply tube

Almost all leaks are caused by malfunctioning faucet valve mechanisms. Whether your sink faucet is a one-handle cartridge type (above) or a two-handle compression type or anything in between, the solution to fixing the leak is to clean or replace the parts that seal off the hot and cold water inlets from the spout.

TERMS YOU NEED TO KNOW

COMPRESSION VALVE—a valve type in which a spindle moves a washer up and down to stop or allow water flow through a valve seat.

CARTRIDGE VALVE—a valve type containing a cartridge, usually made of plastic or plastic and metal, in which a channel is slid open and closed by rotating a handle (see the example above).

NEOPRENE—a rubber-like, usually black material from which washers, rings, gaskets, and other seal-forming valve parts are made.

TELEPHONE—an invaluable tool used to contact your faucet's manufacturer, a font of information specific to the repair of your particular faucet.

TOOLS & SUPPLIES YOU'LL NEED

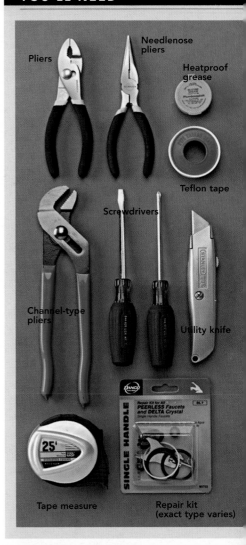

- Pliers
- Needlenose pliers
- Heatproof grease
- Teflon tape
- Channel-type pliers
- Screwdrivers
- Utility knife
- Tape measure
- Repair kit (exact type varies)

SKILLS YOU'LL NEED

- Using channel-type pliers
- Tracking the order and arrangement of parts
- Phone or computer research

DIFFICULTY LEVEL

SKILLS LEVEL

EASY   MODERATE

Time: 30 minutes to 1 hour plus research and shopping

HOW TO FIX A COMPRESSION FAUCET

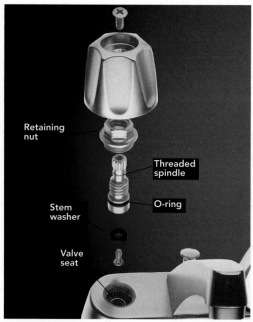

Most compression valves have a threaded metal spindle with a disc-shaped stem washer on the end. When the spindle is screwed all the way in, the stem washer covers a hole, and water flow to the spout is stopped. Drips from the spout happen when the seal between the stem washer and the rim of the hole (called the "valve seat") is imperfect. Usually, replacing the stem washer is enough to stop the drip.

1 Turn off the water at the stop valves for the faucet you are fixing then open the faucet and let the water drain out. Remove the handles by prying an index cap off the top with a dull knife or screwdriver and removing the screw hidden underneath.

2 Use channel-type pliers to unscrew a retaining nut or the entire stem assembly from the faucet body. If what you find looks similar to the stem assembly shown in step 3, you're in the right place.

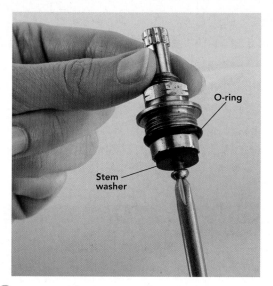

3 Unscrew the stem screw and remove the stem washer. You must find an exact replacement. A flat washer should always be replaced with a flat washer, for example, even if a profiled washer fits. Your washer may have a size code printed on the back, but it's usually easiest to bring the whole stem into the hardware store or home center and try on new neoprene parts there.

Stem washer

O-ring

4 Pry or cut off the O-ring on the stem with a utility knife. This keeps water from leaking under the handle when the faucet is on.

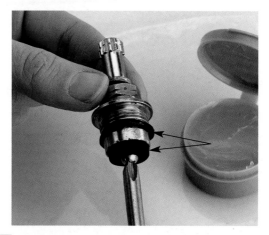

5 Coat the new O-ring and washer with heat-proof grease and install them. Tighten the stem screw enough to hold the washer in place, but do not distort the washer by overtightening. Coat the large threaded spindle threads with heatproof grease to lubricate the action of the faucet valve.

Aerator

6 Wrap Teflon tape onto the retaining nut threads and screw it onto the faucet body. Tighten lightly with channel-type pliers. Replace the handle, the handle screw, and the index cap. **TIP:** Unscrew the aerator at the tip of the spout and open the faucet before turning the water back on. This will flush debris from the system.

HERE'S HOW

There are many ways to classify sink faucets, but perhaps the most useful distinction is compression style versus washerless. These names refer to the type of mechanism inside the faucet. Many older faucets are compression type, but most newer ones are washerless, which can be one of three principal types: cartridge, ball, or disc. All one-handle faucets are washerless. The best way to tell if your faucet is a compression type or washerless is to turn the handle. With compression faucets you can feel the compression building as you crank the handle, even after the water flow has stopped. On washerless models, the handle comes to an abrupt stop.

HOW TO FIX A CARTRIDGE FAUCET

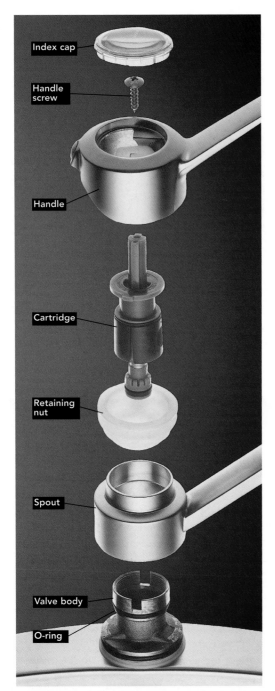

Index cap

Handle screw

Handle

Cartridge

Retaining nut

Spout

Valve body

O-ring

Both one- and two-handle faucets are available with replaceable plastic cartridges inside the faucet body. These cartridges (used by Price-Pfister, Sterling, Kohler, Moen, and others) regulate the flow of water through the spout, and in single-handle faucets they also mix the hot and cold water to alter the temperature out of the spout. To locate the correct replacement cartridge for your faucet, knowing the manufacturer and model number is a great help.

Index cap

1 Turn off the water at the stop valves. To avoid losing small parts, put a rag in the drain if it has no stopper. Some cartridge faucets have an index cap covering a handle screw. Other handles, especially on one-handle faucets, are secured with a recessed set screw that can be loosened with a $3/32$" or $7/64$" hex wrench. A lever type handle with no set screw may be removed with channel-type pliers.

SHOPPING TIP

Replacement cartridges are not interchangeable among brands or sometimes even among models from the same manufacturer. It's always a good idea to bring the old cartridge with you to the hardware store to help you select the correct replacement.

Retaining nut

2 Remove the retaining nut, if there is one, with channel-type pliers. A recessed nut with notches can be removed with open needlenose pliers or a tool provided by the faucet manufacturer. With other kinds, you'll remove a sleeve and three screws before extracting the cartridge.

3 Record the direction the cartridge is facing by noting the orientation of some distinctive part of the cartridge (some are cast with an orientation tab that generally should point straight forward). Pull the cartridge straight up and out with pliers. You may need to twist the cartridge back and forth to break the seal.

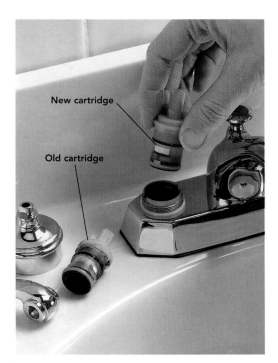

New cartridge

Old cartridge

4 Purchase a replacement cartridge. Apply heatproof grease to the valve seat and O-rings, then install the cartridge in the correct orientation and with its tabs seated in the slotted body of the faucet.

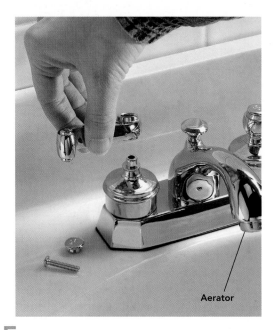

Aerator

5 Reattach the handle, remove the aerator, turn on the water, and test. If the faucet doesn't work, the cartridge may be facing the wrong direction. Remove it and reinsert it facing the other way, still making sure the tabs fit into the slots on the valve body.

HOW TO FIX A BALL FAUCET

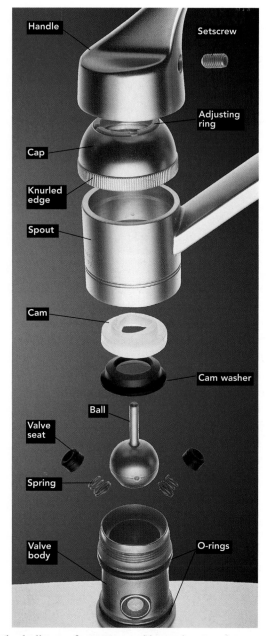

Handle

Setscrew

Adjusting ring

Cap

Knurled edge

Spout

Cam

Cam washer

Ball

Valve seat

Spring

Valve body

O-rings

Ball faucet tool

1 Turn off the hot and cold water at the stop valves and open the faucet to let any water drain from the pipes. Plug the sink drain with a towel to avoid losing small parts. Pry off a red and blue hot/cold button or a knob-handle button, if present, with a small screwdriver or dull knife. Loosen the setscrew hidden underneath with the hex wrench on the ball faucet tool. Now remove the handle.

The ball-type faucet is used by Delta, Peerless, and a few others. The ball fits into the faucet body and is constructed with three holes (not visible here)—a hot inlet, a cold inlet, and the outlet, which fills the valve body with water that then flows to the spout or sprayer. Depending on the position of the ball, each inlet hole is open, closed, or somewhere in-between. The inlet holes are sealed to the ball with valve seats, which are pressed tight against the ball with springs. If water drips from the spout, replace the seats and springs. Or go ahead and purchase an entire replacement kit and replace all or most of the working parts.

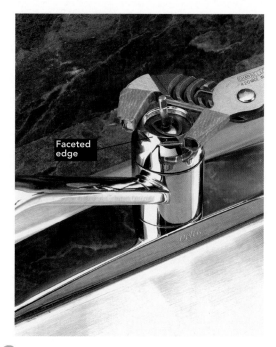

Faceted edge

2 Wrap the jaws of your channel-type pliers with masking tape to protect the faucet finish. Grasp the faceted or knurled edges of the round ball cap with the pliers and twist to remove.

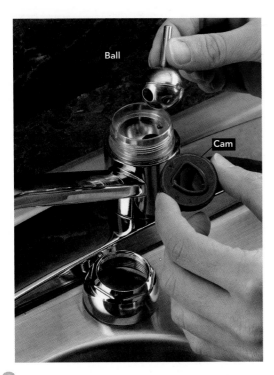

3 Pull out the ball, noticing for later how a pin in the faucet body fits in a slit in the ball. Clean the ball with white vinegar and a toothbrush or replace it if it is scratched.

4 If your faucet drips from the spout, it's because the seal between the ball and the hot- or cold-water intake has failed. Pull the neoprene valve seats and springs from the intakes with a screwdriver. Note how the cupped sides of the valve seats fit over the narrow sides of the springs and how the wide base of the springs fit into holes in the intakes.

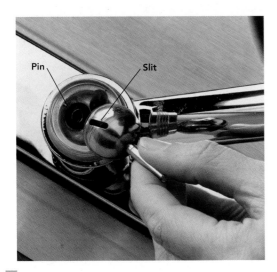

5 Replace parts in the reverse order they came off. Each spring/seat washer combo can be lined up on a screwdriver, set in place, and pushed in with a finger. The pin in the faucet body fits in a slit on the ball. The pointy side of the cam faces forward, and lugs on the sides of the cam fit in notches in the valve body.

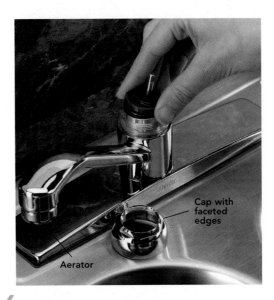

6 Make sure the adjusting ring is partly backed off before screwing the cap on. After the cap is on, gently tighten down the adjusting ring with the ball faucet tool. Remove the aerator, turn on the water supply and test. If water leaks from under the handle or if the handle action is stiff, tighten or loosen the adjusting ring. Replace the aerator.

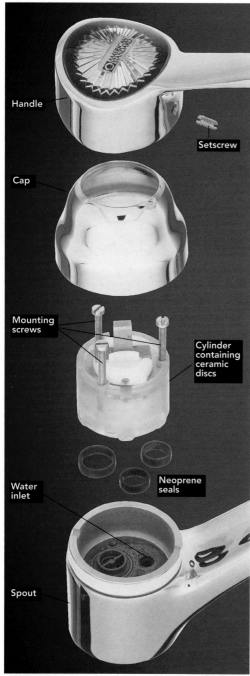

The disc-type faucet used by American Standard, among others, has a wide disc cartridge hidden beneath the handle and the cap. Mounting screws hold the cartridge in the valve body. Two tight-fitting ceramic discs with holes in them are concealed inside the cartridge. The handle slides the top disc back and forth and from side to side over the stationary bottom disc. This brings the holes in the disks into and out of alignment, adjusting the flow and mix of hot and cold water.

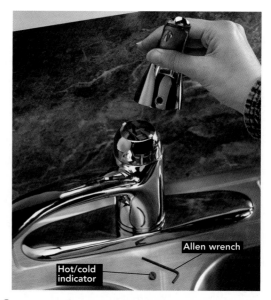

1 Turn off the hot and cold water at the stop valves, open the faucet to let any water drain out, and plug the sink drain. Pry the index cap (and possibly a hot/cold indicator) off the handle with a small screwdriver or a dull knife. Loosen the handle setscrew with a Phillips or slotted screwdriver or an Allen wrench and remove the handle.

2 Remove the chrome cap and/or a plastic or metal retaining ring with channel-type pliers (cover the jaws with masking tape). Remove the cylinder containing the discs, generally by first removing three long retaining screws. Take time to line up parts in the orientation and order in which they were installed.

3 If your faucet leaks under the handle, remove the three neoprene seals from the underside of the disc cylinder. Bring them to the hardware store and find matching replacements. For a leak out of the spout, you need to replace the entire cylinder.

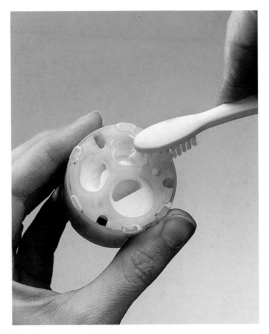

4 If you are reusing the cylinder, clean the water inlets, scouring with a toothbrush and white vinegar if they are crusty.

5 Lightly coat the new neoprene seals with heatproof grease and insert them in the appropriate openings in the cylinder. The seals will be slippery and you'll need to contort them a bit to fit the shapes of the openings, so be sure to do this over a clean, light colored surface so you don't lose the seals.

6 Insert the cylinder and secure it to the faucet body with the cylinder screws. Reattach the retaining nut. Reattach the handle, then turn on the hot and cold supplies and test the faucet. Remove the aerator from the spout to allow debris to escape.

My Bathroom Sink Drains Slowly

5

If your bathroom sink drains slowly, or not at all, the plug is most likely right under the pop-up stopper.

HAIR, SOAP, SOAPY HAIR, HAIRY SOAP—there are any number of things that can plug up a bathroom sink drain, but a couple of materials seem to show up a lot. Hair likes to tangle on the shaft of the pop up stopper, and soap likes to join in the fun by congealing on the hair. Eventually, you can get a long icky rope that snakes down into the trap. So the first thing is to figure out how to remove the pop-up stopper. While you're at it, withdraw the horizontal pivot arm that actuates the stopper. Nine times out of ten, you can vanquish the soap rope by removing and cleaning these two snags. A plunger can flush the beast from a deeper lair. Or you can remove that bend of pipe under the sink called the trap and give this a good cleaning. Finally, with a miraculous tool called an auger, you can pursue the soap rope beyond the trap into the dark and mysterious reaches of your drainage system.

In the event that your pop-up stopper drain needs replacement, see pages 126 to 129.

POP-UP STOPPERS 101

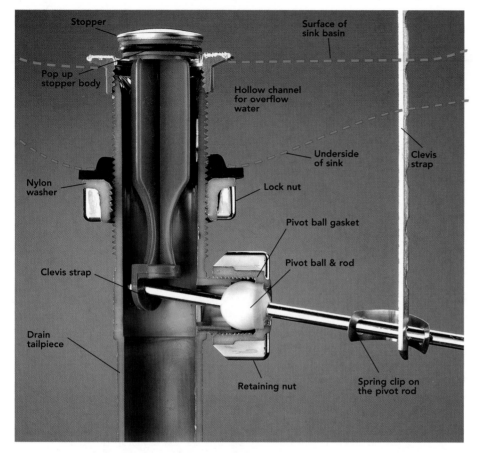

Labels on figure:
- Stopper
- Surface of sink basin
- Pop up stopper body
- Hollow channel for overflow water
- Underside of sink
- Clevis strap
- Nylon washer
- Lock nut
- Pivot ball gasket
- Pivot ball & rod
- Clevis strap
- Drain tailpiece
- Retaining nut
- Spring clip on the pivot rod

Pop-up stoppers keep objects from falling down the drain, and they make filling and draining the sink easy. They also accumulate hair and soap and require periodic cleaning. Cleaning the pop-up stopper provides an opportunity to adjust the actuating mechanism so the stopper works better.

TERMS YOU NEED TO KNOW

POP-UP STOPPER—the drain stopper and the shaft attached to the bottom of the stopper.

PIVOT BALL & ROD—The ball is a fulcrum and the rod a lever, which allows the pop-up stopper to be moved up and down.

TAILPIECE—takes the waste from the pop-up-stopper body to the trap.

TRAP—a bend of drainpipe below the sink. It's always full of water to keep sewer gases from rising into the house.

TRAP ARM—receives waste from the trap and takes it to the fixture drain line in the wall.

FIXTURE DRAIN LINE—begins at the wall and eventually joins with larger drain pipes. On older houses, the drain line may come vertically from the floor.

TOOLS & SUPPLIES YOU'LL NEED

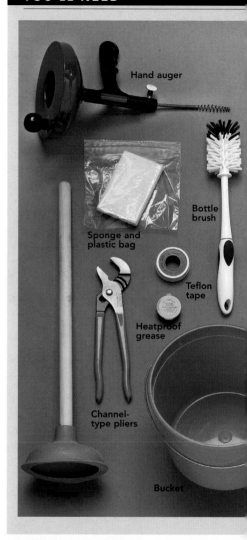

Labels:
- Hand auger
- Bottle brush
- Sponge and plastic bag
- Teflon tape
- Heatproof grease
- Channel-type pliers
- Bucket

SKILLS YOU'LL NEED

- Making pipe connections
- Using plungers
- Auger cranking

DIFFICULTY LEVEL

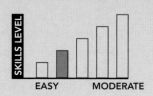

SKILLS LEVEL

EASY   MODERATE

Time: about 1 hour

HOW TO CLEAN A POP-UP STOPPER

1 If the bathroom sink drain is clogged, first bail most of the water out of the sink. Remove the pop-up stopper, noticing as you do how its shaft was oriented in the sink. To remove, try rotating the stopper a quarter turn while tilting the shaft of the stopper away from the pivot arm. If it cannot be freed through gentle manipulation, proceed to step 2.

3 Clean the gunk off the pop-up stopper and rod with hot soapy water and a brush. Clear accessible parts of the drain hole with a long screwdriver or a bottlebrush. Temporarily put the washers, the ball and rod, and the nut back on, but leave the stopper off. Run hot tap water down the drain. If the sink won't drain, plunge as described on the next page.

2 Put a bucket under the drain works. Unscrew the retaining nut attached to the drain tailpiece. Remove the pivot ball and rod, the beveled gasket that seals the ball, and any other washers. You may need to squeeze a spring clip on the pivot rod to move the rod in the clevis.

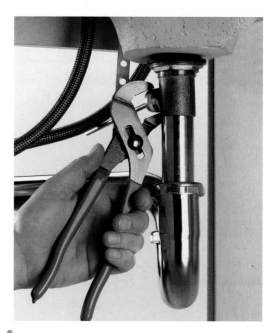

4 Once the water is draining well, remove and replace the pop-up assembly pieces in the correct order. Apply pipe joint compound to the inside of the pop-up stopper body where the beveled washer sits, and onto the threads that receive the retaining nut. The pivot rod must penetrate a hole at the bottom of the pop-up stopper shaft, which is put in before or after the rod, depending on your faucet model.

HOW TO PLUNGE A BATHROOM SINK

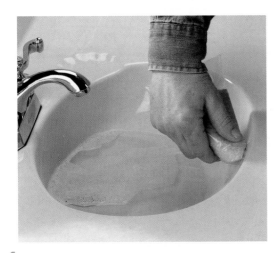

1 Plunging a plugged bathroom sink is usually the next step after cleaning the pop up mechanism. Be prepared to get the bathroom and yourself wet. The stopper should be removed and the pivot ball in place (see previous page). Put a wet sponge in a plastic bag and stuff this in the overflow opening. You may need to have somebody hold this in place while you plunge.

2 Put enough water in the sink to cover the plunger. Rhythmically thrust the plunger up and down with an occasional extra hard thrust up or down. It can take a bit of work. When you've cleared the drain, pour a large pot of boiling water down the drain and follow that with hot tap water. If the plunging doesn't work, remove and clean the trap (see page 172). If the clog wasn't in the trap, follow the steps on the following pages to auger the waste line beyond the trap.

TOOL TIP

The standard redheaded plunger seen in step 2 is the most commonly used plunger for sinks, but the flare-cup style plunger seen here also works. All you need to do is fold the flaps on the working end of the plunger up into the plunger head to create a flat bottom capable of producing ample suction for clearing a sink.

SINK DRAIN MAINTENANCE

Pour a large pot of boiling water down your bathroom sink every so often. Very hot water melts soap better than just about anything.

HOW TO CLEAN A SINK DRAIN TRAP

HOW TO CLEAR A FIXTURE DRAIN LINE WITH AN AUGER

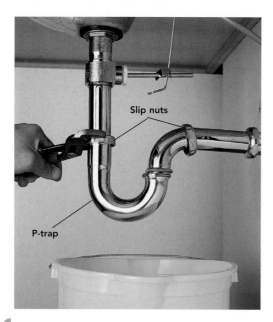

Slip nuts

P-trap

1 Position a bucket under the trap to catch water and debris. Loosen the slip nuts on the trap bend with channel-type pliers. Unscrew the nuts, slide them away from the connections, and pull off the trap bend.

Drain opening (trap arm removed)

1 A hand auger (often called a snake) is used to clear clogs in drain lines when they occur after the trap. To access the drain line, remove the trap arm and push the end of the auger cable into the drain line opening until resistance is met. This resistance usually indicates that the cable has reached a bend in the drain line.

2 Empty the trap into the bucket and use a small wire brush or a bottlebrush to ream out and clean the trap. Soak the trap in very hot water to dissolve and remove any blockages from soap buildup. Reassemble the trap.

2 Set the auger lock so that at least 6" of cable extends out of the opening. Crank the auger handle in a clockwise direction to move the end of the cable past the bend in the drain line.

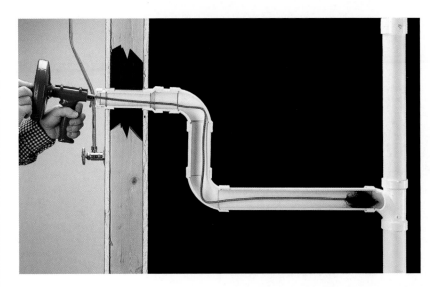

3 Release the lock and continue pushing the cable into the opening until firm resistance is felt. Set the auger lock and crank the handle in a clockwise direction. Solid resistance that prevents the cable from advancing indicates a clog. Some clogs, such as a sponge or an accumulation of hair, can be snagged and retrieved. Continuous resistance that still allows the cable to advance at a very slow rate is probably a soap clog.

RETRIEVAL OPTION: Pull an obstruction out of the line by releasing the auger lock and cranking the handle counter-clockwise while manually feeding the cable back into the auger drum. Removing the whole obstruction may take a number of tries. Call a plumber or go to "Advanced clog cleaning" pages 210 to 211 if the clog can't be cleared.

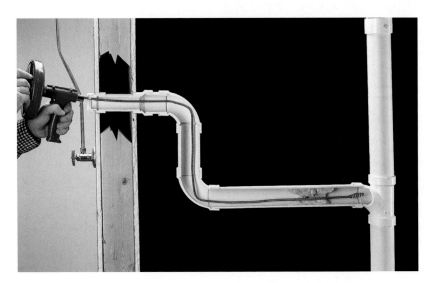

BREAK APART OPTION: Built-up clogs (as opposed to objects) can be broken into small pieces with the auger head and then flushed from the system. Bore through the clog by cranking the handle clockwise while applying steady pressure on the hand grip of the auger. Repeat the procedure two or three times, then reel in the cable. Reconnect the trap and flush the line with boiling hot water.

My Water Pressure
is Low or Uneven

6

**Restoring vigorous water pressure to your water outlets can be as simple
as cleaning a filter in a faucet or showerhead.**

CORRECTING LOW WATER PRESSURE AT A SINK OR SHOWER MAY BE EASIER
THAN YOU'D EXPECT. Minerals and rust can collect in the finely perforated screens and
sprayers in sink spouts and showerheads. Clean these out and, voilà, the water flows with
vigor; no plumber needed. Before water reaches any fixture or appliance, it passes through a
shutoff valve or two. Make sure these are fully open. Washing machines also draw water
through filters. Clean these screens and your washer may fill faster. Old iron water pipes are
subject to mineral buildup. A professional can replace these with modern copper or plastic
pipes that resist buildup and corrosion.

WATER FLOW 101

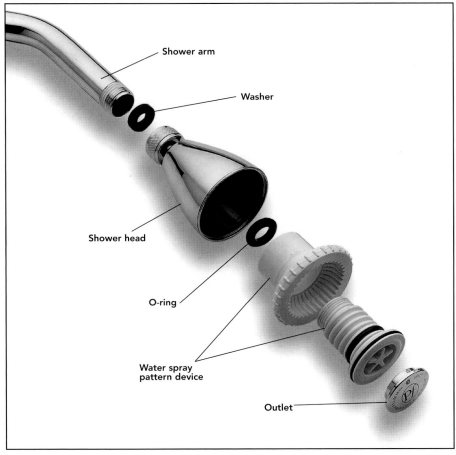

Shower arm

Washer

Shower head

O-ring

Water spray
pattern device

Outlet

A showerhead is easy to remove for cleaning or repair. Once you remove it from the shower arm, you take it apart, clean the parts (you may need to check the flow restrictor), and then reassemble it and reattach it to the arm.

TERMS YOU NEED TO KNOW

AERATOR—a small cylinder on the end of a bathroom or kitchen sink spout that breaks up the water stream so it doesn't splash.

FLOW RESTRICTOR—a disc-shaped part on the inlet side of a showerhead with a small hole or holes designed to restrict water flow and conserve water.

TOOLS & SUPPLIES YOU'LL NEED

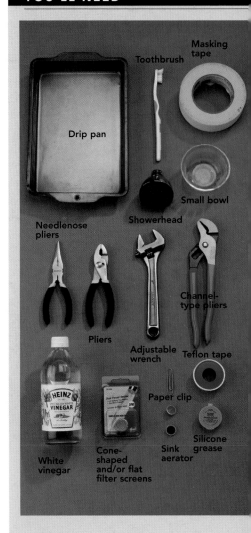

Masking tape

Toothbrush

Drip pan

Small bowl

Needlenose pliers

Showerhead

Pliers

Channel-type pliers

Adjustable wrench

Teflon tape

Paper clip

HEINZ VINEGAR

Sink aerator

Silicone grease

White vinegar

Cone-shaped and/or flat filter screens

SKILLS YOU'LL NEED

• Using channel-type pliers

• Using a wrench

DIFFICULTY LEVEL

SKILLS LEVEL

EASY   MODERATE

Time: less than ½ hour per fixture

HOW TO CLEAN A SHOWERHEAD

Water may flow through two or three shutoff valves between the city water line or the well and your shower or sink. Make sure all the shutoff valves are functioning properly and are opened fully. If the valves are all open, the problem could be in the internal working of your outlet valves. Check the filters and aerators first, as we show you in this project. If the water flow is still subpar, refer to the project that show you how to repair and replace faucets.

1 Remove the showerhead from the shower arm by unscrewing the collar nut that houses the swivel ball and is threaded onto the shower arm. You may need to grip the shower arm with channel-type pliers to keep it from twisting. Wrap the jaws of the pliers with masking tape to protect shower parts.

2 Once the showerhead is fully removed, run water through the shower arm for a couple of minutes to clear it.

3 Disassemble the showerhead. On newer showerheads, the swivel ball or the inlet side of the showerhead will have flow restriction parts. These contain one or more small holes and exist mainly to conserve water. Remove these parts, if you can, with a small knife or screwdriver.

4 Keep all parts in order and oriented in the correct up/down position. If the house water pressure is very poor, you may leave the flow restriction parts (inset photo) out when you put the showerhead back together. **WARNING:** Removing flow restrictor parts can dramatically increase your water and energy bills.

5 Use a paper clip or pin to clean the outlet holes on the showerhead then flush all parts clean with water. Soak encrusted parts overnight in white vinegar to soften mineral deposits.

6 Coat the rubber O-ring that contacts the swivel ball with silicone grease before reassembling the head. Hand-tighten the collar nut that holds the swivel fitting to the showerhead.

7 Wrap the shower arm threads with two or three layers of Teflon tape in a clockwise direction before replacing the head. Tighten the head to the shower arm a little more than hand tight using your adjustable wrench. Tighten a little more if the joint drips with the shower on. If the showerhead does not work to your satisfaction, replace it.

HOW TO CLEAN A FAUCET AERATOR

1 Dry and wrap the aerator with masking tape to protect the finish. Adjust channel-type pliers to fit comfortably over the aerator and twist the aerator counterclockwise to loosen.

2 Finish unscrewing the aerator by hand then gently prod apart its components with your finger or a needle or other pointed tool. Be careful to lay out pieces in the order they fit together and in the correct up/down orientation. **TIP:** Turn on the water while the aerator is removed to flush any built-up materials out the spout.

3 Clean parts with white vinegar and a toothbrush. Soften mineral deposits by soaking overnight in the vinegar. Replace the aerator at a hardware store or home center if parts are damaged or difficult to clean. A standard replacement aerator has both male and female threads and fits most faucets, but take in your old aerator in case yours is a non-standard size.

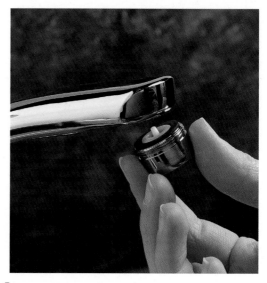

4 Reassemble the aerator exactly as it came apart and hand-tighten it onto the spout. Remove the tape. Replace the aerator if it still doesn't work right.

WASHING MACHINE FILLS SLOWLY?

1 Turn off hot and cold water to the machine and unscrew supply hoses where they join the machine or at the first accessible coupling.

2 Some water supply hoses for washing machines contain filter screens in the hose couplings that connect to the water supply and to the water inlets in the washing machine. If you find these filters, carefully remove and clean them.

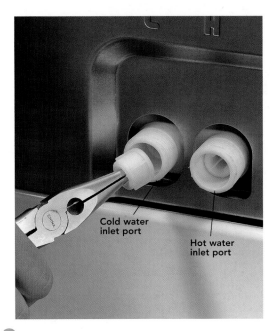

Cold water inlet port

Hot water inlet port

3 Most washing machines contain filter screens at the water inlet port. Remove the cone filter with needlenose pliers and clear debris from the filter screen. If the filter is in poor condition, replace it.

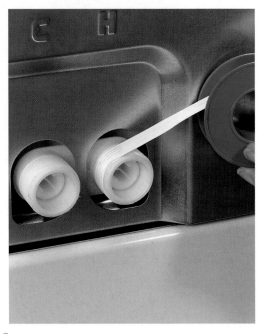

4 Apply Teflon tape to the male pipe threads at the water inlet connection and retighten all hoses.

Runaway Toilet

7

Jiggling the handle can make a running toilet stop, but it's only a temporary solution. Making real repairs is a lot easier than you might think.

SNORING, TICKING CLOCKS, DRIPPING FAUCETS, AND RUNNING TOILETS are perhaps the four greatest nighttime annoyances. Together they conspire to keep you from the blissful slumber you deserve. For help on fixing leaky faucets, see pages 158 to 167. If your toilet runs and runs and you just can't seem to catch up with it, you're in the right place. This project will show you how to diagnose and remedy the most common causes for the perpetually running toilet.

TOILET TROUBLE SHOOTING 101

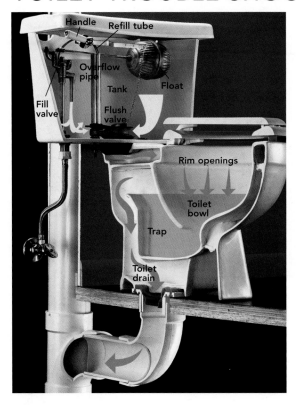

Five steps of a perfect flush: 1.The *handle* opens the *flush valve,* emptying the *tank* into the *toilet bowl.* 2. Water races through *rim openings* and the *siphon jet* at the base of the bowl. 3. The sudden surge causes the water to exit the *trap* and bowl as a unit, siphoning itself down the *toilet drain.* 4. The *ballcock* (fill valve) opens when the *float* drops to refill the tank. The *refill tube* directs some of the water down the *overflow pipe* to refill the bowl. 5. The *float* turns off the *fill valve* when enough water has entered the *tank.*

Most toilets can be fixed with generic replacement parts. However, some brands require special parts, especially newer models, which may have larger flush valves. Contact your manufacturer or go to a well-equipped plumbing-supply house. Identify your toilet brand, which is often written behind (not on) the seat, and its model number (usually stamped inside the tank or tank lid). Always bring old parts with you to the store for reference.

TERMS YOU NEED TO KNOW

BALLCOCK/FILL VALVE—These terms both refer to the valve that fills the tank after you flush the toilet. Traditionally, the ballcock is turned on and off by a float ball on a rod. Modern cup-float fill valves can be used to replace most old ballcocks.

FLUSH VALVE—the assembly that releases water from the tank into the bowl when the toilet is flushed. It includes the overflow pipe, the valve seat (hole), and the flapper or tank ball that covers the hole. Universal flapper-style flush valves can replace old tank ball or flapper flush valves on most toilets.

STOP VALVE—the valve that turns off water to the toilet. Turn to page 235 to replace (widespread faucet installation).

SUPPLY—the hose or tube that takes water from the stop valve to the tank.

TOOLS & SUPPLIES YOU'LL NEED

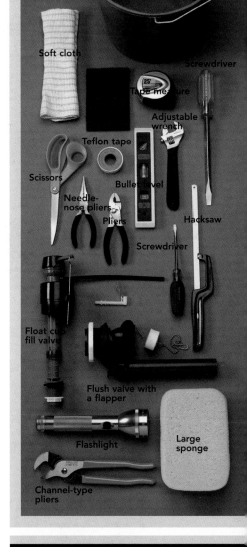

Soft cloth

Screwdriver

Tape measure

Teflon tape

Adjustable wrench

Scissors

Needle-nose pliers

Bullet level

Pliers

Hacksaw

Screwdriver

Float cup fill valve

Flush valve with a flapper

Flashlight

Large sponge

Channel-type pliers

SKILLS YOU'LL NEED

- Patience
- Observation
- Willingness to call a manufacturer help center if you get into trouble

DIFFICULTY LEVEL

EASY   MODERATE

Time: 5 minutes or hours depending on problem

HOW TO RESET TANK WATER LEVEL

1 Perhaps the most common cause of running toilets is a minor misadjustment that fails to tell the water to shut off when the toilet tank is full. The culprit is usually a float ball or cup that is adjusted to set a water level in the tank that's higher than the top of the overflow pipe, which serves as a drain for excess tank water.

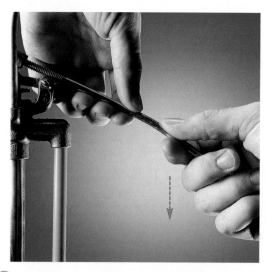

2 A ball float is connected to a float arm that's attached to a plunger on the other end. As the tank fills, the float rises and lifts one end of the float arm. At a certain point, the float arm depresses the plunger and stops the flow of water. By simply bending the float arm downward a bit you can cause it to depress the plunger at a lower tank water level, solving the problem.

3 A diaphragm fill valve usually is made of plastic and has a wide bonnet that contains a rubber diaphragm. Turn the adjustment screw clockwise to lower the water level and counter-clockwise to raise it.

Spring clip

4 A float cup fill valve is made of plastic and is easy to adjust. Lower the water level by pinching the spring clip with fingers or pliers and moving the clip and cup down the pull rod and shank. Raise the water level by moving the clip and cup upward.

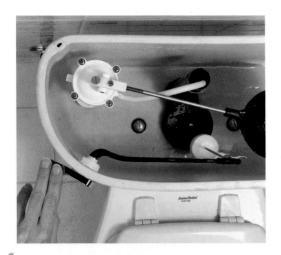

1 Sometimes there is plenty of water in the tank, but not enough of it makes it to the bowl before the flush valve shuts off the water from the tank. Modern toilets are designed to leave some water in the tank, since the first water that leaves the tank does so with the most force. (It's pressed out by the weight of the water on top). To increase the duration of the flush, shorten the length of the chain between the flapper and the float (yellow in the model shown).

2 The handle lever should pull straight up on the flapper. If it doesn't, reposition the chain hook on the handle lever. When the flapper is covering the opening, there should be just a little slack in the chain. If there is too much slack, shorten the chain and cut off excess with the cutters on your pliers. Turn the water back on at the stop valve and test the flush.

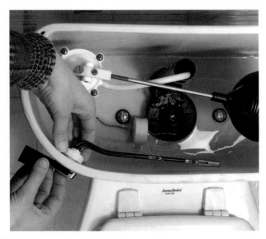

3 If the toilet is not completing flushes and the lever and chain for the flapper or tank ball are correctly adjusted, the problem could be that the handle mechanism needs cleaning or replacement. Remove the chain/linkage from the handle lever. Remove the nut on the backside of the handle with an adjustable wrench. It unthreads clockwise (the reverse of standard nuts). Remove the old handle from the tank.

4 Unless the handle parts are visibly broken, try cleaning them with an old toothbrush dipped in white vinegar. Replace the handle and test the action. If it sticks or is hard to operate, replace it. Most replacement handles come with detailed instructions that tell you how to install and adjust them.

HOW TO REPLACE A FILL VALVE

1 Toilet fill valves degrade eventually and need to be replaced. Before removing the old fill valve, shut off the water supply at the fixture stop valve located on the tube that supplies water to the tank. Flush the toilet and sponge out the remaining water. Then, remove the old fill valve assembly by loosening and removing the mounting nut on the outside of the tank wall that secures the fill valve.

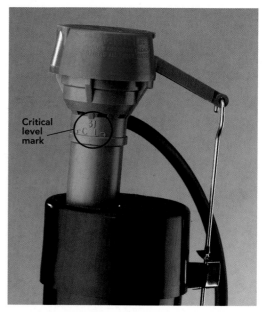

Critical level mark

2 Fill valves need to be coordinated with the flush valve so the tank water level is not higher than the overflow pipe and so the fill valve is not low enough in the tank that it creates a siphoning hazard. New fill valves have a "critical level" mark ("CL") near the top of the valve.

3 The new fill valve must be installed so the Critical Level ("CL") mark is at least 1" above the overflow pipe. Slip the shank washer on the threaded shank of the new fill valve and place the valve in the hole so the washer is flat on the tank bottom. Compare the locations of the CL mark and the overflow pipe.

4 Adjust the height of the fill valve shank so the "CL" line and overflow pipe will be correctly related. Different products are adjusted in different ways—the fill valve shown here telescopes when it's twisted.

Threaded valve stem

5 Position the valve in the tank. Push down on the valve shank (not the top) while hand tightening the locknut onto the threaded valve stem (thread the mounting nut on the exterior side of tank). Hand-tighten only.

6 Hook up the water by attaching the coupling nut from the supply riser to the threaded shank at the bottom end of the new fill valve. Hand-tighten only.

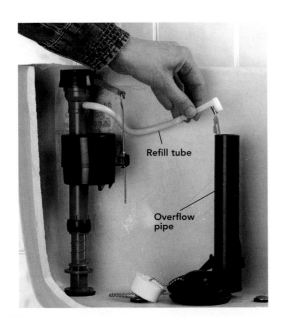

Refill tube

Overflow pipe

7 If the overflow pipe has a cap, remove it. Attach one end of the refill tube from the new valve to the plastic angle adapter and the other end to the refill nipple near the top of the valve. Attach the angle adapter to the overflow pipe. Cut off excess tubing with scissors to prevent kinking. WARNING: Don't insert the refill tube into the overflow pipe. The outlet of the refill tube needs to be above the top of pipe for it to work properly.

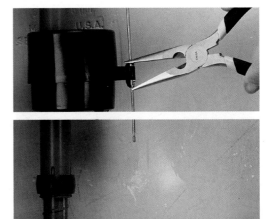

8 Turn the water on fully. Slightly tighten any fitting that drips water. Adjust the water level in the tank by squeezing the spring clip on the float cup with needlenose pliers and moving the cup up or down on the link bar. Test the flush.

HOW TO REPLACE A FLUSH VALVE

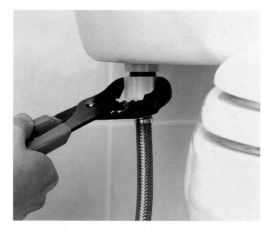

1 If the fixes on the previous pages still do not stop your toilet from running, the next step it to try replacing the flush valve. Before removing the old flush valve, shut off the water supply at the fixture stop valve located on the tube that supplies water to the tank. Flush the toilet and sponge out the remaining water. To make this repair you'll need to remove the tank from the bowl. Start by unscrewing the water supply coupling nut from the bottom of the tank.

2 Unscrew the bolts holding the toilet tank to the bowl by loosening the nuts from below. If you are having difficulty unscrewing the tank bolts and nuts because they are fused together by rust or corrosion, apply penetrating oil or spray lubricant to the threads, give it a few minutes to penetrate and then try again. If that fails, slip an open-ended hacksaw (or plain hacksaw blade) between the tank and bowl and saw through the bolt (inset photo).

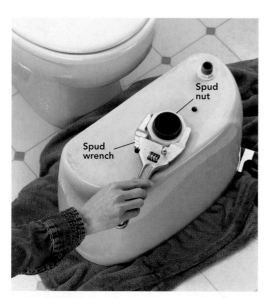

3 Unhook the chain from the handle lever arm. Remove the tank and carefully place it upside-down on an old towel. Remove the spud washer and spud nut from the base of the flush valve using a spud wrench or large channel-type pliers. Remove the old flush valve.

4 Place the new flush valve in the valve hole and check to see if the top of the overflow pipe is at least 1" below the Critical Level line (see page 184) and the tank opening where the handle is installed. If the pipe is too tall, cut it to length with a hacksaw.

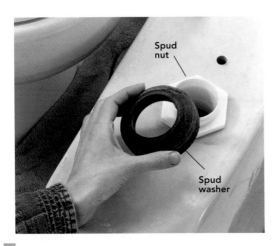

Spud nut

Spud washer

Intermediate nut goes between tank and bowl

5 Position the flush valve flapper below the handle lever arm and secure it to the tank from beneath with the spud nut. Tighten the nut one-half turn past hand tight with a spud wrench or large channel-type pliers. Over tightening may cause the tank to break. Put the new spud washer over the spud nut, small side down.

6 With the tank lying on its back, thread a rubber washer onto each tank bolt and insert it into the bolt holes from inside the tank. Then, thread a brass washer and hex nut onto the tank bolts from below and tighten them to a quarter turn past hand tight. Do not overtighten.

Intermediate nut

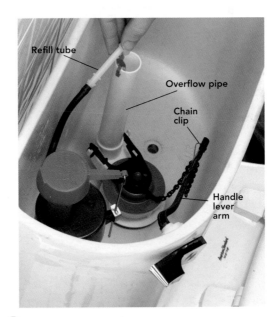

Refill tube

Overflow pipe

Chain clip

Handle lever arm

7 With the hex nuts tightened against the tank bottom, carefully lower the tank over the bowl and set it down so the spud washer seats neatly over the water inlet in the bowl and the tank bolts fit through the holes in the bowl flange. Secure the tank to the bowl with a rubber washer, brass washer, and nut or wing nut at each bolt end. Press the tank to level as you hand-tighten the nuts. Hook up the water supply at the fill valve inlet.

8 Connect the chain clip to the handle lever arm and adjust the number of links to allow for a little slack in the chain when the flapper is closed. Leave a little tail on the chain for adjusting, cutting off remaining excess. Attach the refill tube to the top of the overflow pipe the same way it had been attached to the previous refill pipe. Turn on the water supply at the stop valve and test the flush. (Some flush valve flappers are adjustable.)

Toilet Clogged. Overflowing!

8

A blockage in the toilet bowl leaves flush water from the tank nowhere to go but on the floor.

THE TOILET IS CLOGGED AND HAS OVERFLOWED, or perhaps its gorge has simply risen, lapped the canyon walls but not yet topped the rim. Have patience. Now is the time for considered action. A second flush is a tempting but unnecessary gamble. First, do damage control. Mop up the water if there's been a spill. Next, consider the nature of the clog. Is it entirely "natural" or might a foreign object be contributing to the congestion? Push a natural blockage down the drain with a plunger. A foreign object should be removed, if possible, with a closet auger. Pushing anything more durable than toilet paper into the sewer may create a more serious blockage in your drain and waste system. If the tub, sink, and toilet all become clogged at once, the branch drainline that serves all the bathroom fixtures is probably blocked and your best recourse is to call a drain clearing service.

CLOGGED TOILETS 101

Trap

The *trap* is the most common catching spot for toilet clogs, Once the clog forms, flushing the toilet cannot generate enough water power to clear the trap, so flush water backs up. Traps on modern 1.6-gallon toilets have been redesigned to larger diameters and are less prone to clogs than the first generation of 1.6 gallon toilets.

Not all plungers were created equal. The *standard plunger* (left) is simply an inverted rubber cup and is used to plunge sinks, tubs, and showers. The *flanged plunger*, also called a *force cup,* is designed to get down into the trap of a toilet drain. But in a pinch you can fold the flange up into the flanged plunger cup and use it as a standard plunger.

TERMS YOU NEED TO KNOW

WATER SEAL—Because of the loop-like shape of a toilet's plumbing, there is always water in the bowl and in the passage directly behind the bowl. This water seal keeps sewer gases from rising into the house.

TOILET TRAP—A "trap" in plumbing refers to a bend that holds a water seal, so technically, the toilet bowl is part of the trap. But usually people are talking about the back, hidden portion of that bend when they speak of the toilet trap.

FLUSH VALVE—is the flapper covering the hole in the bottom of the tank that sits behind the bowl. The toilet flushes when this is opened.

CONTROLLED FLUSH—the letting of water from the tank to bowl by manually lifting and closing the flush valve. This prevents bowl overflow when you're not sure the clog is gone.

TOOLS & SUPPLIES YOU'LL NEED

Towels

Plunger with foldout skirt (force cup)

Closet auger

SKILLS YOU'LL NEED

- Vigorous plunging
- Using a closet auger

DIFFICULTY LEVEL

SKILLS LEVEL

EASY   MODERATE

Time: 15 to 30 minutes

HOW TO PLUNGE A CLOGGED TOILET

A flanged plunger fits into the mouth of the toilet trap and creates a tight seal so you can build up enough pressure in front of the plunger to dislodge the blockage and send it on its way.

1 Plunging is the easiest way to remove "natural" blockages. Take time to lay towels around the base of the toilet and remove other objects to a safe, dry location, since plunging may result in splashing. Sometimes, allowing a very full toilet to sit for twenty or thirty minutes will permit some of the water to drain to a less precarious level, or you can bail it out. **WARNING:** Don't use a plunger if the toilet is plugged with a diaper, washcloth, or other object that could get pushed into the drainpipe. It may create a worse clog in a pipe that's beyond your reach. Try to remove the object with a closet auger.

2 There should be enough water in the bowl to completely cover the plunger. Fold out the skirt from inside the plunger to form a better seal with the opening at the base of the bowl. Pump the plunger vigorously half-a-dozen times, take a rest, and then repeat. Try this for 10 to 15 cycles.

3 If you force enough water out of the bowl that you are unable to create suction with the plunger, put a controlled amount of water in the bowl by lifting up on the flush valve in the tank. Resume plunging. When you think the drain is clear, you can try a controlled flush, with your hand ready to close the flush valve should the water threaten to spill out of the bowl. Once the blockage has cleared, dump a five-gallon pail of water into the toilet to blast away any residual debris.

HOW TO CLEAR CLOGS WITH A CLOSET AUGER

TOOL TIP

Acloset auger is a semirigid cable housed in a tube. The tube has a bend at the end so it can be snaked through a toilet trap (without scratching it) to snag blockages.

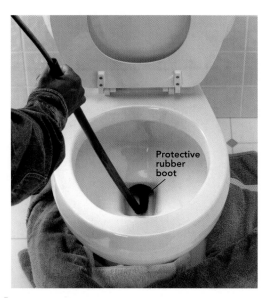

Protective rubber boot

1 Place the business end of the auger firmly in the bottom of the toilet bowl with the auger tip fully withdrawn. A rubber sleeve will protect the porcelain at the bottom bend of the auger. The tip will be facing back and up, which is the direction the toilet trap takes.

2 Rotate the handle on the auger housing clockwise as you push down on the rod, advancing the rotating auger tip up into the back part of the trap. You may work the cable backward and forward as needed, but keep the rubber boot of the auger firmly in place in the bowl. When you feel resistance, indicating you've snagged the object, continue rotating the auger counterclockwise as you withdraw the cable and the object.

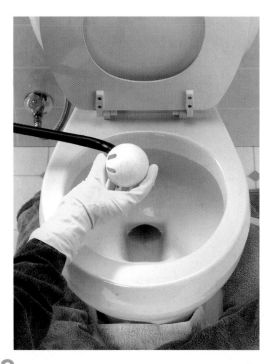

3 Fully retract the auger until you have recovered the object. This can be frustrating at times, but it is still a much easier task than the alternative—to remove the toilet and go fishing.

Fixing a Leaky Tub & Shower

Tub/shower plumbing is notorious for developing drips from the tub spout and the showerhead. In most cases, the leak can be traced to the valves controlled by the faucet handles.

DOES YOUR TUB/SHOWER DRIP, DRIP, DRIP from the spout or the showerhead even when the water is turned off? Chances are, a washer or cartridge in the faucet valve needs attention or replacement. But these parts vary widely by type and by brand name. The most critical part of a good repair job does not involve wrenches and screwdrivers, but the telephone and possibly a computer. That's because finding the brand name, model number, and ultimately part numbers will let you get the exact materials you'll need to do the job right. From there, it's a pretty easy repair.

TUB & SHOWER FAUCETS 101

Showerhead

Faucet

Cold water
supply line

Hot water
supply line

Gate
diverter

Tub spout

If you could make your
tub/shower and the tub
surround above it disappear,
you'd see pipes and plumbing parts similar to this. The
faucet seen here only has
one handle that controls the
water volume and tempera-
ture. The water is directed
to either the *tub spout* or
the *showerhead* with a
diverter located in the tub
spout. Some two-handle
models are joined by a third
handle that serves as a
diverter instead of the
gate on the spout.

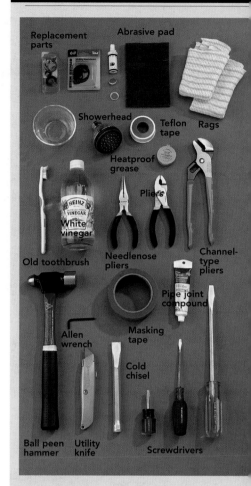
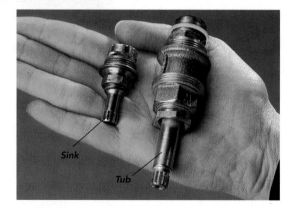

Sink

Tub

As the stem assemblies (right)
demonstrate, sink and tub
compression valves share the
same genetics but vary in size
and the particulars.

SKILLS YOU'LL NEED

- Using channel-type pliers
- Tracking the order and arrangement of parts
- Phone or computer research

DIFFICULTY LEVEL

SKILLS LEVEL

EASY   MODERATE

Time: 1 hour plus research and shopping

TERMS YOU NEED TO KNOW

COMPRESSION FAUCET—a two-or three-handle faucet that uses a simple stem
and washer compression valve.

CARTRIDGE FAUCET—a one-, two-, or three-handle faucet with a valve or valves
that uses a narrow, cylinder-shaped cartridge, which is moved in the valve body
by the handle to channel hot and cold water.

HOW TO FIX A LEAKY ONE-HANDLE FAUCET

Water supply line to showerhead

Built-in shutoff valves

Control valve

Hot water supply line

Cold water supply line

Escutcheon

Gate diverter

1 Single-handle tub and shower faucets have one valve controlling both hot and cold water. This valve sits directly behind the one large knob or lever. If your tub spout drips all the time, you need to fix this valve. The first step involves information and materials gathering (see "Steps to Successful Shopping" on page 197). Next, turn off the hot and cold water supplies. Make sure the diverter is in the tub-filling position, then drain residual water out of the plumbing by opening the faucet to hot and cold water. Lay towels in the tub to prevent damaging the finish with tools and losing small parts.

2 Remove the handle of the damaged valve by first prying an index cap off the front with a dull knife or screwdriver and removing the screw hidden underneath. Pull off the handle. Remove any other parts obstructing the escutcheon, then remove the escutcheon. Keep parts in a safe place. Line them up and orient them as they sit in the faucet. If it's helpful, take digital pictures to remember how the parts went together.

3 Many one-handle tub and shower faucets have hot and cold shutoffs built in to the faucet body. Turn these off clockwise with a large slotted screwdriver. Integral stops are useful if you need to leave the water off for some time during a repair, and the only other turnoff to the tub and shower takes other fixtures out of commission. If you'd rather, you may turn off water at the nearest shutoff valves instead.

4 Remove the threaded retaining ring that secures the cartridge or stem and bonnet assembly (some models may use retaining screws to hold the stem). This unit is what turns the water on and controls the mix of hot and cold water.

5 Remove the cartridge, pulling gently on the stem with a pair of pliers if necessary. With the cartridge out, now is a good time to flush out the system by opening the shutoffs in the valve or in the supply line. Watch out, though, the water will come out of the valve opening, not the spout.

6 Clean the cartridge by flushing with warm water and replace the O-ring at the end (coat the new O-ring with heatproof grease). If the cartridge is old or visibly damaged, replace it. Reinstall the faucet parts in reverse order.

HOW TO FIX A LEAKY TWO- OR THREE-HANDLE FAUCET

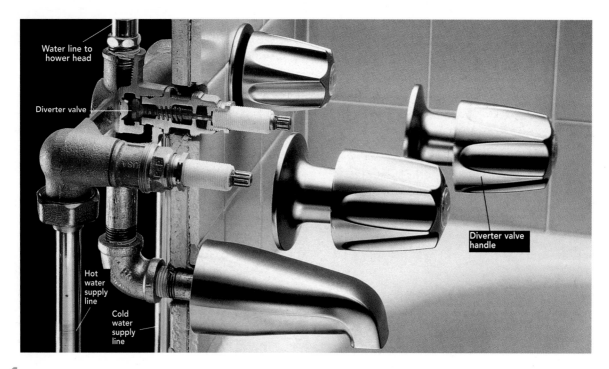

Water line to shower head

Diverter valve

Hot water supply line

Cold water supply line

Diverter valve handle

1 Both three-handle and two-handle faucets have a hot-water valve and a cold-water valve behind their hot and cold faucet handles. If water drips from the spout when the faucet is off, you need to determine which valve isn't working by shutting off the water supply on each line in turn at the shutoff valve. Two- and three-handle faucets are repaired in the same manner, except that the middle handle on the three-handle models is a diverter valve (the diverter on two-handle models is in the spout). If the showerhead on your three-handle system drips, or if you continue to get a high volume of water through the spout when it should be coming out the showerhead, it's the diverter handle that needs attention.

2 Determine which valve is causing the leak (see previous step) and remove the handle cover for that valve (in this case, the diverter valve is being worked upon). Also remove the escutcheon that covers the wall opening for that valve.

3 Remove the bonnet nut from the stem assembly using an adjustable wrench. If your faucet has cartridges, not compression valves as shown here, simply remove the cartridge (see p. 195).

4 Unscrew the stem assembly using a deep-set socket and a ratchet wrench. You may need to enlarge the opening in the wall slightly with a cold chisel and ball-peen hammer to gain clearance for the socket. TIP: You can purchase a shower valve socket wrench at most hardware stores. The most common sizes are $^{29}/_{32}$" and $^{31}/_{32}$".

5 Remove the brass stem screw from the compression valve. Find an exact match for the stem washer that's held in place by the stem screw. Disassemble the spindle and the valve retaining nut.

SHOPPING TIP

STEPS TO SUCCESSFUL SHOPPING

Identify the brand. This may be written on the faucet handle, on a plate behind the handle or handles, or elsewhere on the hardware of the tub or shower. Be aware that a name on a pop-up stopper, overflow cap, or showerhead may or may not be the manufacturer of your faucet.

Identify the model. The major brands have web sites and toll-free numbers. Use these to identify your model.

Identify replacement parts. It may be that all you will need for replacement parts are washers, screws, and a few common valve parts available at a well-equipped home center or hardware store. But if you need to replace a cartridge or other intricate faucet component, your manufacturer can provide parts numbers and tell you how to order these.

6 Clean the valve parts with white vinegar and a toothbrush or small wire brush. Coat all washers with heatproof grease and reassemble then reinstall the valve.

As with bathroom sinks, tub and shower drain pipes may become clogged with soap and hair. The drain stopping mechanisms can also require cleaning and adjustment.

TUB OR SHOWER NOT DRAINING? First, make sure it's only the tub or shower. If your sink is plugged, too, it may be a coincidence or it may be that a common branch line is plugged. A sure sign of this is when water drains from the sink into the tub. This could require the help of a drain cleaning service, or a drum trap that services both the sink and tub needs cleaning. If the toilet also can't flush (or worse, water comes into the tub when you flush the toilet), then the common drain to all your bathroom fixtures is plugged. Call a drain cleaning service. If you suspect the problem is only with your tub or shower, then read on. We'll show you how to clear drainlines and clean and adjust two types of tub stopper mechanisms. Adjusting the mechanism can also help with the opposite problem: a tub that drains when you're trying to take a bath.

BATH DRAINS 101

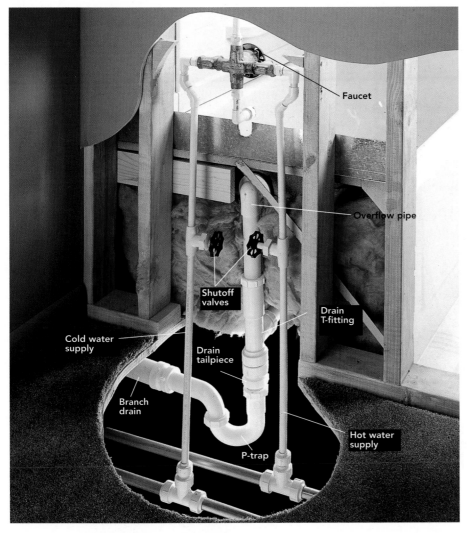

Faucet

Overflow pipe

Shutoff valves

Drain T-fitting

Cold water supply

Drain tailpiece

Branch drain

P-trap

Hot water supply

If you removed the wall behind your tub/shower along with part of the floor, this is pretty much what you would see. From the photo you can tell that having to access your drain for outside the tub is not easy, and that maintaining the drain system to avoid major problems and blockages is well worth the effort. Fortunately, maintenance is not difficult, and minor clogs are relatively easy to track down and eliminate.

TERMS YOU NEED TO KNOW

POP-UP DRAIN—a mechanical drain stopper where a metal drain cover is raised and lowered with a lever mounted on the cover of the overflow opening.

PLUNGER-TYPE DRAIN—another mechanical drain stopper where a plunger is lowered through the overflow pipe to block the drain.

HAND AUGER—a long bendable cable with a crank at one end that is snaked into a drain line to retrieve or break up a blockage.

TOOLS & SUPPLIES YOU'LL NEED

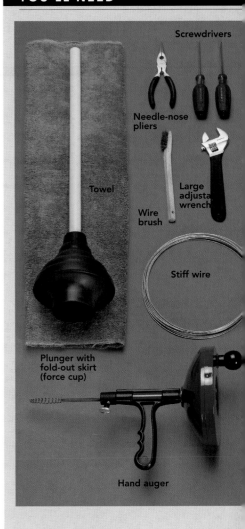

Screwdrivers

Needle-nose pliers

Towel

Wire brush

Large adjusta wrench

Stiff wire

Plunger with fold-out skirt (force cup)

Hand auger

SKILLS YOU'LL NEED

- Vigorous plunging
- Using an auger

DIFFICULTY LEVEL

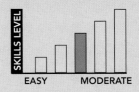

SKILLS LEVEL

EASY   MODERATE

Time: ½ to 1½ hours

HOW TO FIX A PLUNGER-TYPE DRAIN

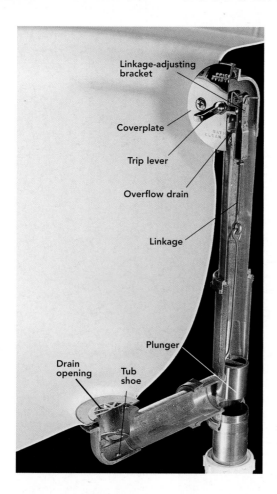

Linkage-adjusting bracket

Coverplate

Trip lever

Overflow drain

Linkage

Plunger

Drain opening

Tub shoe

1 A plunger-type tub drain has a simple grate over the drain opening and a behind-the-scenes plunger stopper. Remove the screws on the overflow coverplate with a slotted or Phillips head screwdriver. Pull the coverplate, linkage, and plunger from the overflow opening.

2 Clean hair and soap off the plunger with a scrub brush. Mineral buildup is best tackled with white vinegar and a toothbrush or a small wire brush.

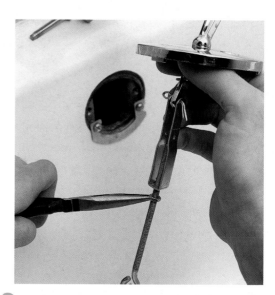

3 Adjust the plunger. If your tub isn't holding water with the plunger down, it's possible the plunger is hanging too high to fully block water from the tub shoe. Loosen the locknut with needlenose pliers then screw the rod down about ⅛". Tighten the locknut down. If your tub drains poorly, the plunger may be set too low. Loosen the locknut and screw the rod in an ⅛" before retightening the locknut.

HOW TO FIX A POP-UP DRAIN

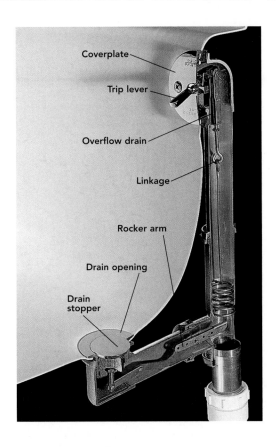

Coverplate
Trip lever
Overflow drain
Linkage
Rocker arm
Drain opening
Drain stopper

1 Raise the trip lever to the open position. Pull the stopper and rocker arm assembly from the drain. Clean off soap and hair with a dishwashing brush in a basin of hot water. Clean off mineral deposits with a toothbrush or small wire brush and white vinegar.

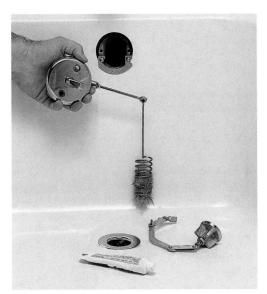

2 Remove the screws from the cover plate. Pull the trip lever and the linkage from the overflow opening. Clean off soap and hair with a dish scrubbing brush in a basin of hot water. Remove mineral buildup with white vinegar and a wire brush. Lubricate moving parts of the linkage and rocker arm mechanism with heatproof grease.

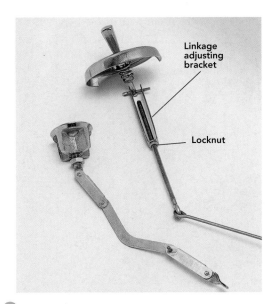

Linkage adjusting bracket

Locknut

3 Adjust the pop-up stopper mechanism by first loosening the locknut on the lift rod. If the stopper doesn't close all the way, shorten the linkage by screwing the rod ⅛" farther into the linkage-adjusting bracket. If the stopper doesn't open wide enough, extend the linkage by unscrewing the rod ⅛". Tighten the locknut before replacing the mechanism and testing your adjustment.

HOW TO CLEAR A SHOWER OR TUB DRAIN

1 To plunge a shower drain, first remove the drain stopper equipment, including the strainer cover (if there is one) from the drain of a tub or shower. Pop the strainer out with a screwdriver, or remove a screw in the middle. Clear any hair from the pipe below the drain with a stiff bent wire.

2 If you can't see and remove an obstruction in the drain, try plunging. Position the plunger over the drain opening. If using a force-cup type of plunger, as seen above, fold the skirt up inside the plunger head. Completely cover the plunger with water. Plunge rhythmically through half-a-dozen ups and downs with increasing vigor, then yank up hard on the plunger. Repeat this cycle for up to 15 minutes. Promising signs: crud from the clog may rise into the tub before the weight of the water pushes the clog down the drain.

TIP: If you can't clear a stubborn clog with a plunger, insert the tip of a hand auger into the drain opening (see next page and pages 172 to 173).

MAINTENANCE TIP

Like bathroom sinks, tubs and showers face an ongoing onslaught from soap and hair. When paired, this pesky combination is a sure-fire source of clogs. The soap scum coagulates as it is washed down the drain and binds the hair together in a mass that grows larger with every shower or bath. To nip these clogs in the bud, simply pour boiling hot clean water down the drain from time to time to melt the soapy mass and wash the binder away.

USING A HAND AUGER ON A SHOWER DRAIN

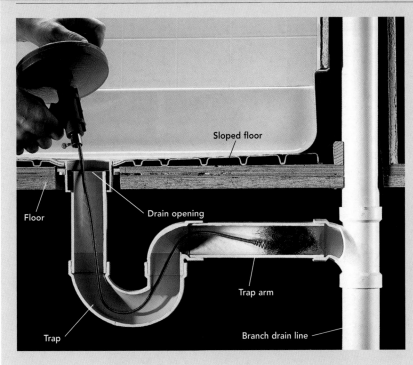

Floor

Sloped floor

Drain opening

Trap arm

Trap

Branch drain line

On shower drains, feed the head of the auger in through the *drain opening* after removing the strainer. Crank the handle of the auger to extend the cable and the auger head down into the trap and, if the clog is further downline, toward the branch drain. When clearing any drain, it is always better to retrieve the clog than to push it further downline. See pages 172 to 173.

USING A HAND AUGER ON A TUB DRAIN

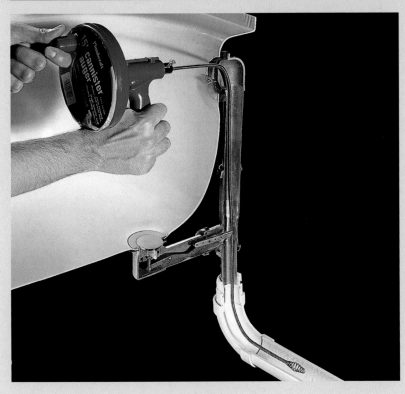

On combination tub/showers, it's generally easiest to insert the auger through the *overflow opening* after removing the coverplate and lifting out the drain linkage (see pages 200 to 201 for more information on drain linkages). Crank the handle of the auger to extend the cable and the auger head down into the trap and, if the clog is further downline, toward the branch drain. When clearing any drain, it is always better to retrieve the clog than to push it further downline. See pages 172 to 173 for more information on using an auger.

Kitchen Sink Stopped (and Disposer Too?)

Drain clearing isn't all drudgery and filth. Some people find the plunger to be as much a tool of personal transformation as an implement for removing clogs.

IT'S A WEEK TO PAYDAY, and that austerity plan you've arranged with your creditors gives you 67 dollars and change to last until then. Alas, the kitchen sink is clogged; you can't afford a plumber! Don't despair—your enemy is merely a wad of coffee grounds and some bacon fat. If plunging doesn't work, you'll go after it where it lives, remove the trap, look in the disposer, explore the fixture drain with a hand auger. With the right tool, you are like Thor and his thunderbolt, Zeus and his trident. You, we are confident, will locate the clog and break it up or drag it into the light, slap it into a basin, and sluice its slimy spawn into the sewer with a triumphant blast of tap water. You. Will. Win.

TIP: Avoid chemical clog removers. They can damage your pipes, your fixtures, and you, and they don't work very well. They're so dangerous to people, in fact, that drain cleaning services often charge extra if you've used them prior to their visit.

KITCHEN SINKS 101

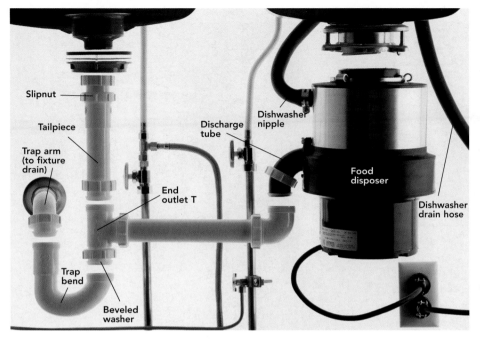

- Slipnut
- Tailpiece
- Trap arm (to fixture drain)
- Discharge tube
- Dishwasher nipple
- End outlet T
- Food disposer
- Dishwasher drain hose
- Trap bend
- Beveled washer

Kitchen sink drain components are usually connected with *slipnuts*, which means everything from the *tailpiece* beneath a basket strainer to the *trap arm* can be removed for cleaning. Clogs commonly occur in the *trap bend* and the *end outlet T*. With the trap arm off, the *fixture drain* can be augered. Make sure your *beveled washers* are facing the right direction when you put things back together. Clogs can happen in the *discharge tube* and *drain chamber* of a disposer. The *impellers* in the grinding chamber of a disposer can get stuck to the *grinding ring* with tough or fibrous waste materials. The *dishwasher drain hose* should be clamped where it joins the disposer if you wish to plunge the sink drain.

TERMS YOU NEED TO KNOW

BASKET STRAINER—This is the typical strainer, plug, and drain found on a kitchen sink that doesn't have a disposer.

TAILPIECE—takes the waste from the basket strainer to the trap.

GRINDING CHAMBER—the chamber visible through the drain of a disposer where wastes are ground.

IMPELLER—one of two or four steel lugs on the metal plate at the bottom of a disposer grinding chamber. Its function is to push food waste against the grinding ring as the plate rotates.

GRINDING RING—a stationary, toothed ring at the bottom perimeter of the disposer grinding chamber. Food wastes are ground against it until they are small enough to be washed into the drain chamber below.

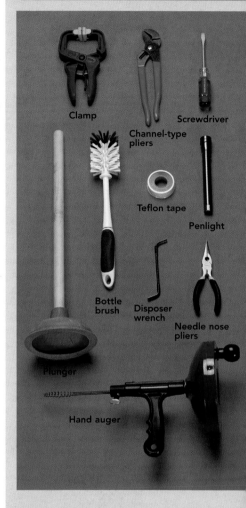
SKILLS YOU'LL NEED

- Working with slip joints
- Plunging
- Flexibility

DIFFICULTY LEVEL

EASY   HARD

Time: ½ to 1½ hours.

KITCHEN SINK STOPPED? PLUNGE IN

CLEARING THE TRAP AND BEYOND

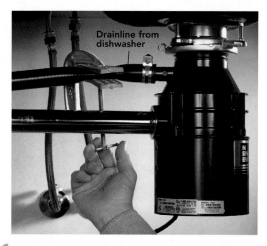

Drainline from dishwasher

1 Plunging a kitchen sink is not difficult, but you need to create an uninterrupted pressure lock between the plunger and the clog. If you have a dishwasher, the drain tube needs to be clamped shut and sealed off at the disposer or drainline. The pads on the clamp should be large enough to flatten the tube across its full diameter (or you can clamp the tube ends between small boards).

2 If there is a second basin, have a helper hold a basket strainer plug in its drain or put a large pot or bucket full of water on top of it. If you just set the strainer plug in place, the pressure of your plunging will pop the plug instead of the clog. Unfold the skirt within the plunger and place this in the drain of the sink you are plunging. There should be enough water in the sink to cover the plunger head. Plunge rhythmically for six repetitions with increasing vigor, pulling up hard on the last rep. Repeat this sequence until the clog or you are vanquished. Flush out a cleared clog with plenty of hot water.

1 If plunging doesn't work, remove the trap and clean it out. With the trap off, see if water flows freely from both sinks (if you have two). Sometimes clogs will lodge in the T-fitting or one of the waste pipes feeding it. These may be pulled out manually or cleared with a bottlebrush or wire. When reassembling the trap, apply Teflon tape clockwise to the male threads of metal waste pieces. Tighten with your channel-type pliers. Plastic pieces need no tape and should be hand-tightened only.

2 If you suspect the clog is downstream of the trap, remove the trap arm from the fitting at the wall. Look in the fixture drain with a penlight. If you see water, that means the fixture drain is plugged. Clear it with a hand auger (p. 203).

DISPOSER NOT GRINDING?

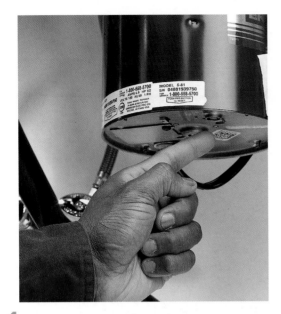

1 Press the reset button located on the base of the disposer and switch the appliance on. If the motor hums but cannot move, the grinders are clogged and need to be cleared.

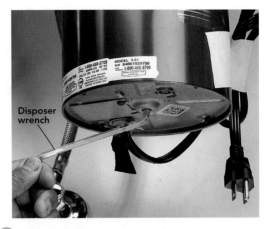

2 Unplug the disposer. Look for a wrench with a hex shaped head that came with the disposer. Stick this in a fitting in the base of the disposer. This manipulates the metal plate that holds the impellers. Typically, some hard or fibrous object is binding an impeller to the grinding ring. Rock the plate back and forth with the wrench to unbind the impeller. You can also attempt to rotate the plate from above by pushing against an impeller with a broom handle.

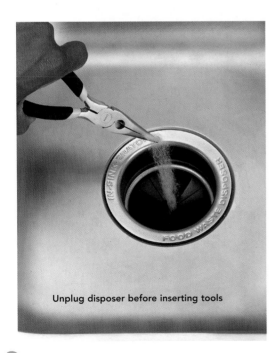

Unplug disposer before inserting tools

3 Look for and remove any material that's keeping the metal plate from rotating. Make sure the disposer is unplugged and then shine a light into the disposer and look for hard or fibrous debris between the impellers and the grinding ring. Use needlenose pliers to pull debris free.

DRAINING SLOWLY?

Discharge elbow

Waste buildup in the drain chamber beneath the impeller disc can lead to a slow-draining disposer. Remove the discharge elbow from the disposer body by withdrawing one or two screws or bolts. These may require a screwdriver or an adjustable wrench. Clear debris from the discharge elbow then shine a light into the drain chamber. Reach into the drain chamber with needlenose pliers to remove any fibrous buildup.

12

Leaky Sink Strainer

If your waste water takes a wrong turn on the way to the sewer, it may be time to reseat, or replace, your sink strainer.

THE SINK STRAINER IS THE PERFORATED BASKET IN THE BOTTOM OF YOUR KITCHEN SINK THAT CATCHES SPAGHETTI AND BROCCOLI SPEARS BEFORE THEY DIVE DOWN THE DRAIN. If your sink is simply not holding water, you may need to replace only the basket. These are available at any hardware store. If water is leaking onto the floor in the cabinet, you may need to reseat or replace the sink strainer body. A replacement includes the basket and the metal well that cradles the basket and forms a seal with your sink and the drain pipe.

FIXING A LEAKY SINK STRAINER

1 Clear out the cabinet under the sink. Unscrew slipnuts from both ends of the drain tailpiece with channel-type pliers. Lower the tailpiece into the trap bend or remove the tailpiece. NOTE: If you have a double sink and your tailpiece is very short, you may need to loosen slipnuts elsewhere and remove a larger piece of the drain assembly to access the strainer body.

2 Loosen the locknut with a spud wrench or channel-type pliers. Unthread the locknut completely, then push the strainer body up out of the sink.

3 Remove old putty from the drain opening with a putty knife. If reusing the old strainer body, clean off the old putty from under the flange. Knead plumber's putty into a warm, soft snake and apply to the lip of the drain opening. Press the strainer body into the drain opening. Any writing on the strainer should be read from the front.

4 From under the sink, place the rubber gasket and the friction washer over the strainer body and secure the body to the sink deck with the locknut. Tap the nubs on the locknut with a screwdriver to tighten it. Reattach the drain by tightening the slipnut over the threaded end of the tailpiece.

TOOLS & SUPPLIES YOU'LL NEED

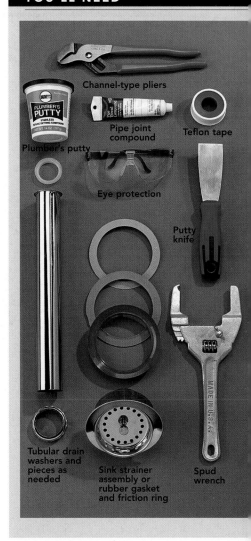

Channel-type pliers

Plumber's putty

Pipe joint compound

Teflon tape

Eye protection

Putty knife

Tubular drain washers and pieces as needed

Sink strainer assembly or rubber gasket and friction ring

Spud wrench

NSKILLS YOU'LL NEED

- Using wrenches
- Putty rolling
- Making slip-joint connections

DIFFICULTY LEVEL

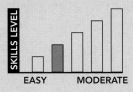

Time: ½ to 1 hour plus shopping

TERMS YOU NEED TO KNOW

PLUMBER'S PUTTY—a clay-like material used to seal metal hardware to the sink.

TEFLON TAPE—a thin white tape used to lubricate and seal threaded fittings and keep them from sticking together.

PIPE JOINT COMPOUND—a paste that may be used instead of Teflon tape.

BASKET STRAINER—another name for a sink strainer.

Advanced Clog Clearing

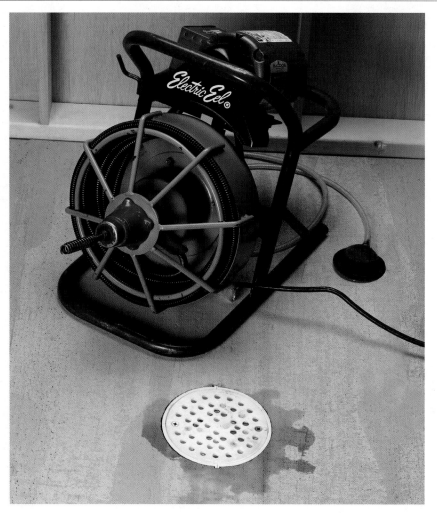

13

When the going gets tough, the tough rent power tools. The medium duty auger shown here is perfect for augering the 2-inch-diameter floor drainlines and branch drainlines.

WHEN PLUNGERS AND HAND AUGERS MEET A CLOG THEY CAN'T DISLODGE, you have one more DIY option before you call a professional drain cleaning service. Most rental centers stock power augers in several sizes. These electric tools work in much the same manner as a hand auger, but with much more tenacity. With spear tools, cutting tools, and spring tools, they can push or cut through a clog, or snag an object and drag it out from your floor or branch drainline.

Always read the instructions carefully and be sure to get through operating instructions at the rental center. If used improperly, power augers can cause major damage to your plumbing system. They are designed to be inserted beyond the trap or through cleanouts in the drainline, so they do not need to be forced through the drain trap. Never run a power auger through a toilet—it could scratch the porcelain or even break the fixture.

POWER AUGERING 101

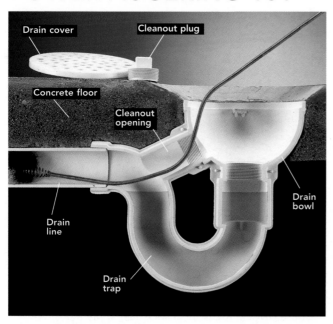

Drain cover
Cleanout plug
Concrete floor
Cleanout opening
Drain bowl
Drain line
Drain trap

Floor drains can develop extremely robust clogs, especially if the drain cover is absent. A *power auger* that's inserted through the cleanout opening can travel 50 feet or more to hunt down and remove stubborn clogs. These rental tools come in several sizes and may also be used to clear tub/shower drainlines, branch drainlines and even a 3- to 4-inch diameter soil stack or house drain.

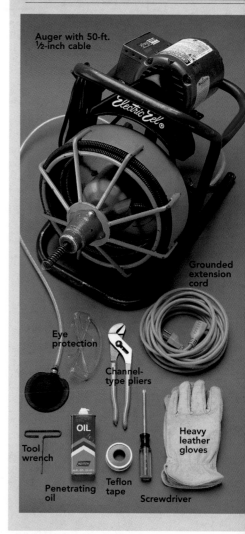
TOOL TIP

Power augers can be fitted with three different head styles. The spring tool is affixed to the cable end to snag and retrieve an obstruction. The spear tool is used to penetrate a clog and puncture it to create a starter hole for the cutting tool, which can cut apart very resistant clogs (often tree roots).

Spring tool
Spear tool
Cutter tool

TERMS YOU NEED TO KNOW

TRAP—a U-shaped bend of drain pipe behind or under every fixture. It's always full of water to keep sewer gases from rising into the house. If possible, remove the trap before augering the drainline to a fixture. With the floor drain, you bypass the trap by opening a cleanout plug.

CLEANOUTS—are access ports in drain pipes kept covered with threaded caps.

CLEANING TOOL—the spring, spear, or cutter attached to the tip of a cable auger. These are interchangeable.

BRANCH OR FIXTURE DRAIN—the run of pipe in the wall or floor that drains a fixture (except a toilet). It's usually 1½ to 2-inches in diameter. It may join with a toilet drain, a stack, or the house drain.

HOW TO POWER-AUGER A FLOOR DRAIN

If you choose to auger a larger line, you may find yourself opening a cleanout with 10 or 20 vertical feet of waste water behind it. Be careful. The cap may unexpectedly burst open when it's loose enough, spewing noxious waste water uncontrollably over anything in its path, including you! Here are some precautions:

Whenever possible, remove a trap or cleanout close to the top of the backed-up water level. Run your auger through this. Make sure the auger and its electric connections will not get wet should waste water spew forcefully from the cleanout opening.

Use the spear tool on the power auger first, to let the water drain out through a smaller hole before widening it with a larger cutting tool. If you are augering through a 3- or 4-inch cleanout, use three bits: the spear, a small cutter, and then a larger cutter to do the best job.

1 Remove the cover from the floor drain using a slotted or Phillips screwdriver. On one wall of the drain bowl you'll see a cleanout plug. Remove the cleanout plug from the drain bowl with your largest channel-type pliers. This cleanout allows you to bypass the trap. If it's stuck, apply penetrating oil to the threads and let it sit a half an hour before trying to free it again. If the wrench won't free it, rent a large pipe wrench from your home center or hardware store. You can also auger through the trap if you have to.

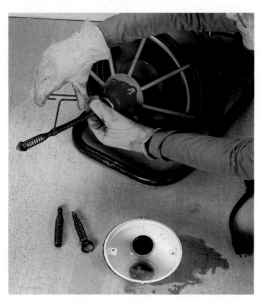

2 Rent an electric drum auger with at least 50 feet of ½-inch cable. The rental company should provide a properly sized, grounded extension cord, heavy leather gloves, and eye protection. The auger should come with a spear tool, cutter tool, and possibly a spring-tool suitable for a 2-inch drainline. Attach the spearhead first (with the machine unplugged).

3 Wear close-fitting clothing and contain long hair. Place the power auger machine in a dry location within three feet of the drain opening. Plug the tool into a grounded, Ground Fault Interrupted (GFI) protected circuit. Put on eye protection and gloves; you will be holding a rotating metal cable and may be exposed to dangerous bacteria and caustic drain cleaning chemicals. Position the footswitch where it is easy to actuate; visualize using the machine without having to overreach the rotating drum or exposed belts. Make sure the FOR/REV switch is in the Forward position (inset photo). Hand feed the cleaning tool and some cable into the drain or cleanout before turning the machine on.

4 Stationary power augers (as opposed to pistol-grip types) are controlled by a foot pedal called an actuator so you can turn the power on and off hands-free.

6 Gradually work through the clog by pulling back on the cable whenever the machine starts to bog down and pushing it forward again when it gains new momentum. Again, never let the cable stop turning when the motor is running. When you have broken through the clog (or if you are using the spring head and believe you have snagged an object) withdraw the cable from the line. Manually pull the cable from the drain line while continuing to run the drum Forward. If it's practical, have a helper hose off the cable as its withdrawn and recoiled. When the cleaning tool is close to the drain opening, release the foot actuator and let the cable come to a stop before feeding the remaining two or three feet of cable into the drum by hand.

5 With both gloved hands on the cable, depress the foot actuator to start the machine. Gradually push the rotating cable into the drain opening. If the rotation slows or you cannot feed more cable into the drain, pull back on the cable before pushing it forward again. Don't force it. The cable needs to be rotating whenever the motor is running or it can kink and buckle, destroying the cable (although a clutch on the drum should prevent this). If the cleaning tool becomes stuck, turn the FOR/REV switch to Reverse and back the tool off the obstruction before switching back to Forward again.

7 After clearing the drain pipe, run the auger through the trap. Finish cleaning the auger. Wrap Teflon tape clockwise onto the plug threads and replace the plug. Run hot water through a hose from the laundry sink or use a bucket to flush remaining debris through the trap and down the line.

Repairing Outside Faucets

14

A leaky outside faucet on a house (called a sillcock or a hose bib) usually is easier to repair than to replace. Because they must withstand cold temperatures, you won't find plastic cartridges in outdoor faucet bodies. Repairs are made in much the same way as for interior compression faucets (see pages 160 to 161).

COMMON AILMENTS OF OUTSIDE FAUCETS include broken or loose handles, dripping spouts, and dripping handles. In the north, outside faucets and their pipes can crack when the water inside them freezes. Outside faucets with hoses or sprinkler systems attached pose another hazard: if water pressure is lost in the house or the community, water may flow backwards in the pipes, drawing potentially polluted water through the hose and into the house or even into the municipal system. For this reason, local plumbing codes often require that a vacuum breaker be attached to faucets that are threaded for hoses. In this section we'll show you how to identify and fix the most common leak causes.

OUTSIDE FAUCETS 101

- Handle screw
- Handle
- Packing nut
- Packing washer
- Packing ring
- Spindle
- Stem washer
- Stem screw

Outside faucets come in different forms, but their valves, which are the mechanism that turns off the water, are always compression style. Ordinary outdoor faucets, like the *hose bib* above, need to be shut off and drained before winter in cold climates. This is done inside the house at a stop and waste valve.

- Pipe joint compound
- Utility knife
- Adjustable wrench
- Slotted and Phillips screwdrivers
- Heatproof grease
- Teflon tape
- Stem washer
- Stem screw
- O-ring
- Packing washer

TERMS YOU NEED TO KNOW

HOSE BIB—a faucet with male threads on the spout to accept female hose threads.

SILLCOCK—a hose bib with a wide flange at the base allowing it to be attached to an exterior wall with screws.

COMPRESSION VALVE—a valve type with the components shown above.

STEM WASHER—When the faucet is off, it is pressed over the intake hole in the faucet by the spindle. Drips at the spout usually involve a worn stem washer.

VALVE SEAT—This forms the rim of the hole plugged by the stem washer. A damaged seat will wear out the stem washer.

PACKING—the neoprene washer or other material pressed below the packing nut that prevents water from leaking out below the handle when the faucet is on.

SKILLS YOU'LL NEED

- Using an adjustable wrench
- Using a screwdriver

DIFFICULTY LEVEL

SKILLS LEVEL

EASY   MODERATE

Time: less than an hour plus shopping

HOW TO REPAIR A LEAKY OUTSIDE FAUCET

1 Turn off the water to your outside faucet and open the faucet to drain any remaining water (this step may be skipped if you are only replacing the handle). The shutoff valve is usually located on the water supply line, close to the faucet on the interior side of the wall. Outdoor faucets have only one supply pipe (cold).

2 Remove the handle from an outside faucet by removing the handle screw and pulling the handle straight off. If the handle is damaged, bring it to the hardware store and find a replacement with the same size spindle hole. Screw the new handle on if the faucet does not leak.

Valve stem

Packing nut

3 Unscrew the packing nut that secures the spindle to the valve body, using an adjustable wrench. If the nut resists, hold the faucet body with a pipe wrench to stabilize it while you bear down on the nut.

Packing washer

4 Pry off the packing washer and packing ring from the top of the spindle and inspect their general condition. If they are worn or damaged, bring them to the hardware store to purchase a replacement. NOTE: Instead of a washer, some older compression faucets (including hose bibs) have a wad of packing string stuffed into the packing nut to seal the spindle (see page 219).

Stem sleeve

5 Pull out the spindle. With some faucets, a stem sleeve holding the spindle will also need to be unscrewed to remove the spindle. Be careful not to damage the male threads of the packing nut when removing this sleeve.

7 Secure the stem washer to the spindle using the stem screw. Coat the new stem washer with heatproof grease and coat the threads of the stem screw with pipe joint compound.

6 Remove the stem screw on the other end of the spindle with a screwdriver and remove and inspect the stem washer (the stem washer is the most likely suspect if the faucet is dripping). Bring the screw and spindle along with the washer to a hardware store or home center to get a matching washer and, if needed, a new screw that fits your spindle. A replacement washer needs to fit within the brass cup on the spindle and have the same profile (typically flat) as the old washer.

SAFETY TIP

An anti-siphon device is required for outdoor faucets and indoor hose bibs. The requirement doesn't apply to old faucets being repaired, but it's still a good idea to use one. The most popular retrofit anti-siphon devices are simply twisted onto the nozzle of the hose bib.

Anti-siphon device

WHAT IF...?

What if I have a freezeless faucet?

Take apart and replace washers and O-rings on a freezeless faucet as you would a regular outside faucet, but with some differences noted as follows:

Stabilize the valve body of the faucet with channel-type pliers before twisting off the packing nut with an adjustable wrench. This will help you avoid torquing the long body of the faucet.

You may need to put the handle back on the spindle after removing the packing nut in order to rotate the spindle into an orientation that will allow it to be pulled out of the valve body.

The stem washer is on the end of a very long spindle with this type of faucet. This allows the water to be shut off in the above-freezing part of the house. Take the spindle to a hardware or plumbing store to get the right replacement washers and O-ring.

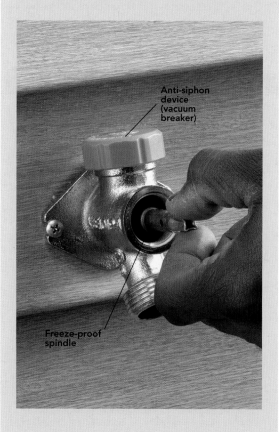

Anti-siphon device (vacuum breaker)

Freeze-proof spindle

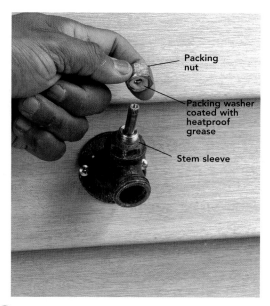

Packing nut

Packing washer coated with heatproof grease

Stem sleeve

8 Install the valve stem, replacing the stem sleeve. Coat the new packing washer with heat-proof grease and slip it and the packing ring, if present, onto the free spindle end (or install it in the packing nut). Apply pipe joint compound to the valve body threads and refasten the packing nut. **NOTE:** Instead of packing, some faucets use an O-ring on the spindle to keep water in the valve. Remove and replace it.

9 Slip the new faucet handle onto the spindle end and secure it with the handle screw.

VARIATION: USING PACKING STRING

1 Wrap two or three layers of Teflon tape clockwise around the male threads on the valve body before tightening on the packing nut with your adjustable wrench. Complete the repair as in the previous sequence. If the faucet drips from the handle, remove it and add more packing string (along with fresh Teflon tape).

2 If your old faucet is sealed with packing string and not a packing washer or an O-ring (or if you can't find a packing washer that fits), remake the seal between the valve stem and the packing nut with new packing string. Packing string is impregnated with graphite. Wrap the new packing string onto the valve stem above the stem sleeve so it's about $1\frac{1}{2}$ times as thick as the thickness of the gap between the stem and the packing nut. You may need to adjust the amount of string you use to create a seal but still leave enough room to tighten on the packing nut.

WINTERIZING YOUR HOSE BIB

Even if you have a freezeless faucet, you need to take the hoses off your outdoor faucets, since these can hold water in the faucet, which can freeze and crack the valve or pipe. Unless you have a freezeless faucet, you also need to turn off your outside faucet from the inside and drain the faucet before below-freezing temperatures settle in. Find the shutoff valve on the branch pipe leading to your outside faucet and close it. Check to see if the valve has a waste valve on the side. If so, use it to drain the water in the line between the valve and the hose bib after opening the outside hose bib. You can also add a cover to the hose bib (see page 225).

WARNING: If you have a sprinkler system, its lines should be professionally cleared for the winter with pressurized air.

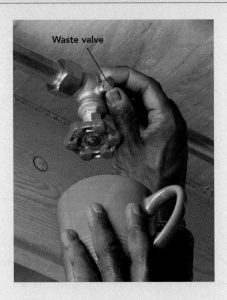

Waste valve

Adding a Shower to a Tub

15

Converting a plain bathtub into a tub/shower is a relatively easy task when you use a flexible shower adapter that fits onto a special replacement tub spout.

FORGET THE LAZY 8 TRUCK STOP. Forget the locker room at the health club. You may be able to enjoy the luxury of a real shower right in your own home or apartment. If you have an old built-in tub but no shower, we'll show you how you can remove the spout and replace it with one equipped with an adapter hose outlet. A flexible shower hose can be screwed to this. We'll also show you how to install a mounting bracket so you can hang the showerhead and free up your hands. Add a telescoping shower curtain rod and a shower curtain and your new shower stall is ready for duty.

SHOWER ADAPTERS 101

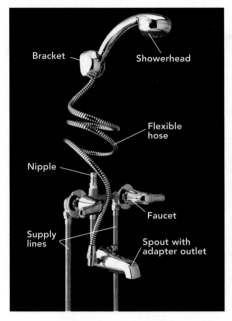

Bracket
Showerhead
Flexible hose
Nipple
Faucet
Supply lines
Spout with adapter outlet

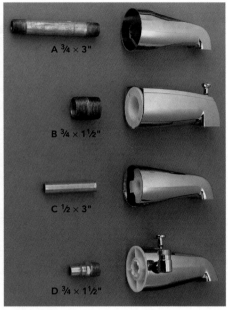

A ¾ × 3"

B ¾ × 1½"

C ½ × 3"

D ¾ × 1½"

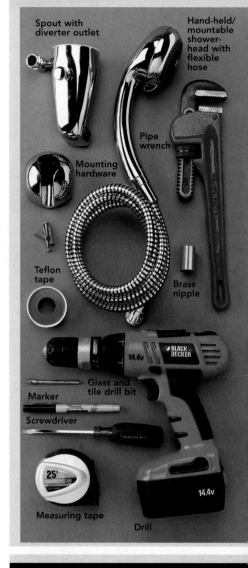
The appearance of the spout gives good clues as to which kind of nipple it is connected to. A) Spout with no diverter is probably connected to a 3" long threaded nipple. To install a diverter spout you'll need to replace the 3" threaded nipple with a shorter threaded nipple that sticks out no more than ½" from the wall—not too big of a job. B) If the spout already has a diverter knob, it already has a showerhead, and you're doing the wrong project (although there is no reason you couldn't hook up a shower adapter if you want a handheld shower). C) If the spout has a small setscrew in a slot on the underside, it is probably attached with a slip fitting to a ½" copper supply nipple. Unless you are able to solder a new transition fitting onto the old pipe after cutting it, call a plumber to install the new spout here. D) Spouts with outlets for shower adapters require a short threaded nipple (or comparable union) that sticks out from the wall no more than ¾".

NTERMS YOU NEED TO KNOW

NIPPLE—a short piece of iron or brass pipe that's threaded on both ends. It may be unscrewed from the wall.

COPPER STUB—a short piece of copper pipe with or without a threaded adapter on the end. It cannot be unscrewed from the wall.

REDUCING BUSHING—a little piece of pipe with interior and exterior threads. In this case, to allow a ¾-inch tub spout to screw onto a ½-inch nipple.

TEFLON TAPE—a white or thin tape wound on pipe threads to seal and lubricate the joint.

SKILLS YOU'LL NEED

- Making pipe connections
- Cutting tile or tileboard
- Working with wall anchors

DIFFICULTY LEVEL

SKILLS LEVEL

EASY   MODERATE

Time: 1 to 2 hours

HOW TO ADD A SHOWER WITH AN ADAPTER SPOUT

1 Make sure the old spout is not held in place with a setscrew (see previous page) and then remove it by wrapping it with a cloth and turning the spout with channel-type pliers or a pipe wrench.

2 If you have a long iron or brass nipple like this, you need to replace it with a short one. Threaded nipples have threads at each end, so you can usually unscrew the old ones. Mark the nipple at the face of the wall and write "front" on your side. Unscrew it counterclockwise with a pipe wrench. Get a threaded brass nipple of the same diameter that is about half an inch longer than the distance from the back of your old nipple to your line.

TOOL TIP

A long-bladed screwdriver or a dowel inserted into the mouth of the spout can be used to spin the spout free from the nipple.

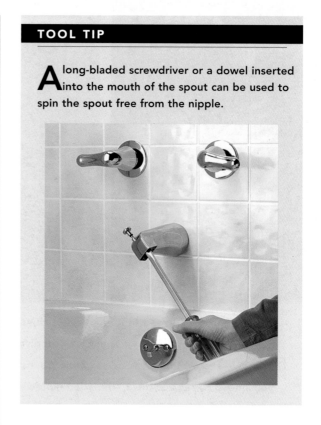

3 Wrap six layers of Teflon tape clockwise on the nipple and thread into the wall. Thread the reducing bushing onto the nipple if it will fit. Thread the adapter spout on. Tighten further with a screwdriver or dowel to orient the spout correctly.

4 Attach flexible shower hose to the adapter hose outlet. Tighten with an adjustable wrench.

5 Determine the location of showerhead bracket. Use hose length as a guide, and make sure showerhead can be easily lifted off the bracket.

6 Mark hole locations. Obtain a glass-and-tile drill bit for your electric drill in the size recommended by the shower bracket manufacturer. Put on eye protection and drill holes in ceramic tile on your marks.

7 Insert anchors into holes, and tap in place with a wooden or rubber mallet. Fasten showerhead holder to the wall using a Phillips screwdriver and the mounting screws.

Preventing Frozen Pipes

16

Spending a little time and money on protecting your water pipes from freezing is one of the best investments a homeowner can make.

BURST FREEZING PIPES lead to about a quarter million families suffering catastrophic water damage to their houses each year. That's the big picture. The small picture works like this: A section of one of your hot or cold water pipes is exposed to below freezing temperatures. You don't use the water in that pipe during the time it takes for an ice plug to develop. As the ice plug grows, it compresses the water between the plug and the faucet(s) at the end of that line. The pressure becomes extreme and bursts the pipe, sometimes in an area away from the ice plug. The plug thaws. Water spews out of the crack, irreparably damaging walls, floors and your possessions. Another scenario goes like this: You take immediate action to thaw and relieve pressure on frozen pipes and then take short- and long-term steps to prevent refreezing. We'll give you pointers here.

FREEZE-PROOFING 101

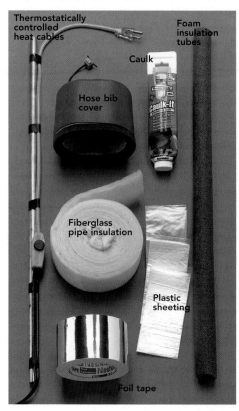

Thermostatically controlled heat cables

Foam insulation tubes

Caulk

Hose bib cover

Fiberglass pipe insulation

Plastic sheeting

Foil tape

Paintable acrylic caulk is good for sealing small gaps, especially in areas where appearance is important. Pipe insulation products include narrow strips of *fiberglass*, *foam insulation tubes* sized to fit common pipe sizes, and *preformed valve covers* for protecting outdoor faucets (hose bibs). *Foil tape* may be used to secure and seal pipe insulation products. *Thermostatically controlled heat cables* prevent pipes that are exposed to long periods of below freezing temperatures from freezing. Expanding foam (not shown here) is effective for stopping large cold air leaks, although it can be unsightly.

HOW TO THAW PIPES:

Open the faucet affected by the frozen pipe. Beginning at the faucet, use a hair dryer to warm the pipe, working back toward the likely area of the freeze. Leave water on until full flow is restored, then take steps to prevent refreezing. If the pipe has burst, see pages 246 to 249. WARNING: Never use an open flame to thaw pipes.

pages 246 to 249.

TERMS YOU NEED TO KNOW

CPVC—This is a kind of plastic water pipe that's incompatible with some kinds of foam insulation (which cause it to soften) and needs to be protected with foil if heat tape is used.

THERMAL ENVELOPE—is the sometimes-murky boundary that divides heated from unheated space. Inside spaces that may be outside the thermal envelope include crawl spaces, attics, garages, basements, and three-season rooms. Pipes that may need your attention are those near or outside the thermal envelope.

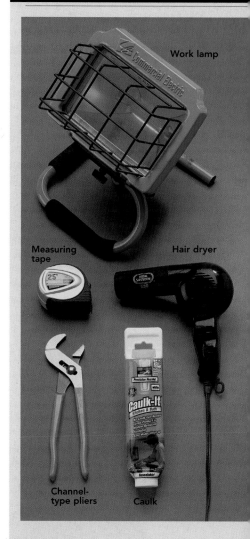

Work lamp

Measuring tape

Hair dryer

Channel-type pliers

Caulk

SKILLS YOU'LL NEED

- Investigative skills
- Cutting and fitting

DIFFICULTY LEVEL

SKILLS LEVEL

EASY   MODERATE

Time: variable

HOW TO FROST-PROOF YOUR PLUMBING

OUTDOOR FAUCETS. Remove hoses from all outside faucets when freezing weather approaches. Shut off the water to the faucet at the shutoff valve inside. Drain the pipe from the shut off to the spout by opening a waste nut on the shutoff and the outside faucet itself. (See "Replacing an Outside Faucet with a Frost Proof Sillcock," pages 268 to 269.)

PIPES NEAR EXTERIOR WALLS. Permit air to circulate from the heated interior of the house to plumbing near outside walls. This could mean opening the dishwasher door and service panel, sink cabinet doors, and plumbed rooms that aren't heated directly. WARNING: Inappropriate warming of pipes is a major cause of house fires.

IMMINENT DANGER OF FREEZING. Leave vulnerable lines open to a fast drip if you suspect any of your supply pipes may be in imminent danger of freezing. Even slowly moving water will not freeze. This may not be water and energy efficient (although if you're around, you can collect water in a bucket), but it gives you time to come up with a permanent solution.

AIR LEAKS NEAR PIPES. Seal gaps that can jet cold air onto pipes. Use caulk for small gaps and expanding foam or fiberglass for large gaps. WARNING: Expanding foam expands more than you think it will and cures to an unsightly rust color when exposed to sun.

INSULATE SUPPLY PIPES. Insulate pipes that pass through unavoidably cold spaces like crawl spaces and attics. Measure a pipe's diameter by closing an adjustable wrench on it and then measuring the span of the wrench jaws. Measure the length of pipes to be insulated so you know how many linear feet of insulation to buy. Buy self-sealing side-slit foam tubes for pipes of your diameter(s). Cut double 45-degree notches with a scissors to turn corners (inset photo). Seal all slits and joints that are not self-adhering with foil tape.

PIPE UNIONS. For irregular and jointed pipes, use fiberglass strip insulation secured with foil tape. Wind the insulation in an overlapping spiral. The tape should not compress the fiberglass too tightly and should form a continuous vapor seal to prevent condensation on the pipes in the summer.

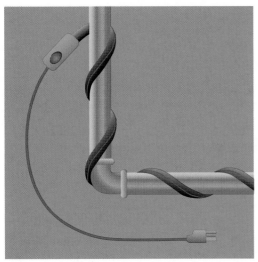

PIPES EXPOSED TO BELOW FREEZING TEMPERATURES for long periods will freeze, insulated or not. Wrap your most vulnerable pipes with U.L. approved thermostatically controlled heat cables according to manufacturer instructions. In the long run, these pipes should be moved to a more protected location or the thermal envelope should be extended to include the pipes.

WHILE YOU'RE AWAY. Don't set the thermostat below 55 degrees F, and have somebody who knows how to shut off the water check on the house daily.

17

Replacing a Bathtub Spout

The bathtub spout may need replacing for many reasons, including a failed diverter like the one above. You also may want to add a flexible shower adapter (see pages 220 to 223), or the old spout could just be disgusting beyond repair.

IN MANY SITUATIONS, REPLACING A BATHTUB SPOUT can be almost as easy as hooking up a garden hose to an outdoor spigot. There are some situations where it is a bit more difficult, but still pretty simple. The only time it's a real problem is when the spout is attached to a plain copper supply nipple, rather than a threaded nipple. You'll know this is the case if the spout has a setscrew on the underside where it meets the wall. Many bathtub spouts are sold in kits with a matching showerhead and handle or handles. But for a simple one-for-one replacement, spouts are sold separately. You just need to make sure the new spout is compatible with the existing nipple (see next page).

TUB SPOUTS 101

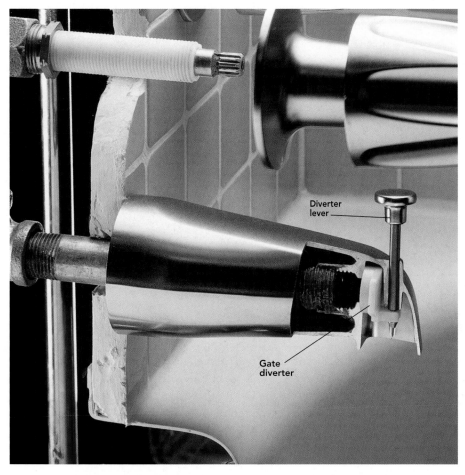

Diverter lever

Gate diverter

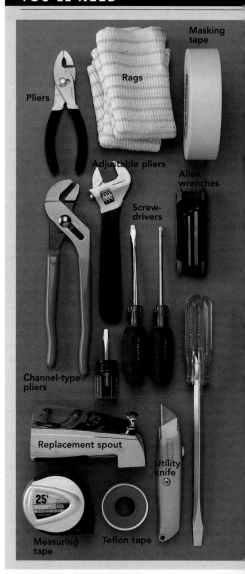

Pliers

Rags

Masking tape

Adjustable pliers

Allen wrenches

Screw-drivers

Channel-type pliers

Replacement spout

Utility knife

Measuring tape

Teflon tape

In many bathtub/shower plumbing systems, the *spout* has the important job of housing the diverter switch—a *gate* inside the spout that is operated by a lever with a knob for pulling. When the gate is open, water comes out of the spout when the faucet is turned on. When the *diverter* is pulled shut, the water is redirected up a *riser pipe* and to the *showerhead*. Failure of the diverter is one of the most common reasons for replacing a spout.

SKILLS YOU'LL NEED

- Using channel-type pliers
- Tracking the order and arrangement of parts

TERMS YOU NEED TO KNOW

TUB SPOUT GATE DIVERTER—a knob-operated gate valve on the tip of a tub spout. When it's pulled up, water cannot pass through the spout and is forced to rise to the showerhead.

HANDLE-OPERATED DIVERTER VALVE—the diverter valve behind the central handle on a three-handle faucet. It uses a compression stem and washer or a cartridge to divert water from the spout so the shower can be used.

DIFFICULTY LEVEL

SKILLS LEVEL

EASY   MODERATE

Time: 1 hour plus research and shopping

HOW TO REPLACE A SLIP-FIT SPOUT

1 Slip fitting: Check underneath the tub spout to look for an access slot or cutout, which indicates the spout is a slip-fit style that is held in place with a setscrew and mounted on a copper supply nipple. Loosen the screw with a hex (Allen) wrench. Pull off the spout.

2 Clean the copper nipple with steel wool. If you find any sharp edges where the nipple was cut, smooth them out with emery paper. Then, insert the O-ring that comes with spout onto the nipple (see the manufacturer's instructions) and slide the spout body over the nipple in an upside-down position.

3 With the spout upside down for ease of access, tighten the setscrews on the clamp, working through the access slot or cutout, until you feel resistance.

4 Spin the spout so it's right-side up and then tighten the setscrew from below, making sure the wall end of the spout is flush against the wall. Do not overtighten the setscrew.

HOW TO REPLACE A THREADED SPOUT

1 If you see no setscrew or slot on the underside of the spout, it is attached to a threaded nipple. Unscrew the tub spout by inserting a heavy-duty flat screwdriver into the spout opening and spinning it counterclockwise.

Copper nipple with threaded adapter

2 Wrap several courses of Teflon tape clockwise onto the pipe threads of the nipple. Using extra Teflon tape on the threads creates resistance if the spout tip points past six o'clock when tight.

3 Twist the new spout onto the nipple until it is flush against the wall and the spout is oriented properly. If the spout falls short of six o'clock, you may protect the finish of the spout with tape and twist it a little beyond hand tight with your channel-type pliers—but don't over do it; the fitting can crack.

Replacing a Widespread Bathroom Faucet

18

Three-piece (widespread) faucets are as classy as a good three-piece suit, and the styles are virtually unlimited.

WIDESPREAD FAUCETS COME IN THREE PIECES INSTEAD OF ONE: a hot tap, a cold tap, and the spout. Each piece is mounted separately in its own hole in the sink. The hot and cold taps (valves) are connected to hot and cold water supplies respectively. The spout is connected to the valves with reinforced flexible hoses. The great advantage to this configuration is that you gain flexibility when locating your spout and handles. If your faucet set has a long enough hose, you can even create arrangements such as locating the handles near one end of the tub and the spout near the other so you can turn the water on and off or adjust the temperature without getting up. Even models made for bathroom lavatories, like the one you see here, offer many creative configuration options.

TIP: Save your paperwork. Should you ever need to service your faucet, the product literature will be useful for troubleshooting and identifying and replacing parts.

WIDESPREAD FAUCETS 101

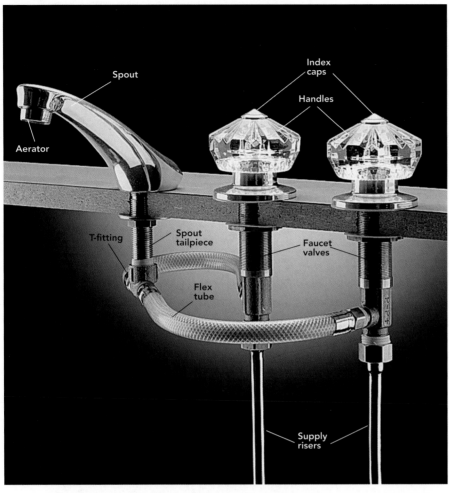

Widespread faucets come in three pieces, a *spout* and two *valves*. *Supply risers* carry hot and cold water to the valves, which are turned to regulate the amount of water going to the spout, where the water is mixed. Water travels from the valves to the spout through *flex tubes,* which attach to the *spout tailpiece* via a *T-fitting.* Three-piece faucets designed to work with a pop-up stopper have a *clevis* and a *lift rod* (see pages 256 to 259). The *handles* attach with *handle screws* that are covered with *index caps.* An *aerator* is screwed on the faucet spout after debris is flushed from the faucet.

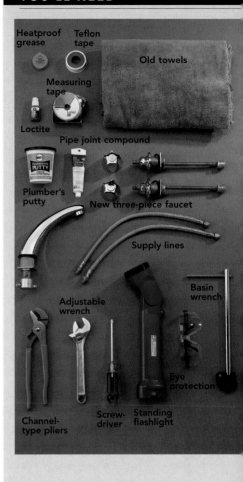

SKILLS YOU'LL NEED

- Using a basin wench
- Working in confined spaces
- Making compression unions

DIFFICULTY LEVEL

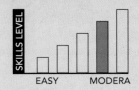

Time: 1 to 3 hours

TERMS YOU NEED TO KNOW

PLUMBER'S PUTTY—a soft clay-like material used to seal faucet parts to sink parts.

TEFLON TAPE—a thin, white tape used to lubricate and seal threaded fittings.

PIPE JOINT COMPOUND—a paste that may be used instead of Teflon tape.

LAVATORY—another name for a bathroom sink.

HOW TO REMOVE A WIDESPREAD FAUCET

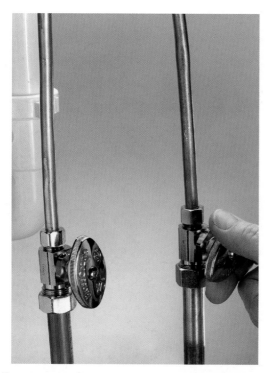

1 Clear out the cabinet under the sink and lay down towels. Turn off the hot and cold stop valves, and open the hot and cold taps. If you have difficulty turning the water off, turn to page 146.

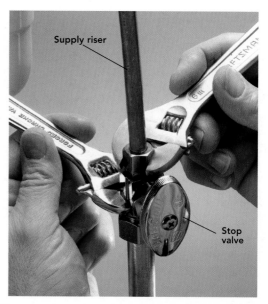

Supply riser

Stop valve

2 Unthread the compression nuts that connect the hot and cold supply risers to the stop valves. If a compression nut is frozen, stabilize the valve body with another wrench before applying more force.

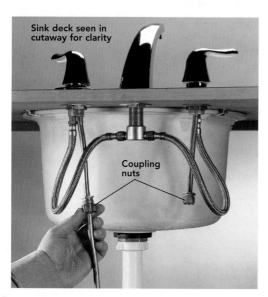

Sink deck seen in cutaway for clarity

Coupling nuts

3 Remove the coupling nuts holding the risers to the supply tubes from the faucet, stabilizing the tubes with a second wrench. Don't reuse old metal supply risers; the soft metal ends have been press-formed to the supply tubes of the old faucet.

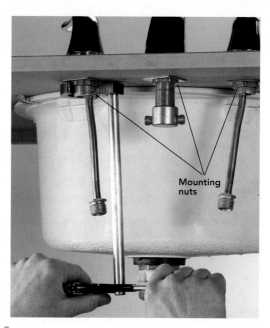

Mounting nuts

4 Using a basin wrench, disconnect all three mounting nuts holding the two faucet handles and the spout. You may need to have somebody hold the spout or valve steady from above. Remove the old faucet parts and clean the installation area in preparation for the new faucet.

HOW TO INSTALL A WIDESPREAD FAUCET

1 Insert the shank of the faucet spout through one of the holes in the sink deck (usually the center hole but you can offset it in one of the end holes if you prefer). If the faucet is not equipped with seals or O-rings for the spout and handles, pack plumber's putty on the undersides before inserting the valves into the deck. NOTE: If you are installing the widespread faucet in a new sink deck, drill three holes of the size suggested by the faucet manufacturer (see page 232 for tips on locating the holes).

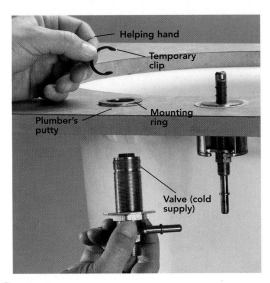

3 Mount the valves to the deck using whichever method the manufacturer specifies (it varies quite a bit). In the model seen here, a mounting ring is positioned over the deck hole (with plumber's putty seal) and the valve is inserted from below. A clip snaps onto the valve from above to hold it in place temporarily (you'll want a helper for this).

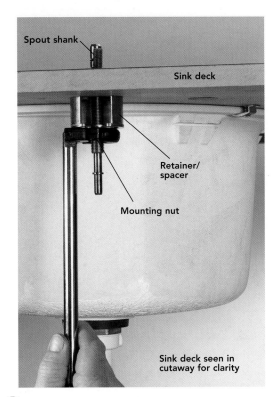

Sink deck seen in cutaway for clarity

2 In addition to mounting nuts, many spout valves for widespread faucets have an open retainer fitting that goes between the underside of the deck and the mounting nut. Others have only a mounting nut. In either case, tighten the mounting nut with pliers or a basin wrench to secure the spout valve. You may need a helper to keep the spout centered and facing forward.

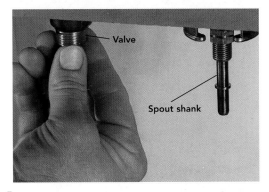

4 From below, thread the mounting nuts that secure the valves to the sink deck. Make sure the cold water valve (usually has a blue cartridge inside) is in the right-side hole (from the front) and the hot water valve (red cartridge) is in the left hole. Install both valves.

HOW TO INSTALL A WIDESPREAD FAUCET (CONTINUED)

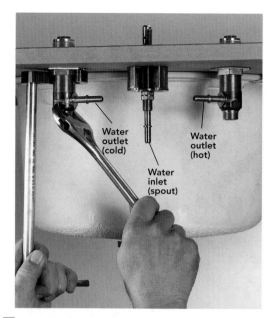

5 Once you've started the nut on the threaded valve shank, secure the valve with a basin wrench squeezing the lugs where the valve fits against the deck. Use an adjustable wrench to finish tightening the lock nut onto the valve. The valves should be oriented so the water outlets are aimed at the inlet on the spout shank.

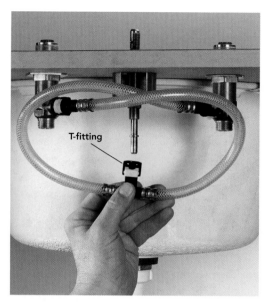

6 Attach the flexible supply tubes (supplied with the faucet) to the water outlets on the valves. Some twist onto the outlets, but others (like the ones above) click into place. The supply hoses meet in a T-fitting that is attached to the water inlet on the spout.

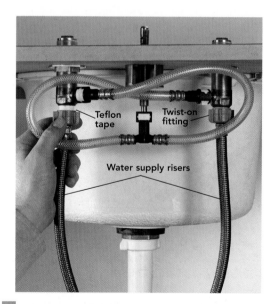

7 Attach flexible braided metal supply risers to the water stop valves and then attach the tubes to the inlet port on each valve (usually with Teflon tape and a twist-on fitting at the valve end of the supply riser).

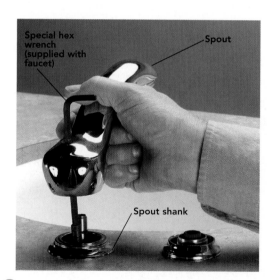

8 Attach the spout. The model shown here comes with a special hex wrench that is threaded through the hole in the spout where the lift rod for the pop-up drain will be located. Once the spout is seated cleanly on the spout shank you tighten the hex wrench to secure the spout. Different faucets will use other methods to secure the spout to the shank.

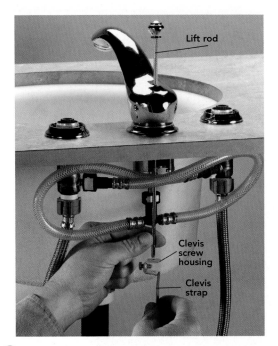

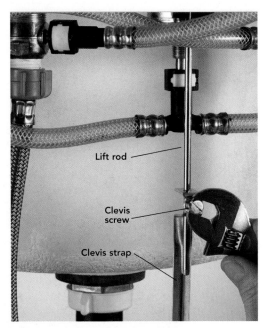

9 If your sink did not have a pop-up stopper, you'll need to replace the sink drain tailpiece with a pop-up stopper body (often supplied with the faucet). See pages 250 to 255. Insert the lift rod through the hole in the back of the spout and, from below, thread the pivot rod through the housing for the clevis screw.

10 Attach the clevis strap to the pivot rod that enters the pop-up drain body and adjust the position of the strap so it raises and lowers properly when the lift rod is pulled up. Tighten the clevis screw at this point. It's hard to fit a screwdriver in here, so you may need to use a wrench or pliers.

11 Attach the faucet handles to the valves using whichever method is required by the faucet manufacturer. Most faucets are designed with registration methods to ensure that the handles are symmetrical and oriented in an ergonomic way once you secure them to the valves.

12 Turn on the water supply and test the faucet. Remove the faucet aerator so any debris in the lines can clear the spout.

Installing a
New Bathroom Faucet

19

Standard one-handle, deck-mounted bathroom faucets are interchangeable with two-handle models, fitting in the same two or three holes in the bathroom sink.

ONE-PIECE BATHROOM FAUCETS ARE EASY TO REPLACE. They're attached to the sink with a couple of mounting nuts and to the water supply with coupling nuts. With the faucet gone, you'll be looking at two or three holes in the faucet deck. The outside holes take tailpieces or mounting posts for the faucet, and the middle hole is for the pop-up stopper lift rod. The outside holes are spaced four inches apart and will accept any standard deck-mounted, one-piece bathroom faucet, except if you don't have a middle hole, you can't have one with a pop-up stopper. We'd advise you to buy a heavy, quality faucet made of brass (chrome or another metal on the outside). Cheap chromed-plastic faucets tend to wear out at the handle attachments, and chrome-plated steel tends to rust. Faucets usually come with a pop-up stopper mechanism. We show you how to replace these on pages 256 to 259.

ONE-PIECE FAUCETS 101

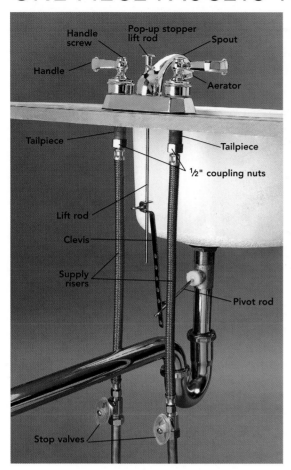

The tailpieces of a standard deck-mounted, one-piece bathroom sink faucet are 4" apart on center. As long as the two outside holes in the back of your sink measure 4" from center to center, and you have a middle hole for a pop-up stopper, you can put in any standard one-piece bathroom faucet with *pop-up stopper.*

The faucet is secured to the sink with *mounting nuts* that screw onto the tailpieces from below. Also get two *flexible stainless steel supply risers* for sinks, long enough to replace the old tubes.

These typically attach to the stop valves with ⅜-inch *compression-sized coupling nuts* and to the faucet with standard *faucet coupling nuts.* But take your old tubes and the old compression nuts from the stop valves to the store to ensure a match. The *clevis, lift rod,* and *pivot rod* are parts of the pop-up stopper assembly. (Replaced on pages 256 to 259.) The handles attach with *handle screws* that are covered with *index caps.* An *aerator* is screwed on the faucet spout after debris is flushed from the faucet.

TERMS YOU NEED TO KNOW

PLUMBER'S PUTTY—a soft clay-like material used to seal faucet parts to sink parts.

TEFLON TAPE—a thin white tape used to lubricate and seal threaded fittings.

PIPE JOINT COMPOUND—a paste that may be used instead of Teflon tape.

DECK-MOUNTED FAUCET—another name for a one-piece faucet.

LAVATORY—another name for a bathroom sink.

TOOLS & SUPPLIES YOU'LL NEED

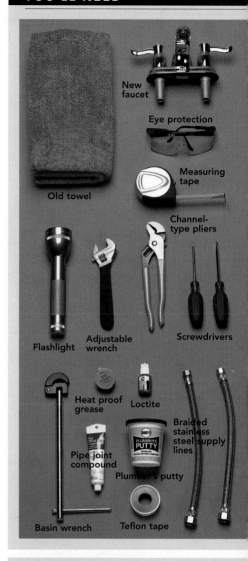

SKILLS YOU'LL NEED

- Making plumbing connections
- Ability to work in confined space

DIFFICULTY LEVEL

TIME: 1 to 2 hours plus shopping

HOW TO REPLACE A ONE-PIECE FAUCET

1 Clear out the cabinet under the sink and lay down towels. Turn off the hot and cold stop valves and open the faucet. Unscrew the compression nuts that are holding the hot and cold supply tubes in the stop valves. Remove the coupling nuts holding the supply tubes to the tailpieces of the faucet and remove the tubes.

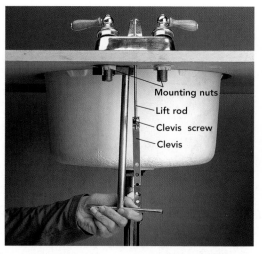

Mounting nuts
Lift rod
Clevis screw
Clevis

2 Put on protective eyewear! Debris will be falling in your face. Loosen the clevis screw (counterclockwise) holding the clevis strap to the lift rod. Remove the mounting nuts on the tailpieces of the faucet with a basin wrench or channel-type pliers. If the mounting nuts are rusted in place, apply penetrating oil, let stand ten minutes, and try again. TIP: Attach locking pliers to the basin wrench handle for greater leverage.

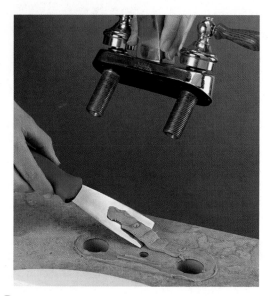

3 Pull the faucet body from the sink. Scrape off old putty or caulk with a putty knife and clean off the sink with a scouring pad and an acidic scouring cleaner like Barkeeper's Friend. Take your old supply tubes and the stop valve compression nuts to the home center so you'll know what size flexible supply risers to get.

4 Most faucets come with a plastic or foam gasket to seal the bottom of the faucet to the sink deck. These gaskets will not always form a watertight seal. If you want to ensure no splash water gets below the sink, discard the seal and press a ring of plumber's putty into the sealant groove built into the underside of the faucet body.

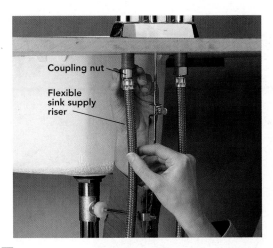

5 Insert the faucet tailpieces through the holes in the sink. From below, thread washers and mounting nuts over the tailpieces, then tighten the mounting nuts with a basin wrench until snug. Put a dab of pipe joint compound on the threads of the stop valves and thread the metal nuts of the flexible supply risers to these. Wrench tighten about a half turn past hand tight. Overtightening these nuts will strip the threads. Now tighten the coupling nuts to the faucet tailpieces with a basin wrench.

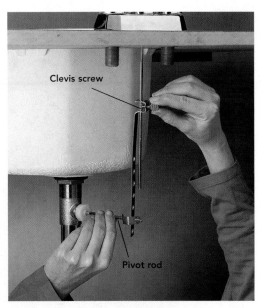

6 Slide the lift rod of the new faucet into its hole behind the spout. Thread it into the clevis past the clevis screw. Push the pivot rod all the way down so the stopper is open. With the lift rod also all the way down, tighten the clevis to the lift rod.

7 Grease the fluted valve stems with heatproof grease, then put the handles in place. Put a drop of Loctite on each handle screw before tightening it on. (This will keep your handles from coming loose). Cover each handle screw with the appropriate index cap—Hot or Cold.

8 Unscrew the aerator from the end of the spout. Turn the hot and cold water taps on full. Turn the water back on at the stop valves and flush out the faucet for a couple of minutes before turning off the water at the faucet. Check the riser connections for drips. Tighten a compression nut only until the drip stops.

Dealing with Kitchen Sprayers

20

When most of us think of kitchen sprayers, the image that comes to mind doesn't closely resemble the powerful stream of accurately directed water that's cleansing the fresh apples in the photo above. For a variety of reasons, sink sprayers seldom seem to function as designed. But improving the performance of your kitchen sprayer is a simple job with a high likelihood of success.

IF THE FLOW TO YOUR SPRAYER IS WEAK, first make sure the hose under the sink isn't kinked. If the hose is damaged, you will need to replace the hose and sprayer. If the screen at the base of the sprayer is clogged with debris, remove it and flush it clean. If you dislodged other parts from the base of the sprayer, clean these and put them back in the order in which they were removed. If the sprayer leaks from the base, replace the neoprene washer. If the sprayer doesn't turn off fully, replace the sprayer. If water isn't fully diverted from spout to sprayer, you may need to replace the diverter.

KITCHEN SPRAYERS 101

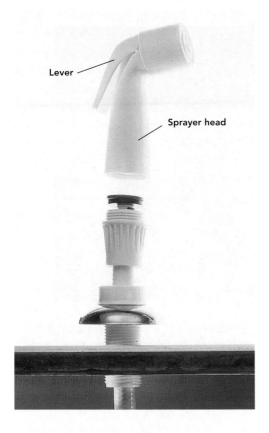

Lever

Sprayer head

When you squeeze the *lever* on your properly functioning kitchen sprayer, water flows out through the *sprayer head,* which causes a diverter valve in the faucet to close off water to the spout.

Plumber's putty

Channel-type pliers

New aerator

Diverter valve and O-rings

Replacement sprayer head

Replacement hose

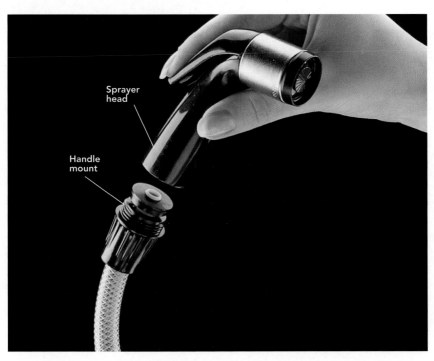

Sprayer head

Handle mount

Older spray hoses are easy to work with—you simply grasp the *sprayer head* and twist counterclockwise. The screen inside can then be removed and cleaned or replaced. Twist the sprayer head back on in a clockwise direction.

SKILLS YOU'LL NEED

• Making pipe connections

• Working with putty

DIFFICULTY LEVEL

SKILLS LEVEL

EASY   MODERATE

Time: About an hour

HOW TO REPAIR A SPRAYER DIVERTER VALVE

1 Shut off the water at the stop valves and remove the faucet handle to gain access to the faucet parts. Disassemble the faucet handle and body to expose the diverter valve. Ball-type faucets like the one shown here require that you also remove the spout to get at the diverter.

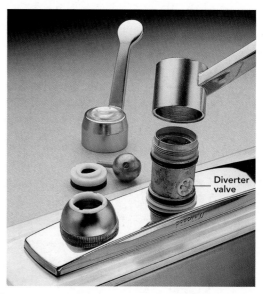

2 Locate the diverter valve, seen here at the base of the valve body. Because different types and brands of faucets have differently configured diverters, do a little investigating beforehand to try and locate information about your faucet. The above faucet is a ball type (see page 164).

3 Pull the diverter valve from the faucet body with needlenose pliers. Use a toothbrush dipped in white vinegar to clean any lime buildup from the valve. If the valve is in poor condition, bring it to the hardware store and purchase a replacement.

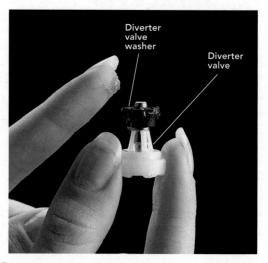

4 Coat the washer or O-ring on the new or cleaned diverter valve with heatproof grease. Insert the diverter valve back into the faucet body. Reassemble the faucet. Turn on the water and test the sprayer. If it still isn't functioning to your satisfaction, remove the sprayer tip and run the sprayer without the filter and aerator in case any debris has made its way into the sprayer line during repairs.

HOW TO REPLACE A KITCHEN SPRAYER

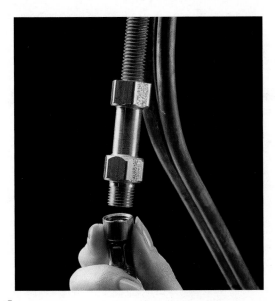

1 To replace a sprayer hose, start by shutting off the water at the shutoff valves. Clear out the cabinet under your sink and put on eye protection. Unthread the coupling nut that attaches the old hose to a nipple or tube below the faucet spout. Use a basin wrench if you can't get your channel-type pliers on the nut.

2 Unscrew the mounting nut of the old sprayer from below and remove the old sprayer body. Clean the sink deck and then apply plumber's putty to the base of the new sprayer. Insert the new sprayer tailpiece into the opening in the sink deck.

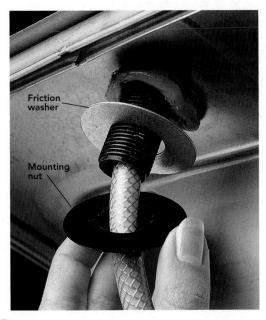

3 From below, slip the friction washer up over the sprayer tailpiece. Screw the mounting nut onto the tailpiece and tighten with a basin wrench or channel-type pliers. Do not over-tighten. Wipe away any excess plumber's putty.

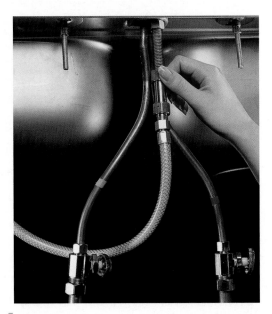

4 Screw the coupling for the sprayer hose onto the hose nipple underneath the faucet body. For a good seal, apply pipe joint compound to the nipple threads first. Tighten the coupling with a basin wrench, turn on the water supply at the shutoff valves, and test the new sprayer.

Repairing a Burst Pipe

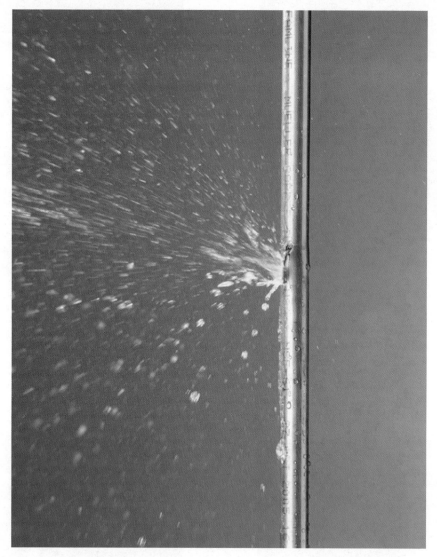

21

Water supply pipes can burst for many reasons, but the most common cause is water freezing and expanding inside the pipe. First turn off the water, then apply a fix.

IF A WATER PIPE FREEZES AND BREAKS, your first priority may be getting it working again—whatever it takes. There are a number of temporary fix products out there, some involving clamps and sleeves, others, epoxy putties and fiberglass tape. These repairs usually can get you through a weekend okay. We also show you how to apply full slip repair couplings, a more permanent fix. Whatever repair approach you take, please, please, please, don't leave for the store without first determining a) the diameter of your pipe and b) the material of your pipe.

TIP: Pipes frozen? Don't let it happen again. Turn to page 224 to find out how.

WATER PIPE REPAIR PRODUCTS 101

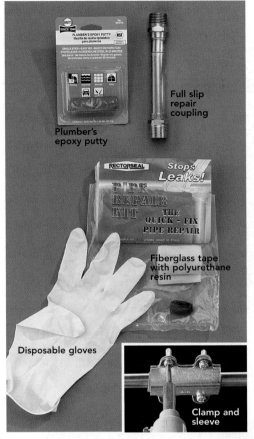

Plumber's epoxy putty

Full slip repair coupling

Fiberglass tape with polyurethane resin

Disposable gloves

Clamp and sleeve

Plumber's epoxy putty may stem a leak at a fitting, at least partially or temporarily. *Fiberglass tape with polyurethane resin* can produce a durable patch; it's sometimes used in conjunction with epoxy putty. A *clamp and sleeve* is quick and cheap. A *full slip repair coupling* is the closest to a permanent fix, but it requires straight and unblemished pipes of the right diameter and material. All of these products require that you carefully follow manufacturer's directions, or they simply will not work.

WARNING: A damaged pipe section with a patch should be replaced as soon as possible. Because of the natural movement of pipes, patches may leak again in time.

If a water supply pipe bursts, your first stop should be a shutoff. If there is a shutoff near the burst pipe, go ahead and turn off the water there or shut off the water to the whole house (right). Open faucets on every floor of the house to drain the supply system if your repair product requires dry pipe.

TERMS YOU NEED TO KNOW

OUTSIDE DIAMETER—clamps and slip couplings require that you know the outside diameter of the pipe. Close an adjustable wrench on the pipe then measure the distance between the jaws.

PIPE MATERIAL—Certain repair products work on certain pipe types. Make sure you know yours before heading out to the home center.

TOOLS & SUPPLIES YOU'LL NEED

Metal file

Channel-type pliers

Adjustable wrench

Screwdriver

Tubing cutter

Tape measure

SKILLS YOU'LL NEED

• Using a tubing cutter

• Making compression joint

DIFFICULTY LEVEL

SKILLS LEVEL

EASY   MODERATE

Time: a few minutes plus shopping

HOW TO APPLY A SLEEVE AND CLAMP REPAIR

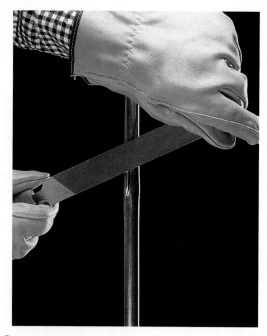

1 Make temporary repairs to a burst copper supply pipe with a sleeve clamp repair kit, available at most hardware stores. With the water supply shut off at the main, smooth out any rough edges around the damage with a metal file.

2 Center rubber sleeve of repair clamp over the rupture. If the sleeve enfolds the pipe, the seam should be opposite the rupture.

3 Place the two metal repair clamps around the sleeve.

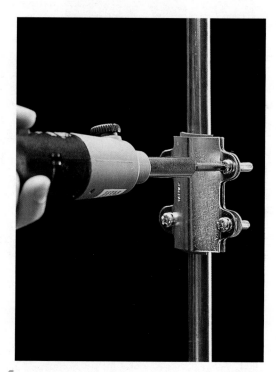

4 Tighten the screws with a Phillips screwdriver. Open water supply and watch for leaks. If it does leak, start from the beginning with the sleeve in a slightly different place. Have the section of ruptured pipe replaced as soon as possible.

HOW TO APPLY A REPAIR COUPLING
TO A COPPER PIPE

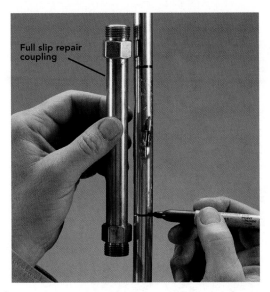

Full slip repair coupling

1 For a longer-lasting (not permanent) repair, use a compression-fit, full slip repair coupling (these come with parts to make a compression union—you can also buy a slip coupling that's just a piece of copper tubing with an inside diameter equal to the outside diameter of the tubing being repaired, but these require soldering). Turn off water at the meter. Mark the boundaries of the pipe to be replaced. This should include pipe beyond the damaged area. The cutout section must fall within the bare copper section of the repair coupling.

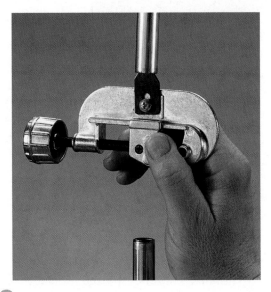

3 Deburr the inside of the pipes with the triangular blade on the tubing cutter.

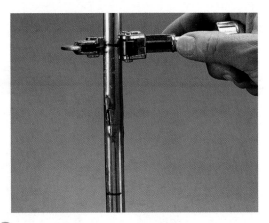

2 Lightly tighten the tubing cutter onto the pipe on a cutting line. Both wheels of the cutter should rest evenly on the pipe. Rotate the cutter around the pipe. The line it cuts should make a perfect ring, not a spiral. Tighten the cutter a little with each rotation until the pipe snaps. Repeat at your other mark.

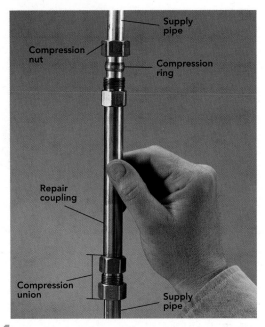

Supply pipe

Compression nut

Compression ring

Repair coupling

Compression union

Supply pipe

4 Slip the compression nuts and rings supplied with the repair coupling onto the cut ends of the pipe being repaired and then slip the repair coupling over one end. Slide the coupling further onto the pipe and then slide it back the other way so it fits over the other pipe section and the repair area is centered inside the coupling. Tighten each compression nut with pliers while stabilizing the coupling with an adjustable wrench.

22

Replacing a Kitchen Faucet

Kitchen faucets don't last forever: in styling or in function. When it's time for you to say goodbye to yours, take comfort in knowing that if you choose one that's the same configuration, the project is quite simple.

MOST MODERN KITCHEN SINK FAUCETS ARE DECK MOUNTED, which means the bulk of the faucet sits on top of the back rim of the sink or counter. Typically, these faucets attach to the sink or counter and to their hot and cold water supplies through three holes. A fourth hole may hold a kitchen sprayer. Standard kitchen sinks (or pre-drilled counters) have three or four holes spaced 4" apart. It's best to look for a new faucet that uses the same number of holes as your current model, although any old holes that aren't used may be covered with a cap or a stand-alone accessory, like a liquid soap dispenser, that doesn't require additional plumbing work (there are several plumbed options, too, such as a water filter spout and a dishwasher air gap).

KITCHEN SINK FAUCETS 101

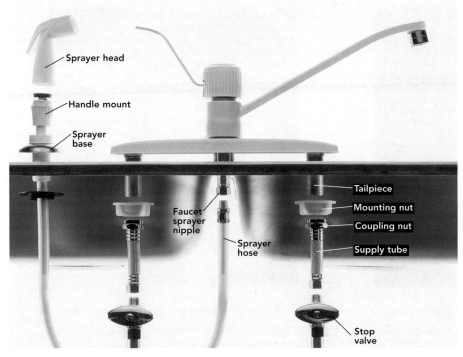

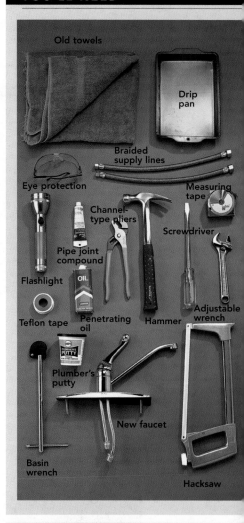

In this section, we show you how to install one of the most popular faucet types for home use: a *single-lever kitchen sink faucet* with *hose sprayer*, configured for a four-hole sink with standard 4-inch spacing between the holes. If the faucet you want to install isn't quite the same type as this, keep reading anyway. The basic installation requirements are the same: the *faucet body* must be secured firmly to the sink or counter, and the *hot and cold supply tubes* must be connected to the *hot and cold water supplies*.

SKILLS YOU'LL NEED

- Working with tools in tight spots
- Making compression joints

TERMS YOU NEED TO KNOW

COMPRESSION FITTING—a way of attaching copper tubes to stop valves.

FLEXIBLE SUPPLY LINES—flexible hoses that are used to attached to the hot and cold stop valves.

PLUMBER'S PUTTY—a soft clay-like material used to seal faucet parts to sink parts.

TEFLON TAPE—a thin, white tape used to lubricate and seal threaded fittings.

PIPE JOINT COMPOUND—a paste that may be used instead of Teflon tape.

DECK-MOUNTED FAUCET—a faucet that mounts on top of a sink or counter, usually in two to four holes spaced 4 inches on center.

DIFFICULTY LEVEL

Time: 2 to 3 hours for removal and installation plus shopping

HOW TO REMOVE THE OLD FAUCET

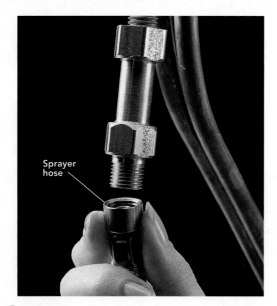

1 To remove the old faucet, start by clearing out the cabinet under the sink and laying down towels. Turn off the hot and cold stop valves and open the faucet to make sure the water is off. Detach the sprayer hose from the faucet sprayer nipple and unscrew the retaining nut that secures the sprayer base to the sink deck. Pull the sprayer hose out through the sink deck opening.

2 Spray the mounting nuts that hold the faucet or faucet handles (on the underside of the sink deck) with penetrating oil for easier removal. Let the oil soak in for a few minutes.

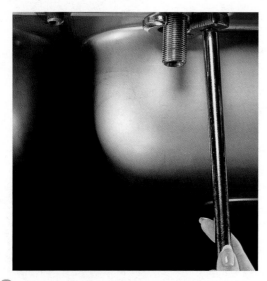

3 Unhook the supply tubes at the stop valves. Don't reuse old chrome supply tubes. If the stops are missing or unworkable, replace them. Then, remove the coupling nuts and the mounting nuts on the tailpieces of the faucet with a basin wrench or channel-type pliers.

4 Pull the faucet body from the sink. Remove the sprayer base, if you wish to replace this. Scrape off old putty or caulk with a putty knife and clean off the sink with a scouring pad and an acidic scouring cleaner like Barkeeper's Friend.
TIP: Scour stainless steel with a back and forth motion to avoid leaving unsightly circular markings.

HOW TO INSTALL A KITCHEN FAUCET

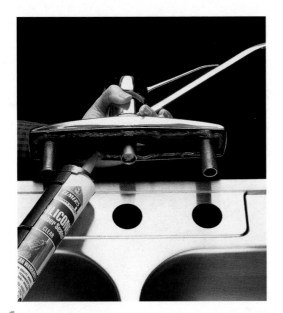

1 Apply a thick bead of silicone caulk to the underside of the faucet base then insert the tailpieces of the faucet through the appropriate holes in the sink deck. Press down lightly on the faucet to set it in the caulk.

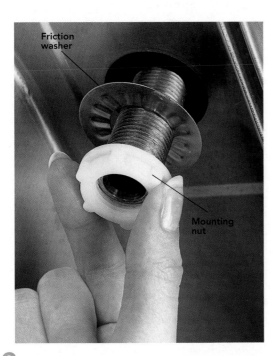

Friction washer

Mounting nut

2 Slip a friction washer onto each tailpiece and then hand-tighten a mounting nut. Tighten the mounting nut with channel-type pliers or a basin wrench. Wipe up any silicone squeeze-out on the sink deck with a wet rag before it sets up.

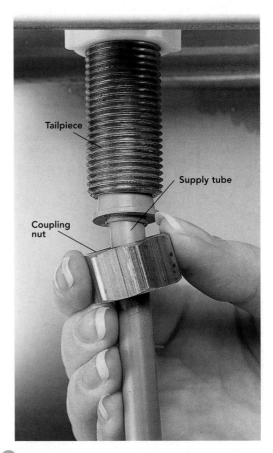

Tailpiece

Supply tube

Coupling nut

3 Connect supply tubes to the faucet tailpieces—make sure the tubes you buy are long enough to reach the stop valves and that the coupling nuts will fit the tubes and tailpieces.

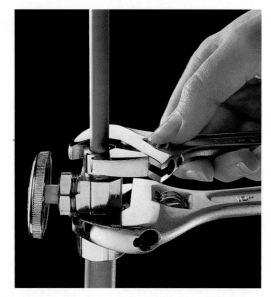

4 Attach the supply tubes to the shutoff valves, using compression fittings. Make sure you connect the hot supply to the hot stop valve. Hand-tighten the nuts, then use an adjustable wrench to tighten them an additional quarter turn. It's a good idea to hold the shutoff valve with another wrench to stabilize it while you tighten the nut. It's also a good idea to wrap some Teflon tape around the threads of the shutoff body.

Sprayer tailpiece

5 Apply a ¼" bead of plumber's putty or silicone caulk to the underside of the sprayer base. With the base threaded onto the sprayer hose, insert the tailpiece of the sprayer through the opening in the sink deck.

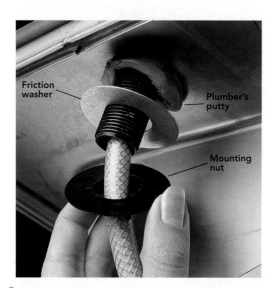

Friction washer

Plumber's putty

Mounting nut

6 From beneath, slip the friction washer over the sprayer tailpiece and then screw the mounting nut onto the tailpiece. Tighten with channel-type pliers or a basin wrench. Wipe any excess putty or caulk on the sink deck from around the base.

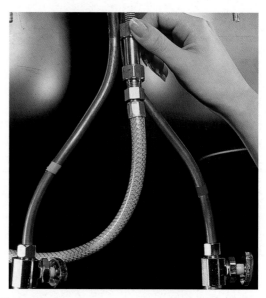

7 Screw the sprayer hose onto the hose nipple on the bottom of the faucet. Hand-tighten and then give the nut one quarter turn with pliers or a basin wrench. Turn on the water supply at the shutoff, remove the aerator and flush debris from the faucet.

VARIATION: INSTALLING A KITCHEN FAUCET WITH PREATTACHED COPPER SUPPLY TUBES

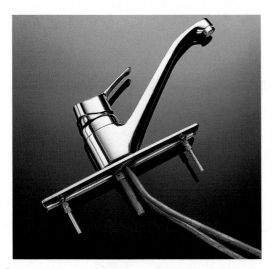

1 Some faucets come with the copper supply tubes preattached to the faucet body. This minimizes the number of connections so you can hook the new faucet directly to the shutoff valves. To install a single-handle lever-type faucet with preattached supply tubes, start by caulking the faucet base and setting it on the deck, as in step 1, on page 253. The copper supply tubes and the sprayer nipple should go through the center hole and then mounting bolts on each side should go through the two outside holes.

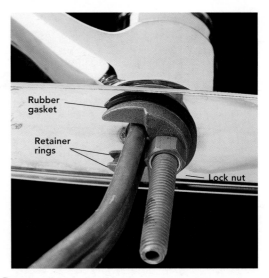

2 Secure the faucet to the sink deck by placing a rubber gasket between the retainer rings and the underside of the countertop. Orient the cutout in the retainer to fit around the supply tubes. Thread a lock nut onto the threaded sprayer nipple and hand-tighten up to the retainer.

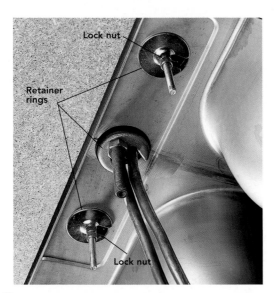

3 Attach retainer rings and washers to the two mounting bolts as well and hand-tighten the mounting nuts. Tighten all nuts with pliers or a basin wrench.

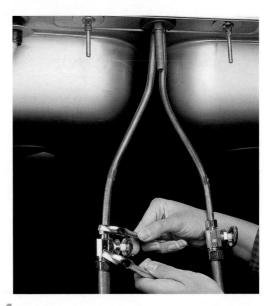

4 Bend the copper faucet tubes so they are in straight up-and-down positions as they meet the stop valves. You may need to trim them with a tubing cutter. Connect the tubes to the stop valves with compression nuts and rings (attach the hot supply tube to the hot supply pipe). Install the sprayer as shown on the previous page. Turn on the water at the shutoffs and test the faucet.

Replacing a Pop-up Stopper

23

A bum pop-up stopper may require complete regime change. Not just the stopper, but the tube and lever apparatus under it may need to be replaced.

POP-UP STOPPERS ARE THOSE CHROME-PLATED, LONG-LEGGED PLUGS IN BATH-ROOM SINKS that are opened and closed with a knob behind the spout. The stopper itself is just the glory guy for a behind-the-scenes assembly that makes sure the stopper sits and stands on cue. New faucets come with their own pop-up stopper assemblies, assuming they use one, but you may also purchase one by itself. This will include everything from the stopper to the pipe that drops into the trap (the trap is that drooping piece of drainpipe under your sink). If you choose to buy a pop-up stopper assembly, we recommend one that's heavy brass under the chrome finish. This will hold up better to time and abuse than a plastic or light-gauge metal model.

POP-UP STOPPERS 101

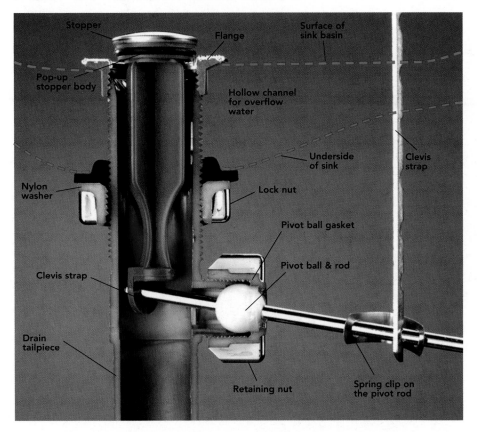

Labels on diagram: Stopper · Flange · Surface of sink basin · Pop-up stopper body · Hollow channel for overflow water · Underside of sink · Clevis strap · Nylon washer · Lock nut · Pivot ball gasket · Pivot ball & rod · Clevis strap · Drain tailpiece · Retaining nut · Spring clip on the pivot rod

Pop up stoppers keep objects from falling down the drain, and they make filling and draining the sink easy. When you pull up on the *lift rod*, the *clevis strap* is raised, which raises the *pivot rod*, which seesaws on the *pivot ball* and pulls the *pop-up stopper* down against the *flange*. This blocks water through the sink drain, but water may still overflow into the *overflow channel*, and get into the stopper body and down the drain through *overflow ports* in the pop-up body, which is a nice feature if you leave the water running in a plugged basin by mistake.

TERMS YOU NEED TO KNOW

PLUMBER'S PUTTY—a soft clay-like material used to seal metal parts to the sink.

TEFLON TAPE—a thin, white tape used to lubricate and seal threaded fittings.

PIPE JOINT COMPOUND—a paste that may be used instead of Teflon tape.

POP-UP WASTE—another term for a pop-up assembly.

TAILPIECE—takes the waste from the pop-up stopper body to the J-bend.

J-BEND—a J-shaped bend of drainpipe below the sink. It's the part of the trap that's always full of water to keep sewer gases from rising into the house.

TOOLS & SUPPLIES YOU'LL NEED

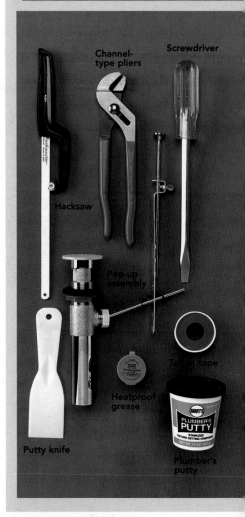

Labels: Channel-type pliers · Screwdriver · Hacksaw · Pop-up assembly · Teflon tape · Heatproof grease · Putty knife · Plumber's putty

SKILLS YOU'LL NEED

- Making slip joints
- Handling small parts
- Cutting metal with a hacksaw

DIFFICULTY LEVEL

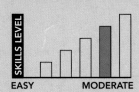

SKILLS LEVEL

EASY   MODERATE

Time: 1 to 2 hours plus shopping

HOW TO REPLACE A POP-UP STOPPER

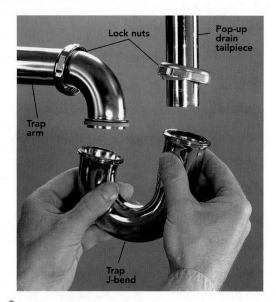

1 Put a basin under the trap to catch water. Loosen the nuts at the outlet and inlet to the trap J-bend by hand or with channel-type pliers and remove the bend. The trap will slide off the pop-up body tailpiece when the nuts are loose. Keep track of washers and nuts and their up/down orientation by leaving them on the tubes.

3 Remove the pop-up stopper. Then, from below, remove the lock nut on the stopper body. If needed, keep the flange from turning by inserting a large screwdriver in the drain from the top. Thrust the stopper body up through the hole to free the flange from the basin, and then remove the flange and the stopper body.

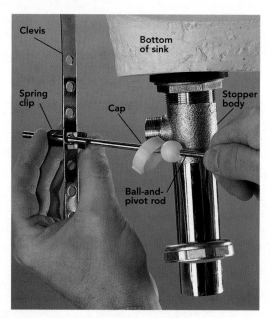

2 Unscrew the cap holding the ball-and-pivot rod in the pop-up body and withdraw the ball. Compress the spring clip on the clevis and withdraw the pivot rod from the clevis.

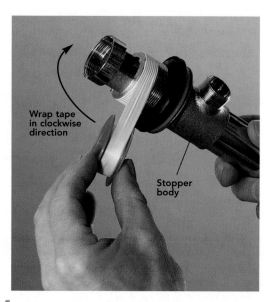

4 Clean the drain opening above and below, and then thread the locknut all the way down the new pop-up body followed by the flat washer and the rubber gasket (beveled side up). Wrap three layers of Teflon tape clockwise onto the top of the threaded body. Make a ½"-dia. snake from plumber's putty, form it into a ring and stick the ring underneath the drain flange.

Plumber's putty

5 From below, face the pivot rod opening directly back toward the middle of the faucet and pull the body straight down to seat the flange. Thread the locknut/washer assembly up under the sink, then fully tighten the locknut with channel-type pliers. Do not twist the flange in the process, as this can break the putty seal. Clean off the squeezeout of plumber's putty from around the flange.

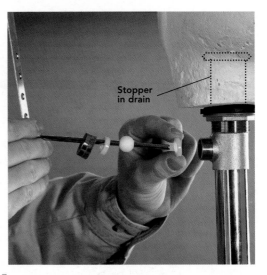

Stopper in drain

6 Drop the pop-up stopper into the drain hole so the hole at the bottom of its post is closest to the back of the sink. Put the beveled nylon washer into the opening in the back of the pop-up body with the bevel facing back.

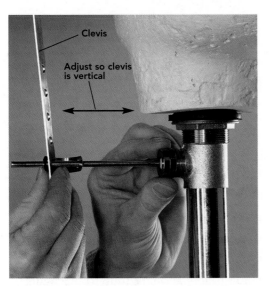

Clevis

Adjust so clevis is vertical

7 Put the cap behind the ball on the pivot rod as shown. Sandwich a hole in the clevis with the spring clip and thread the long end of the pivot rod through the clip and clevis. Put the ball end of the pivot rod into the pop-up body opening and into the hole in the the stopper stem. Screw the cap on to the pop-up body over the ball.

Clevis screw

8 Loosen the clevis screw holding the clevis to the lift rod. Push the pivot rod all the way down (which fully opens the pop-up stopper). With the lift rod also all the way down, tighten the clevis screw to the rod. If the clevis runs into the top of the trap, cut it short with your hacksaw or tin snips. Reassemble the J-bend trap.

24

Replacing a Toilet

Replacing a toilet is simple, and the latest generation of 1.6-gallon water-saving toilets has overcome the performance problems of earlier models.

YOU CAN REPLACE A POORLY FUNCTIONING TOILET WITH A HIGH-EFFICIENCY, HIGH-QUALITY NEW TOILET FOR UNDER TWO HUNDRED AND FIFTY DOLLARS, but don't, as Ben Franklin would say, be penny wise and pound foolish. All toilets made since 1996 have been required to use 1.6 gallons or less per flush, which has been a huge challenge for the industry. Today, the most evolved 1.6-gallon toilets have wide passages behind the bowl and wide (three-inch) flush valve openings—features that facilitate short, powerful flushes. This means fewer second flushes and fewer clogged toilets. These problems were common complaints of the first generation of 1.6-gallon toilets and continue to beleaguer inferior models today. See what toilets are available at your local home center in your price range, then go online and see what other consumers' experiences with those models have been. New toilets often go through a "de-bugging" stage when problems with leaks and malfunctioning parts are more common. Your criteria should include ease of installation, good flush performance, and reliability. With a little research, you should be able to purchase and install a high-functioning economical gravity-flush toilet that will serve you well for years to come.

TOILETS 101

Round front

Floor bolt (cap on)

Rough-in distance 10", 12" or 14" (12" most common)

Buy a toilet that will fit the space. Measure the distance from the floor bolts back to the wall (if your old toilet has two pairs of bolts, go by the rear pair). This is your *rough-in distance* and will be either 10" or approximately 12". Make note of the *bowl shape*, round or oval (long). Oval bowls (also called elongated bowls) are a few inches longer for greater comfort, but may be too big for your space. The safest bet is to buy a replacement with the same bowl shape.

TERMS YOU NEED TO KNOW

CLOSET FLANGE—the metal or plastic slotted ring on the floor around the drain opening to which the toilet is bolted.

CLOSET ELBOW—the drain elbow the closet flange attaches to.

WAX RING—a compressible ring that forms a seal between the toilet and the closet flange; it fits either a 3-inch or 4-inch closet elbow.

CLOSET BOLTS—the pair of bolts that attach the toilet to the flange.

TOOLS & SUPPLIES YOU'LL NEED

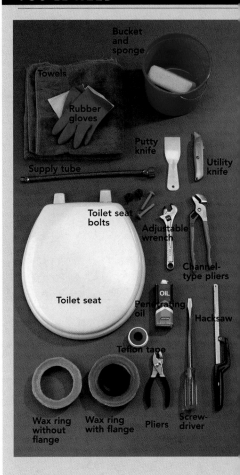

Bucket and sponge

Towels

Rubber gloves

Putty knife

Utility knife

Supply tube

Toilet seat bolts

Adjustable wrench

Channel-type pliers

Toilet seat

Penetrating oil

OIL

Hacksaw

Teflon tape

Wax ring without flange

Wax ring with flange

Pliers

Screwdriver

SKILLS YOU'LL NEED

- Making compression joints
- Lifting 50 pounds
- Hand tool usage

DIFFICULTY LEVEL

SKILLS LEVEL

EASY   MODERATE

Time: Allow about 1 hour for this project

Coupling
nut

Stop
valve

1 Remove the old toilet. First, turn off the water at the stop valve (see pages 148 to 149 if you have trouble). Flush the toilet holding the handle down for a long flush, and sponge out the tank. Unthread the coupling nut for the water supply below the tank using channel-type pliers if needed. **TIP:** If you have a wet vac, use this here and in step three to clear any remaining water out of the tank and bowl.

2 Grip each tank bolt nut with a box wrench or pliers and loosen it as you stabilize each tank bolt from inside the tank with a large slotted screwdriver. If the nuts are stuck, apply penetrating oil to the nut and let it sit before trying to remove them again. You may also cut the tank bolts between the tank and the bowl with an open-ended hacksaw (inset). Remove and discard the tank.

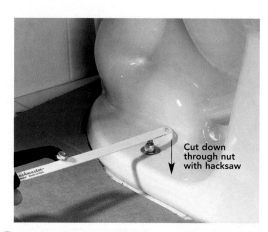

Cut down
through nut
with hacksaw

3 Remove the nuts that hold the bowl to the floor. First, pry off the bolt covers with a screwdriver. Use a socket wrench, locking pliers, or your channel-type pliers to loosen the nuts on the tank bolts. Apply penetrating oil and let it sit if the nuts are stuck, then take them off. As a last resort, cut the bolts off with a hacksaw by first cutting down through one side of the nut. Tilt the toilet bowl over and remove it.

TECHNIQUE TIP

Removing an old wax ring is one of the more disgusting jobs you'll encounter in the plumbing universe (the one you see here is actually in relatively good condition). Work a stiff putty knife underneath the plastic flange of the ring (if you can) and start scraping. In many cases the wax ring will come off in chunks. Discard each chunk right away—they stick to everything. If you're left with a lot of residue, scrub with mineral spirits. Once clean, stuff a rag in a bag in the drain opening to block sewer gas.

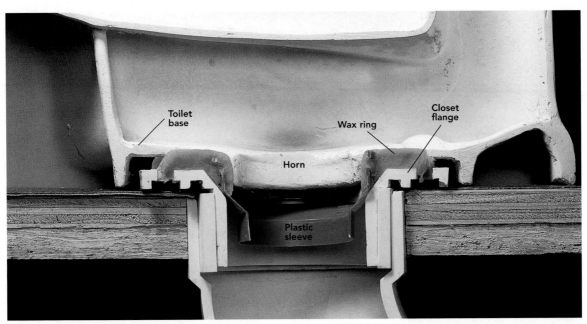

A cross-section of the connection between the toilet stool and the drain reveals that it really is only a ring of wax that makes the difference between a pleasant water closet and something that smells like an open sewer.

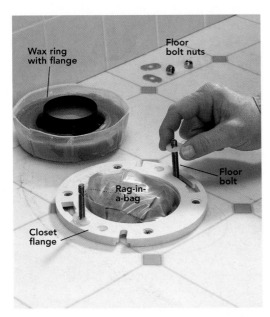

4 Remove the rag-in-a-bag from the drain opening and put new all-brass toilet bolts into the slots on the closet flange at 3 and 9 o'clock and rotate each ¼ turn so the elongated heads cannot be withdrawn. Put the plastic keepers or extra washers and nuts on the bolts to secure them to the flange. Unwrap the wax ring and position it over the flange so it looks like the one in the cross section photo at the top of this page.

5 Lower the new toilet down over the wax ring so the bolts go through the holes on the bottom of the stool (this can be tricky—be patient and get help). Press down on the toilet to seat it in the wax ring and check for level. If the bowl is not quite level, you can shim the low side with a few pennies. Thread washers and nuts onto the floor bolts and tighten them a little at a time, alternating. Do not overtighten. Cut the bolts off above the nuts with a hacksaw and add the caps. Lay a bead of tub and tile caulk around the base of the toilet, but leave the back open to let water escape so you'll know if there's ever a leak.

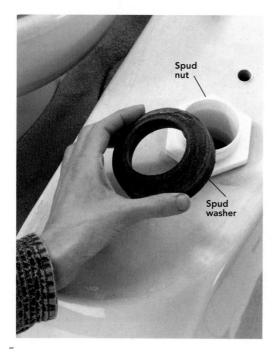

6 Attach the toilet tank. Some tanks come with a flush valve and a fill valve preinstalled, but if yours does not, insert the flush valve through the tank opening and tighten a spud nut over the threaded end of the valve. Place a foam spud washer on top of the spud nut.

7 If necessary, adjust the fill valve as noted in the directions (also see pages 184 to 187).

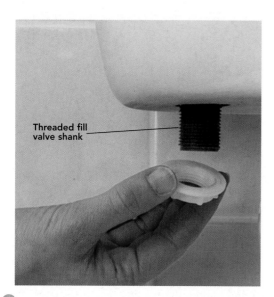

8 Position the valve in the tank. Push down on the valve shank (not the top) while hand-tightening the locknut onto the threaded valve shank (thread the nut on the exterior side of tank). Hand-tighten only.

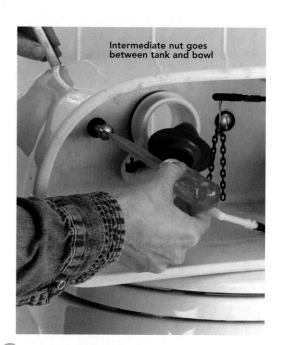

9 With the tank lying on its back, thread a rubber washer onto each tank bolt and insert it into the bolt holes from inside the tank. Then, thread a brass washer and hex nut onto the tank bolts from below and tighten them to a quarter turn past hand tight. Do not overtighten.

10 Position the tank on the bowl, spud washer on opening, bolts through bolt holes. Put a rubber washer followed by a brass washer and a wing nut on each bolt and tighten these up evenly.

11 You may stabilize the bolts with a large slotted screwdriver from inside the tank, but tighten the nuts, not the bolts. You may press down a little on a side, the front, or the rear of the tank to level it as you tighten the nuts by hand. Do not overtighten and crack the tank. The tank should be level and stable when you're done.

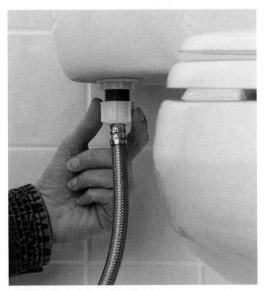

12 Hook up the water supply by connecting the supply tube to the threaded fill valve with the coupling nut provided. Turn on the water and test for leaks.

13 Attach the toilet seat by threading the plastic or brass bolts provided with the seat through the openings on the back of the rim and attaching nuts.

Graduate School:
Installing a Frost-free Faucet

25

That outside faucet freeze again? Replace it with one that you never have to turn off in the winter.

IF YOU LIVE IN A PART OF THE WORLD WHERE SUB-FREEZING TEMPERATURES OCCUR for extended periods of time, consider replacing your old sillcock (outdoor faucet) with a frost-proof model. In this project we show you how to attach the new sillcock using compression fittings, so no torch or molten solder is required. Compression fittings are ok to use in accessible locations, like between open floor joists in a basement. Your building code may prohibit their use in enclosed walls and floors. To see if your sillcock can be replaced according to the steps outlined here, see the facing page.

FROST-PROOF SILLCOCK 101

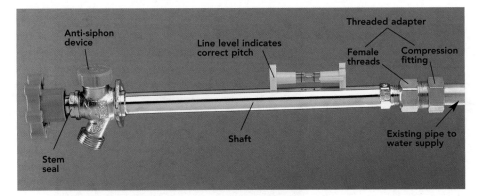

The *frost-proof sillcock* shown here can stay active all winter because the stem washer turns off the water in the warm interior of the house. The *shaft* needs to be pitched slightly down toward the outside to allow water to drain from the shaft. This supply pipe is connected to the *threaded adapter* with a *compression fitting*, which is secured to the pipe with two wrenches.

Do not use the steps that follow if any of the following apply:

- Your pipes are made from steel instead of copper.
- The length of the pipe from the sillcock to where you can comfortably work on it is greater than 12 inches.
- The pipe has a valve or change of direction fitting within ten inches of the existing sillcock.
- The existing supply pipe is ⅝-inch outside diameter as measured with an adjustable wrench, and you are unable to make the hole in the wall bigger to accommodate the thicker shaft of the frost-proof sillcock. (For example, the hole is in a concrete foundation.)

TERMS YOU NEED TO KNOW

SILLCOCK—an outdoor faucet with a threaded spout for a hose and a wide flange at the base allowing it to be attached to an exterior wall with screws.

FROST-FREE SILLCOCK—a sillcock with a long shaft that turns off the water inside the house.

COMPRESSION FITTING—a kind of mechanical pipe connection that allows copper pipes to be fitted without solder or a torch.

OUTSIDE DIAMETER (O.D.)—The outside diameter of the pipe is measured for a compression fitting.

NOMINAL DIAMETER—Valves, sillcocks, pipes, and fittings other than compression fittings go by the nominal diameter. For our purposes here, it's ⅛-inch less than the O.D.

TOOLS & SUPPLIES YOU'LL NEED

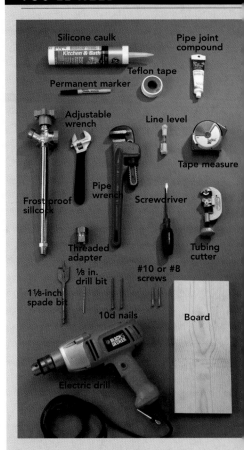

Note: Purchase a sillcock that has the same diameter male-threaded end as your existing pipe (either ½- or ¾-inch). You'll also need a tube-to-FIP (female iron pipe) compression fitting sized for your pipe.

SKILLS YOU'LL NEED

- Using a level
- Using a drill
- Using a tube cutter
- Making accurate measurements

DIFFICULTY LEVEL

Time: 2 hours plus shopping

HOW TO REPLACE AN OUTSIDE FAUCET WITH A FROST-PROOF SILLCOCK

1 Turn off the water to your outside faucet at a shutoff found inside the house or basement behind the faucet (see pages 148 to 149 if you have trouble turning off the water). Open the faucet and a bleeder valve on the shutoff to drain any remaining water from the pipe.

2 When you are sure the water flow has been stopped, use a tubing cutter to sever the supply pipe between the shutoff valve and the faucet. Make this first cut close to the wall. Tighten the tube cutter onto the pipe. Both wheels of the cutter should rest evenly on the pipe. Turn the cutter around the pipe. The line it cuts should make a perfect ring, not a spiral. If it doesn't track right, take it off and try in a slightly different spot. When the cutter is riding in a ring, tighten the cutter a little with each rotation until the pipe snaps.

Spot where supply tubing was cut

3/4" I.D. / 7/8" O.D.

3 Remove the screws holding the flange of the old sillcock to the house and pull it and the pipe stub out of the hole. Measure the outside diameter of the pipe stub. It should be either ⅝", which means you have ½" nominal pipe, or ⅞", which means you have ¾" nominal pipe. Measure the diameter of the hole in the joist. (If it's less than an inch, you'll probably need to make it bigger.) Measure the length of the pipe stub from the cut end to where it enters the sillcock. This is the minimum length the new sillcock must be to reach the old pipe. Record all this information.

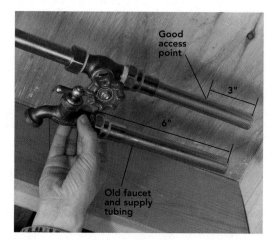

Good access point

3"

6"

Old faucet and supply tubing

4 Find a spot on the supply pipe where you have good access to work with a fitting and wrenches. The point of this is to help you select a new sillcock that is the best size for your project. In most cases, you'll have only two or three 6" to 12" shaft sizes to pick from. In the example above, we can see that the cut section of pipe is 6" long and the distance from the cut end to a spot with good access on the intact pipe is 3", so a new sillcock that's 9" long will fit perfectly.

Drill guide

5 If you need to replace old pipe with a larger diameter size, simplify the job of enlarging the sillcock entry hole into your home with a simple drill guide. First, drill a perpendicular 1⅛" diameter hole in a short board. From outside, hold the board over the old hole so the tops are aligned (you can nail or screw it to the siding if you wish). Run the drill through your hole guide to make the new, wider and lower hole in the wall.

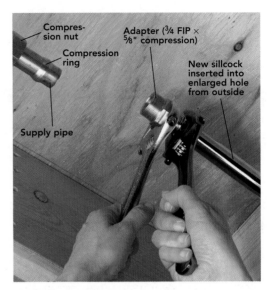

Compression nut

Compression ring

Supply pipe

Adapter (¾ FIP × ⅝" compression)

New sillcock inserted into enlarged hole from outside

6 Insert the sillcock into the hole from the outside. Cut the supply pipe where it will meet the end of the sillcock. From the inside, wrap Teflon tape clockwise onto the threads of the sillcock. Stabilize the sillcock with one wrench and fully tighten the Adapter onto the threaded sillcock with the other wrench.

Apply pipe joint compound here

7 Insert the end of the supply pipe into the Adapter and pull them together. Spin the sillcock shaft so the faucet outside is oriented correctly (there should be a reference line on the bottom or top of the shaft). Apply pipe joint compound to the male threads on the Adapter body. Hand thread the nut onto the Adapter body. Stabilize the Adapter body with one wrench then tighten the compression nut with the other about two full turns past hand tight.

8 Turn the water back on. With the sillcock off and then on, check for leaks. Tighten the compression nut a little more if this union drips with the sillcock off. From outside the house, push the sillcock down against the bottom of the entry hole in the wall. Drill small pilot holes into the siding through the slots on the sillcock flange. Now, pull out on the sillcock handle in order to squeeze a thick bead of silicone caulk between the sillcock flange and the house. Attach the sillcock flange to the house with No. 8 or No. 10 corrosion resistant screws.

INDEX